Practice research in Nordic social work:
Knowledge production in transition

I0127664

Critical Studies
in Socio-Cultural Diversity

Editor-in-Chief: Dr Sara Ashencaen Crabtree

Current and future titles in the same series

Surrender: Connecting to a Global Story.
The larger truth about the intra-cultural world community
Paul Johnson and Bruce St Thomas

A Rainforest Asylum
The enduring legacy of colonial psychiatric care in Malaysia
Sara Ashencaen Crabtree

The Cup, The Gun and The Crescent:
Social welfare and civil unrest in Muslim societies
Sara Ashencaen Crabtree, Jonathan Parker & Azlinda Azman

Practice research
in Nordic social work
Knowledge production in transition

Edited by

Edgar Marthinsen
& Ilse Julkunen

Co-editors:
Lars Uggerhøj, Tove Rasmussen,
& Synnöve Karvinen-Niinikoski

Whiting & Birch
MMXII

© Whiting & Birch Ltd 2012
Published by Whiting & Birch Ltd,
Forest Hill, London SE23 3HZ

ISBN 9781861771308
Printed in England and the United States by Lightning Source

Contents

The Authors

Ilse Julkunen Professor, Department of Social Research, University of Helsinki, Mathilda Wrede Institute, Finland, ilse.julkunen@helsinki.fi

Synnöve Karvinen Niinikoski Professor, Department of Social Research, University of Helsinki, Finland, sykarvin@mappi.helsinki.fi

Karin Kildedal Associate Professor at Department of Sociology and Social Work, Aalborg University, Denmark, kildedal@socsci.aau.dk

Edgar Marthinsen Professor, South Troendelag University College, Trondheim, Norway, edgar.marthinsen@hist.no

Tove Rasmussen Senior Lecturer, Via University College, Aarhus, Denmark. tove@viauc.dk

Erja Saurama Professor, Dept of Social Research, University of Helsinki, Finland. erja.saurama@helsinki.fi

Lars Uggerhøj Associate Professor , Aalborg university,Denmark. lug@socsci.aau.dk

Laura Yliruka Senior Researcher Social Worker, Heikki Waris Institute, Helsinki, Finland. laura.yliruka@hel.fi

Preface

The editors are proud to present this book *Practice research in Nordic Social work: Knowledge production in transition*. The authors have worked together on this theme for more than a decade. The book reflects the strong focus on bridging the gap between academy and practice that are evolving. Authors are all from the Nordic countries, and their particular framework comes from the context in which they work. The project contributes to a wider discourse in social work and social work research but also to a global discourse on reflexive and critical knowledge production as well as evidence based practices. Scholars and practitioners from other countries will be familiar with many of the issues raised here, and will, we are sure, be interested to compare the Nordic experience with their own.

The concept of 'Practice research' may serve as a rhetorical message containing intentions of furthering research different from that which is not practice-based. This polarization may well illustrate the difficulties in defining both ends of the scale – that which is, at one end, research-led and far from practical focus, and at the other the realm of the researching practitioner in her own field and her own work. In discussing the practice research framework we bring forth different conceptions and ways of producing knowledge in social work in relation to practice research.

'Knowledge production' may be a way of reinterpreting the idea of science-based practice, and we have chosen this term, partly because 'knowledging' may be understood as a verb, rather than using the noun 'knowledge'. The authors agree upon an epistemological position where knowledge is understood as based upon the acceptance of different positions as legitimate in understanding knowledge. The client may well be an expert in his/her own field, as much as the social worker or professional may be said to master their work. Knowledge is always positional, and may be conceived as true or valid from one position, but wrong or invalid from another. This situational validation of knowledge refers to knowledge making as social processes of negotiation, especially applied to a field like social work. Social work may be identified as a field where different actors tend to negotiate about what is valid and/or what distinctions should be granted as valid capital within the social field in which they operate or move. This positioning may open a space for democracy – and visible power, in knowledge making.

The opposite position assumes that scientific knowledge operates with truth claims which may not be opposed by those who are unqualified to criticize the holders of power in the field of knowledge making. The latter kind of truth may adopt and use the noun 'truth', while not regarding this as a process of claiming validity and relevance in different life worlds. 'Knowledge making in transition' thus positions this enterprise as a contribution to the ongoing discourse on valid knowledge in the field of social work. A competing position may be nourished from the concept of evidence-based practice. There is, however, not *necessarily* a dichotomy between the concepts of practice research and research-based practice on the one hand, and evidence-based practice and research on the other. It is in the positioning of these concepts within the discourse that the differences, even dichotomous ones, may evolve.

Another question about knowledge making, and how truth claims evolve around certain phenomena, is raised by the role and methods of research and researching. Good research may challenge what we (from different positions) hold as truths and may expose as myths those assumptions about the world that were our guidelines to understanding and performing in practice as well as research. The ongoing discourse on social work and science tend to alternate between a reflexive position and a new positivism – the latter position often advance on the basis of an extremely limited understanding of such concepts as evidence-based research and practice. We do not favour any of these positions since the choice of the method to be used must be dependent on what questions we ask, and some questions are best answered by combining different perspectives.

As will be elaborate further throughout the book, epistemology may be important in this discourse, but what is the relation between social work and science – especially social science? This is not necessarily about epistemology, but about power within the academic world versus power in a social political practice field.

The structure of the book

In Chapter 1, Edgar Marthinsen looks at social work as a part of social sciences as well as social policy in operation in welfare states like the Nordic countries. Social work may be regarded as a 'politics of sociology' the way social work becomes embedded within social policy in practice. Enhancing the research focus and the development of more research based, reflexive practices may be regarded as a response to new claims of legitimacy as well as a new space of possibility enabled by the expansion into the scientific field through access to more social workers with higher education. In this regard social work may profit in different ways to the expansion of mode II knowledge production (scientific knowledge production outside the traditional university and research field – mode I).

In Chapter 2, Synnove Karvinen-Niinikoski takes up the changing paradigms for knowledge production in the emerging knowledge-society. This has changed the relationships of expertise, learning and knowledge production. Research- and learning-mindedness have become central goals for social work education in developing knowledge based social and welfare services. Getting social workers and social care staff to use research knowledge in their day-to-day work is a key aspect of the drive to modernize social care. Expertise and knowledge are understood as more open and dialogical and even conditional for negotiations. Seeing expertise as a dynamic and progressive problem-solving process and as an issue of knowledge creation also opens up new ways of combining practice development and social work education.

In Chapter 3, Tove Rasmussen discusses the development of a more research based knowledge in social work as a response to claims of professionalism. The concept of mode I and mode II knowledge production is further explored. Social work may not give in completely to science, since there is a strong emphasis on user involvement and the need for a critical stance towards expertise. Researching practices may also be complicated through bureaucratic and managerial governance of the field.

In Chapter 4, Lars Uggerhoj focuses on theories, definitions, interests, possibilities and barriers in practice research. He follows practice research down three different paths; practice research, practitioner research and user-controlled research. Practice research is explored as collaboration and as a meeting place for different stakeholders in the field of social work. Uggerhoj explores the different interests at stake and what challenges this development poses for research and practice. He argues that we should not aim for a consensus on the concept of practice research but to explore its possibilities and not restrict the idea to certain activities or meanings.

In Chapter 5, Ilse Julkunen discusses how evaluation research deals with practical questions on practice, how it can be studied and evaluated and how the outcomes can be communicated to practice. In her chapter, critical elements in evaluation practices are scrutinized from a generative perspective. It draws attention to the role of the researcher, the knowledge production and dissemination phases, and how these have changed. It highlights the importance on practice connectedness and how this challenges the knowledge production process. She concludes by stating that to be able to learn from practice, evaluation requires an evolution towards both a more deliberative approach and also an active role in science and society.

In Chapter 6, Laura Yliruka reviews the self and peer evaluation method *Mirror* developed in Finland. How can a peer and evaluation method support client work and well-being at work as well as providing a structure for critical thought and development? The focus is both on the immediate consequences resulting from the method's application and its long-term consequences.

In Chapter 7, Karin Kildedal takes on the challenge of action research and its opportunities for professional development of social work practice. Action research is compared to other types of interactive research. The interesting point however is highlighting the democratic and learning theory principles within an action approach that was applied and scrutinized in the article.

Finally, Erja Saurama and Ilse Julkunen reflect on their approach towards practice research. Critical points are put forward such as: the relationship between the subjects and objects of knowledge; the collective nature of knowledge formation; and, particularly, user-participation. A crucial part of the conceptual awareness of practice research is that different kinds of knowledge stand in equal position with each other. Connecting to the learning and democratic principles reflected in Karin Kildedal's article, the ideal in practice research is that different knowledge forms are respected and different kinds of research and practice-based expertise meet each other as equals.

The authors rely on experience from developing and managing research projects and infrastructure in the Nordic countries, and they are all active in the international drive for new knowledge production in social work.

*

All authors of this book are grateful to colleagues in a wider international network on practice research. Behind this development in the Nordic countries there are much inspiration from fellow researchers and scholars. This is illustrated by the inclusion of the Salisbury Statement on Practice Research which reflects the broad global basis for this development within Social Work. The statement as such is itself part of an on-going process and is due to be revised in Helsinki 2012 at the release of this book. We have been fortunate to receive support from our universities, colleges and from municipal and state grants and cooperation. The network has received funding from Nordplus who support university networks throughout the Nordic Countries. The will to develop social work and support backing from research seems to be strong in many Nordic countries and this may be linked to the ambivalent changes (for social work) in the welfare systems of these countries where quality development may be linked to outsourcing and greater focus on individual responsibility. This challenges the value base and understanding of the content and direction of social work. Tove Rasmussens chapter touches in on this theme, but it may be important to further develop a critical position to this evolving background to some of the more enthusiastic examples we have discussed here.

We thank the *European Journal of Social Work* for allowing Karvinen-Niinikoskis (EJSW vol. 8 No 3 2005) chapter to be published again, and *Social Work and Social Sciences Review* who published all the other material in Vol.15/1 and 15/2 2011.

The material brought together here is aimed at academics, students, practitioners, managers and those interested in social work in practice and research. It is a response to the need for a more thorough discussion on practice related research and to present and critically discuss new experiences in knowledge production collaboration between academy, practice and management.

Edgar Marthinsen
Ilse Julkunen
Trondheim/Helsinki April 2012

I

Social work practice and social science history

Edgar Marthinsen

Introduction

Reading social work literature leaves one with the impression of a troubled relationship between academic and professional practice. Is it possible to envision practice and research as integral parts of social work, and what are the preconditions that make this likely to happen now? In this chapter we explore this theme by reviewing the situation today in regard to social work history.

Like many other disciplines it is difficult to draw clear boundaries around social work. To some extent the field may be distinguished as limited to the profession of social work but this does not clarify the task and methods of social work. 'Social work' as such is not an exclusive word solely limited to the work of professionals. Teaching the discipline of social work is not purely just about social work either – it is about politics, psychology, sociology and so on. To some extent social work may be described as an eclectic field operating within the social milieu. One important feature is that it is often about changing and altering society–involving acts of change. People as individuals and groups may change their ways of living by acts of will (also including the will to want and work for change) – believing this to be a core idea within social work. Our idea is that seeing this possibility and applying this concept of social change and seeing how it operates in politics and in society at large, opened the way for modern social work. In fact there may not have been much social work until this change occurred and this fact marks the birth of the discipline in modernity. The epistemology follows the ontological change from pre-modern to modern societies.

To write the history of social work is also to write about the early work on sociology. It is also about the relationship between humanism,

Christianity and charity – not so much about social science. To some extent we may also regard it as a politization of sociology. When it comes to the application of science to the subject, medical schools relate to natural sciences, in a similar way to social work's relationship to social sciences and humanities. Unlike medicine however, social work may be carried out by anyone as a social activity not just by a professional. As a social practice, anybody helping someone to sort out their relationship to others or renegotiating their own idea of self may say they have done social work. As a professional task it is also a social practice, but it has to relate to education, professional practice rules and methods, politics and research. In order to enter the social field of *professional social work*, one has to complete a basic education, and most professionals also identify with the professional code of ethics and the internationally agreed agenda for social workers (Global standards 2004). The new question arising is to what extent does the professional have to relate to scientific knowledge or scientific methods in practice to be regarded as a legitimate professional in the future? Social workers today seem to turn to colleagues rather than to research when they are in need of knowledge, or lack necessary arguments to support or make their decisions. Examples of the use of scientific texts are scarce in practice (Lie et al. 2005; Socialstyrelsen 2005).

Reading earlier social work literature, such as Perlman (1957), Minahan and Pincus (1973), Compton & Galaway (1975) and Germain (1979), reveals how the authors related to different ideas of science. While Perlman claims her method as scientific due to the use of deduction based on systematic observation, Germain and Compton & Galaway rely on the diffusion of science validating itself through wide acceptance of the understanding it brings to the world (Marthinsen 1997). Habermas (1968) criticises these positions and claims that ideology will always replace the lack of knowledge in time whereas the agent or group of professionals will still claim or defend its scientific base. What is new in the application of the ideas of 'evidence based' practice is that the practitioners themselves may have to defend their own actions as both scientifically based and scientifically applied – which means they will have to be more research minded in their practices.

The position advanced in this collection of papers may be a combination of all of these concepts, since we discuss how better knowledge of research and practice together with users or citizens using services may enhance their knowledge about social work. What separates it from the modern ideas of knowledge building is that we are aiming for a new kind of practice where good actions and good results can be demonstrated and recorded but can never be the final outcome– there is no end to the process of knowledge making, and it reflects a distinct mindset, a thirst for knowledge.

This transition from educated professionals with limited scientific responsibility, to responsible actors within the scientific field, may be the most significant change social work has undergone. Politicians and managers will still be formally responsible but the social worker will look towards adopting the identity of a street level intellectual rather than a bureaucrat. Intellectual in the sense of Said[1] (1996,7) referring to Benda:

> Real intellectuals ... are supposed to risk being burned at the stake, ostracized, or crucified. They are symbolic personages marked by their unyielding distance from practical concerns ... with powerful personalities ... in a state of almost permanent opposition to status quo ...

Such a transformation would come on top of the political and ethical responsibility social workers are already burdened with, and would raise the standard of the whole field of practice.

A brief history of social work

Professional social work in Europe may be said to struggle for intellectual respectability with the traditional training establishments often situated outside universities in polytechnics or colleges. This has become very evident in the wake of the Bologna process introducing a new standard for education with bachelor, master and PhD. Social work did not usually find itself within this framework and has had to adjust in most countries (Labonté-Roset 2005). Professional practices are also facing a simultaneous challenge in the political demands for more scientifically based, or scientifically legitimated welfare practices – lately often confused with the prominently advocated position of evidence based practices and research. Conceptualizing the discipline of social work may be regarded as a look into a troubled and troubling trade.

Looking back

In this chapter we will try to follow social work over a couple of centuries to explore the future boundaries of the subject – an attempt to read the signs and trends social work has to relate to at the outset of a new millennium. History may be an aid to a more critical stance towards dominant discourses. Reading through Nordic social work literature representing the last decade and having scanned through the content of major journals like the *British Journal of Social Work* and the *European Journal of Social Work* for the last five years, one is left with the impression of two significant discourses:

1. how does social work as a discipline respond to the demand for evidence based practice?, and
2. how does practice and academic research and education respond to and relate in general to the knowledge claim?

The chapters which follow present research on practice and debates on organization and politics, and they also often respond to the current knowledge claim or are themselves a practical example of producing legitimate knowledge. Labonté-Roset (2007), representing the Alice-Salomon-University and EASSW, tries to present the kind of action-research-policy guaranteeing close cooperation between professional practice and social work. Karvinen, Pösö and Satka (1999, 11) argue that social work does not have its own theory or research methods but

> we must speak about more or less relevant ways in which they have been adapted to the practice of social work research.

This text is based on the idea that social work is a part of social sciences as well as social policy where it operates in welfare states like the Nordic countries. In many other countries however much of social work practice may rather be related to the actions of NGOs or the church, and/or other religious institutions. This chapter is based on a welfare state context. The question about who is to do the research and who is to do the social work in practice is not discussed here but in other chapters in this book.

Social work developed during a time of strong belief in the human capacity for personal transformation and in the ability of society to improve the opportunities required to do so (Parton 2000). McBeath and Webb (2002) argue that social work is formed within the social and cultural dimension of modernity. It relates to ideology as well as to scientific progress and developing insight into society. To various degrees social work also has to relate to science and research, and, as this collection of papers discusses, this seems to be rather important since it has become a requirement where social work is part of public policy. In his analysis of the origins of social work, Villadsen (2004) draws heavily on the philanthropic discourse and the expressed need to improve the lot of the poor and the weary. The reasons for their difficulties were suggested as being their own wrong decisions and lack of understanding, while the solutions relied heavily upon authoritarian action and punishment.

There is still a lot of ontological disagreement about the explanations for social problems, but while professional social workers may have gained a more complex understanding of the interplay between agent and structure, parts of their discourse still lean towards archaic solutions. On the whole social work has become part of social policy action in the Nordic countries as in many other parts of the western world, although some services are still run by NGOs, the church and other institutions rather than by municipal authorities or the state. We are also witnessing how social work becomes part of the new structures of civil society in former communist and socialist countries. This collection of papers is not about the global expansion of social work, but it is an important factor to take into consideration when one discusses the challenges social work must face. If social work becomes part of the everyday life of more and more people, we have to be very critical of how the power exerted in the field is treated. Åkerstrøm Andersen (2003) are among the new younger writers focusing on the question of how social work ends up as an authoritarian force in society, leaving the citizen with the blame and the responsibility for creating and solving the social problems society has to face. Social work may also be said to play an important role in the construction of ever more sophisticated degrees of client dependency due to the proliferation of problems in people's everday lives (Parton, Thorpe & Wattam 1997; King 1997; Marthinsen 2003).

Is social work a child of modernity and the Enlightenment? – and if so, why so? The etymology of social work may reveal the strongest link to the Enlightenment period, since the word 'social' was reintroduced and used in many different concepts, such as society, socialism, social-antisocial. Webb (2007) asks why we ended up with the word 'social' rather than 'religious', 'philanthropic' or 'civic'. He argues that social was chosen because of the strong link it had to the new dominant ideas of modern society, the idea that society transcended the individual and led us into a discourse concerning the common good. There was a need for focus on self development and the creation of a reasonable and responsible citizen – not someone saved and taken into custody by the church. A responsible citizen was the cement of the social world (the state conceived as the society of societies in which all the claims upon each other are mutually adjusted) (op cit). The etymological base comes from the Latin *socius* meaning 'comrade' in the setting of the city, *civitas*. Civilization and social and society are three concepts very closely linked, and a *safe, predictable* and *just* world is projected into these concepts. The rise of the republic did not start with the revolutions, but with the rise of secret societies all over the western world. Societies which slowly infiltrated the men in power and left their mark on history. The idea of agency is also linked to the word social – the social man is a subject creating to some extent the social world. This philosophy dates back to Aristotle, but was revived through newer philosophers like Aquinas, Vico and later Kant and Hegel, ending up in the existentialism of Heidegger and Sartre, rearranged by Marxist-oriented phenomenologists like Bourdieu and Giddens in our own time. Man replaces God. Man becomes responsible for his own destiny.

Some claim that social work is as ancient as man, since we have always been social and caring beings, but this idea lacks a foundation in the worldviews of earlier times (Soydan 1993). If social work is strongly linked to the idea that man creates its own world(s), social work has to be linked to a discourse on the possibilities of active agency free from religious or mythical views – the idea of a disenchanted world that rose in the wake of the Enlightenment (Taylor 2007). There is a great portion of objective reality in social work, which helps to relate it to science, but the subject is also ambiguous. Habermas (1968) claims we retreat into ideology as soon as we run out of scientific arguments, and this is a boundary we seldom notice passing. As a mainly communicative action, social work has to face the problems of interpretation, uncertainty and all that we do not know in real life – as well as its links to sensibility, the idea of a just world and to religiously founded brotherhood and politically founded solidarity (Parton 2000). Discussing the worldview of the Enlightenment, one should also consider the fact that the world then was regarded as developing into a far better state of existence (Darwin's idea of evolution is just one argument among many), not deteriorating and on its way to Armageddon. This gave man and science the upper hand and there was no need for religious saviours.

Let us have a closer look at history. Based on the above mentioned arguments, social work may be considered as a subject that developed together with sociology during the mid 18th century in Europe and North America. With the language of Kuhn (1962/1996) and Bourdieu (2004) sociology may be regarded as a new social field growing out of philosophy. The development of knowledge about the social sciences was expected to have the same degree of ambition as the natural sciences; it should take a positive stand through objective empirical studies of the social world (Comte). This was a quest for reason in the social life which would leave the social scientist as the major force in the interpretation of the social world. Ideas that proved to be both a weapon and a tool in the hands of politicians and rulers in the centuries to follow. The rise of grand ideas is found in several utopian stories from the early medieval era (Moore 1516; Campanella 1602; Bacon 1627). These ideas threatened the feudal system and the existing monarchies to such an extent that even kings tried to adjust to the rising trend and build the ideas into their existing systems, like Louis XIV trying to be the Sun King, building on a mixture of ancient ideas (Egyptian) of rule, and modern ideas about the state (Campanella). Humans have always had a longing for the good life, but for many centuries this longing was projected into a life after death and based on religious beliefs – a worldview which left the church and its servants with the power of sanctity. All power had to relate to this understanding of the world. Instead of living in time, one lived in high time with the focus on the afterlife and eternity (Taylor 2007). Modernity transformed this worldview and thus religion lost power to politics. Destiny was now in the hands of science.

The fantasies of pre-enlightenment times chart the transition from high time to modern times. Thomas More's *Utopia* was printed in 1512 as one of the first medieval narratives of a better world in real life. Utopias – meaning 'no place' but with strong connotations to the word *Eutopia* meaning the 'good place'. These worlds were usually encountered while lost at sea and finding the perfect place by accident, the society having developed out of reach of the known world. These stories seem to have developed as a risky discourse on changing the structure of the feudal society. Another story of this kind was *The City of the Sun*, by Tommaso Campanella [1568-1639], written in Italian in 1602, just after he was condemned to life imprisonment for sedition and heresy. In 1626 Francis Bacon published *New Atlantis*. Bacon also being one of the founders of the Royal Society (1660), legitimates the discourse on developing a new world based on scientific knowledge and not on belief. The model of the Royal Society was the early *Bureau d'Adresse* in France which inspired the establishment of offices and newspapers with the intention of publishing scientific knowledge and spreading the ideas of the Enlightenment. The discourse on new worlds and new forms of democracy inspired the establishment of societies such as the Quakers and other more short lived collective socialist experiments over the years to follow. Many of these were prosecuted and punished, and many fled to the new world bringing the ideas with them. During the mid 1800 there are thought to have been more than 150 of these societies in existence, living experiments of new ways of life (Frängsmyr 1980).

Ideas of how to rule and treat people developed long before we had any advanced social science analysis of individual, psychological development or social practices. What was to become sociology seems to have developed more as an ideologically based tool for social change and politics, rather than a social science. The idea of organising the whole of society on the basis of the powers contained within social science (the new ontology) seem to have developed before the idea of negotiating with individuals in society. Taylor (2007) claims that some of the first social experiments with socializing large populations were carried out by Bismarck in order to have a strong army with obedient soldiers, a goal he achieved through better education and living conditions – ideas that more often seem to be linked to the history of social democracy and social policy. Taylor's point is that waging war was a far more relevant subject for politics than building a fair and just society, and that we today seem to be confused about what aims really lay behind some of the social changes that occurred during the Enlightenment.

One of the first real life experiments, 'new Lanark', developed in industrial Manchester (1799). Robert Owen was a member of the Manchester Literary and Philosophical Society. Here he was introduced to new ideas and a different class of society and soon became friends with the leading intellectuals of the day, including Dr. Percival - pioneer in public health reform, the poet Coleridge and John Dalton the chemist. As an active member of the Society, Robert Owen took part in debates and presented papers on *'the improvement of the cotton industry, the utility of learning, universal happiness and industrialisation and social influences on belief'*. He left his mark on history as one of the most prominent social reformers of the period, a pioneer of modern British socialism and a source of inspiration to the co-operative and trade union movements.

> My intention was not merely to be a manager of cotton mills, but to change the conditions of the people who were surrounded by circumstances having an injurious influence upon the character of the entire population ... The community was a very wretched society and vice and immorality prevailed to a monstrous extent.

Owen's expectations of man were high;

By my own experience and reflection I had ascertained that human nature is radically good, and is capable of being trained, educated and placed from birth in such manner, that all ultimately (that is as soon as the gross errors and corruptions of the present false and wicked system are overcome and destroyed) must become united, good, wise, wealthy and happy [2].

Simultaneously in France Saint-Simon (1760-1825) developed what Comte later would describe as the first attempt to make a society based on applied social science – sociology.

Henri de Saint-Simon is renowned as the founder of the 'Saint-Simonian' movement, a type of semi-mystical 'Christian-Scientific' socialism that pervaded the 19th Century. Saint-Simon envisaged the reorganization of society with an elite of philosophers, engineers and scientists leading a peaceful process of industrialization tamed by their 'rational' Christian-Humanism. His advocacy of a 'New Christianity' -- a secular humanist religion to replace the defunct traditional religions -- was to have scientists as priests (http://cepa.newschool.edu/het/profiles/saintsimon.htm)

It may be wise to note that there seems to be no reflection upon the problems or challenges related to biological or social diversity – perhaps one of the gross failures of early applied social science and the policies that were derived from the field. Believing in the omnipotent effects of education and good environments of certain kinds, seem to have created a cultural imperialism that led to marginalization and stereotypical ideals of man and society. All differently described people became clients and should be brought within the normal variation of society, or should be rendered extinct to purify the race. Before genetics were very well developed (before DNA history) many myths arising from these views resulted in grave maltreatment, exploitation and humiliation of despised categories of people. History shows we find the extremes in social democracies as well as in totalitarian states (Hirdman 1989).

Any educated social worker will easily see the traces of Owen's and Saint-Simon's scientific-political agenda in the ideas of the founding mothers of social work like Jane Addams and Mary Richmond - although the two had different view on society. They both had the strong belief in enlightenment as a practice, either on a social level in general or as casework with the citizen as such. They seem to converge around the theme of educating the poor. Social work may be as much a child as a stepchild of academe. In most of northern Europe schools of social work were established at the beginning of the 20th century - often associated with philanthropic organisations and women's emancipation. Alice Salomon established the Social School for Women in Berlin in 1899, which is now the Alice-Salomon University. In Chicago the School of Social Work was founded in 1946, today known as the Jane Addams College of Social Work. It still carries the same mission:

> ... to educate professional social workers, develop knowledge, and provide leadership in the development and implementation of policies and services on behalf of the poor, the oppressed, racial and ethnic minorities, and other at-risk urban populations. In doing this, the college values and respects the full range of human diversity (Wikipedia 2008).

It was established after strong controversies within the field of sociology and social anthropology represented by a phenomenologist like Mead (Lewin 2000). Social work in the hands of Jane Addams became politics and eventually earned her the Nobel Peace Prize. In the Nordic countries scattered schools of social work grew up during the early 20th century, but the real expansion came after the post war eras with the investment in building professional services to carry out their ambitious social policy plans. In academe social work may be regarded as a socially concerned subject that departed from sociology and psychology to form a new distinct field of its own – focusing on the applied side of social and psychological knowledge. In Germany and to some extent in the northern European area social pedagogy has developed alongside social work. In the Nordic countries social pedagogy has been related to work with children and young people, often in institutions. Sometimes a struggle surfaces in the discourse on social work where some would rather connect their identity to social pedagogy. The history of childhood thus becomes more visible and the traces of Rousseau and ideas about innocence and possible developments move into the centre of discourse rather than social change as such. Theories of agency in childhood emerged as a dominant view as well as the discussion of how this approach could also be applied to adults. (James, Jenks & Prout 1998).

Through most of the 20th century we may regard social work as a multi-subject field, focusing on developing a practice of social work based on a methodological discourse in the field of social work, but with no empirical science of its own. This may be due to the dominant epistemological view of how knowledge is diffused between science and professionals. Some professions did not evolve within the university, social work among them. The loose connection with the universities may explain some of the lack of research in the field but it is not the whole explanation. Even when social work entered the universities (in Norway and Sweden during the 1970s,) the amount of research on practical issues did not necessarily expand significantly. Many of the studies of the students look into social phenomena and social problems as such, but not at how social work is practised[3]. This may have to do with how the funding of research to some extent also decides what questions are researched. This again relates to the power structures of the academic world and social sciences as such. It took decades to produce professorships where the candidates would come from the field of social work itself. According to Bourdieu (2004) we may regard the establishment of a new subject in social sciences as the evolution of a new academic field creating a situation of tension within the already established system. This produced a situation where social work higher education and research had to fight their way against already established fields within the social sciences. Much of the resources then available for public research were spent on social policy, sociology, political science and other related fields. This research did not focus on social work as such but on the use of resources, how judgement was deployed, and the consequences of policy for individuals and society and other related topics. Outcomes could be studied, but not how different outcomes might be explained in terms of the results of different practices – it was seldom about the process as such.

Social work organizations like FORSA[4] in Sweden and Norway helped to put social work research on the agenda and for many years had to demand more resources for social work before the state would allocate resources in the field. This is not to say that these organizations were crucial to this development, but that they were themselves a sign of the times and could feed on the expanding knowledge claim of public services. Social work research in the Nordic countries has only after the turn of the century received grants to develop services as a result of new knowledge claims. Some of the schools in the Nordic countries have developed research activities during the last decades, and there are research centres focusing on social work in different settings like child protection, work with young people and some with a more general focus on social work practices. The latest development is that of the joint ventures between municipal services and universities and colleges. These institutions aim to develop services through a stronger research focus on practice and knowledge production (Sociorama in Växjö, Sweden; Heikki Waris and Mathilda Wrede -institutes in Helsinki, Finland and the HUSK project in Norway).

Sociology developed into many specialist areas like political science, sociology of knowledge and so on, and became very dependent on the idea that objective social science was best represented by keeping a distance from politics and practice, relying on quantitative methods and leaving the study of the functioning of the human brain and emotions as such to subjects like psychology and neurology. Social work developed mainly as part of the welfare services in the Nordic countries, supported by a growing number of schools of social work, mostly established after the 1950s, but the epistemology was still heavily influenced by the dominant discourses in the social sciences, medicine, biology, chemistry and physics. As you look back in social work history over the last century however, you will find it moving from psychoanalysis, through systems theory and into social constructionism and bioengineering (Parton 2000).

The applied schools of social work have been for most of the period we have been discussing outside of the university sector, concentrating on producing formally qualified professionals, and responding to claims to legitimate practice. Social work as a university subject was established mainly from the 1970s onwards and later in some Scandinavian countries and not necessarily as part of the basic training of social workers. Sweden developed PhD programmes in four universities during the 1980s and has since expanded. Finland has transformed their professional programmes to master programmes in 6 universities and have PhD programmes in all the universities as well as a national PhD programme. Denmark has so far only one master programme in social work (Aalborg University) and no specific PhD programme for social work, but a joint programme between different universities in related areas.

The academic field has to some extent been separate from the world of practice, marking an attractive distinction.. While academic success requires contemplation and individual concentration to acquire honours and promotion, the practice field receives its honours from politicians and administration through a set of complex forms of feedback, from user satisfaction, good budget policy and being efficient according to bureaucratic standards. Practice knowledge of research was often through critique of bad practices, as an illustration the first *Nordic Symposia on Social Work Research and Practice* were about bridging the gap (in Trondheim 1996 and Malmö 1997).

The Department of Social Work at the University of Trondheim (UiT, since 1996 NTNU) may serve as an example. The new schools of social work needed qualified teachers with higher university degrees in order to legitimise public investment in the schools, and therefore they had to be affiliated closer to the universities and the sciences as such through the development of research in the field. Among the arguments to establish the department at the UiT, 1974, was the idea that society needed social engineers who would have the skills to put an end to social problems related to the urbanization of the country. They would have to play a central role in developing sustainable social and physical planning and policies for modern life (Tronvoll & Marthinsen 2000). Social planning was thus the modus operandi of public politics. This tempted young, male social workers to apply in the early 1970s, but alas the world changed. According to one of the teachers at the department, together with her American professors imported to run the institute, she was very frustrated and disappointed because the students would not read the books on the curriculum, and were only interested in politics, attending demonstrations and quarrelling about how to run the university as a democratic and critical base for revolution. The establishment was hit by the impact of the 1968-upheaval. No social engineering developed, young men with 'industrial ambitions' were replaced by women social workers. The first students to receive their post-graduate qualifications were all women. After the first 10 years, with few applications the Department changed its policies and was turned into a regular social science academy with the focus on research and advanced social work theory. The Department now runs a masters and phD programme in social work

Although the situation varies a lot around the world, in contrast to the somewhat offbeat position mentioned above, social work has long been a university degree and we have much of research in the field, journals, books and international conferences. We have professors of social work, we have researchers and we have well qualified teachers. We may rightfully claim that social work is a distinct social field within society as well as within research and academe, but its success is dependent on the symbolic capital acquired by social work within the social sciences (Bourdieu 2004). In the Nordic countries one may be tempted to say that the investment in research in social work is meagre, and representatives of academic social work often draw the short straw in competition for resources. The direct investment in knowledge production aimed at social work from state departments during the last decade may be easing the situation somewhat, but there is still a shortage of funding.

An epistemological turn

The social sciences were all influenced, and to some extent also in charge of the critique of the modern worldview and the idea of a neutral and objective science during the 1970s and 1980s, that changed the focus of research and the idea of what science as well as knowledge was. Positivism moved from domination to a defensive position during the last quarter of the 20th century, partly because of its lack of sensitivity to culture and diversity. It was also a question of method – how do you research society ? Is objectivity a possibility? We experienced a dichotomous struggle between quantitative and qualitative research (Holter & Kalleberg 1972). Science itself came to be regarded as a part of the production of ideology (Habermas 1968), and social science became much influenced by the impact of phenomenology and post-structuralist theory. During the first phase of this scientific revolt, it was dominated by a critical position, but later we may describe the direction of the revolt as an epistemological change? or even maybe as a linguistic change. For the social sciences the discourse on social theory and the social construction of the world became crucial. The label post-modernity may be used to describe the rebellion, but modernity was not ready to be discarded so the terms were soon changed to late modernity or the post-structuralist era. The consequences of late modernity may be illustrated by how concepts change their reference. Modernity may crudely be identified by universalism, monoculture and true and false, the mode of description was the noun. Late modernity sees the global in the local, but not just universalism, but rather multiculturalism, where believing is related to the best argument and negotiable; the mode of description is the verb, and understanding replaces ideas of grand theory, based on acknowledging the socially situated nature of knowledge. This change has affected words related to social work like 'critical'. Critical was often related to or replaced by the word 'radical' implying the notion of a long awaited revolution or reform to move society towards the common good. Critical and radical were applied to leftist policy or political radicalism – it was socialism versus capitalism or conservatism. Words like empowerment came to be associated with radical as well. But radical today may rather be associated with fundamentalism – seeking universal solutions to systems with totalitarianism as an expected result. Not really very different from the way we may regard the radicalism of the 1970s – at least the most extreme forms. We still use the word critical and the discourse on critical social work may even be described as one of the most dominant in the field (Leonard, Dominelli et al., Ferguson, Haley, Olesen, Oltedal). We also operate with critical realism (Bashkar, Olesen). But the word radical seems to be replaced by reflexive as the relevant connotation. Words like empowerment seems to have changed their connotation too, and may also be related to reflexivity and knowledge, or to the mastering of the situation by contextualizing the agent in the structure with the space of possibility in mind. Right and wrong is replaced by an intricate discourse on distinctions and power (or micropower). Foucault and his concept of the archaeology of knowledge and genealogy enter the social work discourse even more often - social work has to relate to Foucaultian concepts like discipline and pastoral power; the latter positioning the social worker in the place of the priest in traditional society – the one who tells you what is right and wrong...and produces a sense of guilt, shame and remorse.

Partly based on the more humble position in relation to science the voice of the user becomes more important as a validation and legitimation of knowledge. Acknowledgement of the subjective element in knowledge production and in the dissemination and implementation of knowledge, leads to a need to listen to user opinions and claims of justice. A new welfare law in Norway illustrate this change by including the word *respect* in its first paragraph. Respect, decency and authenticity have entered the scientific vocabulary and seem to represent paramount values in and for social work. Rawls' (1979/1999) theory of justice, and major works in social philosophy discussing the prerequisites for a sustainable civil society such as those of Nussbaum, Honneth, Sen, Bauman and others, may play a similar role in the discourse of social work today just as Freud and Bateson a generation or two ago.

The linguistic turn

Gadamer (2004 (1986), 447) claims that *being [that] you can conceive, is language*. It is in language that being comes to light, the word opens up the world and sheds light on what is hidden. In order to discover this we have to engage in the play of language, where one word is a metaphor for another. Allegories and symbols serve to expand what is already known. Searching for words and finding them creates meaning. Sharing this with others is communication and at the same time construction of a common frame of reference. To agree to a necessary extent that what is represented by what is said by those words refers to the same thing. Gadamer refers to Hegel in his Phenomenology of the Spirit where he argues that the elementary movement of the spirit is when you have to recognize your own in what is unfamiliar or strange and then feel at home in it. Every person develops a sense of self and identity through the conception of language from a natural stage to a spiritual one where you find yourself within a language, culture(s) and your worlds' institutions. At the same time language never becomes reality; it is always a representation and thus metaphysical. This leaves every one of us in an existential position where we only have our own reference to the world as a worldview – a worldview where we, through language, habits and culture, may have some common understanding, but never identical and never true in a strict sense. This recognition led Derrida to exclaim that all that is solid melts into air – the melodrama of post-modernity soon to be confronted with all those claiming the world also consists of some sort of stability making social life and society possible (Searle 1997). Gadamer himself referred to *language* as the main carrier of tradition. Bourdieu developed the concept of *habitus* to count for some stability within the conception of the world. Both Habermas and Searle operate with the notion of *background* that resembles and represents the same phenomenon as Bourdieu with *habitus*. What makes Bourdieu interesting to social work is that he manages to create a toolbox for deconstructing the way the agent operates in the structure, and on what conditions society operates. Late modernity seems to have settled for some consensus about agency and structure to be able to operate in a world with both stability and movement at the same time. Due to the prevailing uncertainty and to the lack of a thorough disciplinary force within society , we are all able to exert some kind of agency in our lives – there are some margins for freedom within any system. This is also the opportunity for social work – to renegotiate the formation of society , how individuals and groups relate to society, and how society relates to groups and individuals. Social work is thus perfectly fit to work in the field of changing people (Hasenfeld 1992).

The consequences of accepting an existential phenomenology is that no one can claim to know any certainty – one may only *claim* validity. Evidence has to pass through some judgement to become proof, and is as such left to operate within society as a contract.

Arendt (1971) draws in her work *The Life of the Mind* – separated into three themes; Thinking, Willing and Judging - on Husserl's notion of time, where thinking unfolds in the gap between past and future.

> The gap between past and future opens only in reflection, whose subject matter is what is absent – either what has already disappeared or what has not yet appeared. Reflection draws these two 'regions' into the mind's

presence ... a fight against time itself. It is only because 'he' thinks, and therefore is no longer carried along by the continuity of everyday life in a world of appearances, that past and future manifest themselves as pure entities, so that 'he' can become aware of a no-longer that pushes him forward and a not-yet that drives him back. (Arendt 1971, 206)

The language change has consequences for practice and research as well. To practise it may not be a notable and conscious change , but the need to listen to users, to be aware of the experience of the client, the client's view and the client's notion of meaning, represents a language change in the way that the focus of the dialogue has moved from the sender to the receiver. For research it becomes inevitable. It means that any text has to be interpreted; a sentence from one to another may be received with a new meaning differing from that of the speaker. This may produce misinterpretation but it might equally lead to a dialogue that ends in the opening up of a new horizon of understanding to both participants. Even the most stringent scientific article needs interpretation and the notion of *applied social science* sounds suspicious to a critical realist. The science to enhance understanding within such a context then becomes the one which deals with how the spirit operates in society – a far more complex task than applying a manual developed through scientific testing over limited time. In addition to these challenges, many of the tasks undertaken by social work are related to the construction of meaning in everyday life – to experiences of grief, loss, poverty and other socially experienced phenomena – not a broken leg, a house burnt down or a plane crashed. Most social work tasks undertaken are related to the metaphysical sphere – how we experience the world – and how we put words and meanings to it.

This does not mean that social work and research in social work should move in the direction of reflexivity alone, but this may be an important modus operandi for working in the field. Quantitative inquiry should be used to reveal patterns and insight into phenomena where no cognitive grip may be possible and where the volume of observations otherwise leads to the creation of myths about practice. All inquiries are dependent on good categorization and meaningful concepts and thus almost immediately require some good foot work ahead of any attempt to study the questions posed.

From academe to practice

For the period covering the late 19th and early 20th century it may be correct to relate social work closely to the rise of social science. However, the establishment of schools of social work outside the universities permitted a new semi-professional development – as in other fields in health and social affairs. For a long time the schools of social work were organized with teaching in several subjects related to society, health and mental well-being. Subjects like law, medicine, psychiatry, family therapy and so on were taught alongside the methods of social work; defined as work with individuals and groups and later society (*samfunnsarbeid*). Professional legitimacy was guaranteed by the quality of teaching and teaching staff[5]. The establishment of university degrees at post-graduate level was also linked to the need for research on how to cope with the social and individual problems related to urbanization and modernization of traditional societies which were being transforming into modern industrialized civilizations (Marthinsen 2001). The establishment of post-graduate social work studies in universities both in Norway and Sweden during the 1970s created a situation where professional training was provided in schools of social work while post-graduate level studies took place in universities. While Norway chose to hire emeritus professors in social work from the USA, Sweden established its post-graduate curriculum with professors from sociology and psychology. Such a situation did not leave much scope for an autonomous field to emerge. While Sweden established a PhD programme, Norway chose to follow their own system with the 'major' as something in between a master programme and a PhD. In Finland doctoral programmes were established at first in the early 1980s as part of social sciences under the discipline of social policy. In the mid 1990s this ended in the establishment of a national graduate school in social work supported by the Ministry of Education. This occurred some years before social work became a fully established academic discipline of its own as part of social sciences departments.

During the late 1980s and the 1990s we experienced a vast expansion of the welfare systems in much of the western world. In Scandinavia we had an increasing number of clients both in child and family services and as recipients of social services (both income support and services for the elderly). Budgets rose as a result of increasing staff levels as well as from there being more clients and more people reliant on public support for their basic needs. New ideas of management demanded cost efficiency and quality indicators, and this enhanced the demand for research. Related to the growth of social work in general, we have seen, over the last two decades, the establishment of both child and family research centres. During the last decades of the 20th century we had a development of two distinct separate fields, research relating to an international discourse on social science – and a growing number of schools of social work trying to relate to a globalized world. There seemed to be a gap between schools of social work and practice, as well as between practice and research. The international social work organizations became an arena for these discrepancies. To put it bluntly, while IASSW[6] reflected the views of an aging group of teachers discussing education, the IFSW[7] kept in touch with politics and research and attracted more and more attention from practitioners and managers all over the world. Especially in Europe there was a need for cooperation and the European conferences became joint ventures for the two organizations also contributing to bridging the gap. In the Nordic countries the FORSA conferences took a large chunk of the conference time available and there was a need to make a deal to change to biannual arrangements with IASSW.

The request for research based knowledge increased as new public management required quality assurance and efficiency measures. This made the lack of (evidence based) research obvious to politicians and managers, and several countries started to invest in knowledge production and dissemination in social work and related fields. The UK established the first centres of excellence in social work and the first reviews were started to enable a presentation of the scientific basis available[8]. Establishing centres like NC2 and granting money for reviews revealed that there was no or very little of that kind of knowledge available anywhere in the world – not even in the USA. What we are experiencing today are the consequences of this revelation – a need for heavy investment in the development of scientifically sound social work research.

How had this situation developed? What made the scientific field in social work unable to deliver the goods asked of it ? Academic social work in the Nordic countries coincidentally developed during an era of very strong focus on qualitative research. Late 20th century social sciences were challenged by the influence of phenomenology and critical theory. Unlike other established sciences there was little traditional positivist social science to be continued alongside the opposing new ideas in social work. The lack of different competing research agendas within the field may explain some of the problems experienced today and to some extent the lack of resources; researchers, dedicated institutions and funding may also take the blame. The development of work processes was conceptualized with terms such as 'reflective practices' (Karvinen 2001). Many studies have been explorative and there is always a danger of generalizing from small samples to the population, contributing to myths rather than expanding knowledge. In theorizing social work practices we also find a strong influence from the concept of tacit knowledge (Schön 1983) explaining the work processes of the reflexive practitioner. Schön's theorizing of practice in fields where professionals have to act in changing situations requiring the use of judgement while in action, seems to have had a special affinity to social work. His work is frequently quoted among social work academics and not least in master and PhD work (Probably also a consequence of his work being on the curriculum). The combination of qualitative research and focus on theories enhancing the idea of tacit knowledge representing social work, has given insight into many intricate phenomena in social work practice and has enhanced knowledge of how we conceptualize the world. Paradoxically we may say, the writing about tacit knowledge seems to produce understanding based on things not being left unsaid but outspoken – putting words to the notions. A creative language produces knowledge. Very often research cooperation with practice turns the unseen and known into knowledge that may be articulated and used in the communication within the organization (Marthinsen & Clifford 1998).

Explorative research has produced knowledge on clientship and how clients conceive their life and experiences as clients. Sociology has similarly revealed the life and experiences of other oppressed groups and made their lives visible to politics and society (Halvorsen 2002). However, in spite of all the good that came out of this knowledge production, it never managed to solve the questions of efficiency in an expanding welfare system. On the contrary, use of thorough research methods enabling the varied results of practice to come to life, require costly research designs and infrastructure in the field of social work to produce valid and relevant information. Social work lacks much of the categorization developed in other professions to register work and determine what kind of tasks are performed to meet needs – although some systems exist in child protection. Work practices are not identified with stringent methodology, rather as eclectic and creative uses of judgement and personal skills (Engmark & Lundstrøm 2008). All this indicates that there is much work to be done before thorough research on method and practice as such can be introduced. Research in and with practice over the last decade has revealed these challenges in the field.

During the strong positivist era, social work had no position in the field of research politics and had few or no members of the societies with influence within the universities and the government9. Social work lobbying was strongly linked to social policy and run by social politicians and NGOs and had little or no relation to the academic field. They seem to have been concerned mostly with establishing social work and child protection as professional fields in the municipal services as part of developing a strong welfare state. As a new academic subject with little access to research funding, social work became very dependent on the individual's own work and had little or no part in research centres. Academics in social work lacked the resources to engage in social research and could not compete with sociology and political science research submissions that were dominant in the field of social research.

The question of social work research has been contested in the UK as well, and Parton (2000) reflects on some of the struggles from the 1970s and onwards in ways that reveal a very similar situation to Scandinavia. He refers to Sheldon versus Jordan (1978) discussing the negative attitudes of many in the profession towards science. Sheldon argued for a more scientific and cumulative evaluation of the theoretical components of social work, and he also argued that there were many similarities between good research and good social work. He wanted 'a small injection of positivism – counterbalancing emphasis on what can actually be seen to have changed, rather than impressions of change inferred from conversations alone' (Sheldon 1978, 18) [10]. Sheldon's argument seems to be an early stage of the strategies later found under the ideas of evidence-based social work. Jordan disagreed strongly with Sheldon, arguing that social science as well as other sciences is strongly linked to power, and that social work had more to do with caring, changing and living with 'inevitable uncertainty, confusion and doubt'. Parton regards their disagreement along the axis from rational-technical to practical-moral. Parton at that time shared some of Jordan's views and argued that social work was very much about informal negotiation about roles and changing of life as such. What makes people clients of social work is that their lives are not ordinary any more, they do not live up to ideas of respectable and decent citizenship, and social workers are called in to negotiate, and only in rare situations have to apply formal, imposed solutions using their legal power. The challenge is how not to become too moralistic, and to avoid imposing bourgeois moral standards on working class people. Still it is about some kinds of 'normalization', specific norms of living (Parton 2000). This leads social work into a world of good judgement, ideas of reflexivity and change and knowledge of justice in a world of difference (Satka, Karvinen, Pösö 1998; Sennet

2003 etc). Social work is about being virtuous (McBeath & Webb 2002). Along this path, scientification tends to be about mastering knowledge of communication, language, and social constructionism.

Reflexivity and evidence

A brief look at some of the recent social work research literature seems to reveal some dominant discourses. Scientification may be achieved either through development of a sound reflexive position studying the agency of the social worker and enhancing their ability to think and judge, while the other alternative seems to be focusing on evidence based research and practices. Within the reflexivity-discourse we also find the idea of social work as reflection-in-action (Schön 1983) and the ideas of agency and structure and the world as a site of globalization and late modernity (Giddens, Beck, Bourdieu, Baumann, Payne, Dominelli et al.). This discourse is partly identified as an opposition towards the discourse of evidence-based research and practice. Reflexive positions may lead to discussions of virtue and ethical considerations and to the opening up of more democratic ways of service development, since users may have a distinct voice in this kind of research based practice. Other positions may look at other traits, such as how critical may social work be? or to what extent does social work become a tool for new managerialism? In relation to scientification, there may be disagreement about how strongly social work practice should be involved in research, or what kind of research may produce sound results in practice. There are examples of quite large investments in building knowledge data bases (SCIE and Campbell), but little investment in discovering how practitioners use this knowledge, to what extent reading science produces better practices or whether it necessarily make practice scientific. Focusing on reflection, judgement and the development of a decent and just society may be regarded as one of the dominant discourses in social work.

Even though the epistemological turn helped social work re-enter the academic world without changing its practice, it may not have given social work the scientific legitimacy it may need to stay within the realm of the public in western society. Since all welfare policies are becoming very costly to taxpayers, all services have to prove their right to existence. Reflexivity and virtue does not seem to deliver the arguments necessary to allocate the resources needed, and they cannot support the arguments with the need to know what you get for the money – *how many bangs for the buck* is one of many slogans used by politicians and economists to illustrate this[11].

Social work has to be able to respond also to managerialism and new public management. This means no development of social work can solely focus on understanding and searching for insight into social phenomena. We also have to respond to the claim for a deconstruction of work whereby it is possible to answer questions of efficiency, and we may require social work also to ask questions about what kind of services we are developing. Are the services treating citizens with decency and respect? This requires a will to spend money on research in practice and to develop practices with feedback loops that allows for both first and second order analysis. What works for whom, and what kind of world are we creating with and for these people? Whose interests are research and practice in social work defending?

At last the expansion of knowledge production into practice does not only seem like a system demand. Gibbons et al. (2007) explains the expansion of knowledge production outside universities as a result of the vast expansion in higher level education. The demand for scientifically oriented knowledge has increased and become a symbolic capital within management and also a necessity in order to be competitive and develop efficiency. Knowledge production in this new setting is categorized as mode II knowledge production. This mode encompasses practice and knowledge while mode I refers to scientists and science. The concept is further elaborated on by Tove Rasmussen in the next chapter in this book.

Further throughout this book we discuss how the gap between research and practice may be bridged, we look at some experiences of research in and with practice – even with users involved. Under what conditions may one create knowledge, for whom and to serve what interests? What do we mean by practice research and how can the concept be operationalized?

References

Åkerstrøm Andersen, Niels (2003): *Borgerens kontraktliggørelse*, København: Hans Reitzels Forlag.

Arendt, Hannah (1971): *The Life of the Mind*. Harcourt.

Bourdieu, Pierre (2004): *Science of Science and Reflexivity*. Polity press.

Compton, Beluah, R. & Galaway, Burt 1975 (1979): *Social work Processes*. Dorsey press.

Frängsmyr, Tore (1990): *Framsteg eller förfall. Framtidsbilder och utopier i västerländsk tanketradition.* Allmänna Förlaget.

Gadamer, Hans-Georg (2004): *Sandhed og metode.* Systime Academic.

Germain, Carel B. (1979): *Social work practice, people and environments.*

Gibbons, Michael, Limoges, Camille, Nowotny, Helga, Schwartzman, Simon, Scott, Peter, Trow, Martin (2007): *The New Production of Knowledge.* Sage.

Habermas, Jürgen (1968): *Vitenskap som ideologi.* Fakkel.

Halvorsen, Rune (2002): *The Paradox of Self-Organization among Disadvantaged People: A study of Marginal Citizenship.* Doctoral Thesis NTNU, Dept of Sociology.

Hasenfeld, Y. (1992): *Human services as complex organizations.* Newbury Park, CA: Sage Publications.

Hirdman, Yvonne (1989): *Att lägga livet tillrätta: studier i svensk folkhemspolitik.* Carlsson bokförlag.

Holter, Harriet & Kalleberg, Ragnvald (1982): *Kvalitative metoder i samfunnsforskning.* Oslo: Universitetsforlaget.

James, Allison, Chris Jenks and Alan Prout (1998): *Theorizing Childhood.* Polity press.

Karvinen, Synnöve (2001): Socialt arbete på veg til reflexiv expertis. In Tronvoll & Marthinsen (eds) *Sosialt arbeid, refleksjoner og nyere forskning. Tapir Akademiske forlag.*

King, Michael (1997): *A better world for children? Explorations in morality and authority.* Routledge.

Kuhn, Thomas S. (1996): *The structure of scientific revolutions.* 3rd ed. University of Chicago Press.

Labonte´ -Roset, Christine (2005): The European higher education area and research-orientated social work education. *European Journal of Social Work* 8 (3) pp. 285-296.

Labonte´ -Roset, Christine (2007): Status and Special Features of Social Work Research within the Canon of the Social Sciences and Humanities: Open and Hidden Asymmetries. Research Note. *European Journal of Social Work* 10 (3) pp. 417 – 421.

Lie, Benedicte, Rud, Mons Georg, Innvær, Simon, Steiro, Asbjørn, Smedslund, Geir, Sjøholm, Ingunn Bekken & Hind, Roar (2005): *Bruk av, holdninger til og behov for kunnskap i sosialkontortjenesten-BAKST.* Oslo: Sosial- og helsedirektoratet.

Marthinsen, Edgar (1997): Sporene av det moderne i sosialt arbeid. S.27-40 in Marthinsen, Edgar & Karin Ekberg (eds): *Nordisk symposium om forskning i sosialt arbeid – et møte mellom forsking og praksis.* NOSEB.

Marthinsen, Edgar & Graham Clifford (1998): *Mellom forsorg og sosialt arbeid.* BUS rapport nr. 5. 1998.

Marthinsen, Edgar (2001): Sosialt arbeid - et fag i det sosiales grense. In Tronvoll, Inger M. & Marthinsen, Edgar (eds) *Sosialt arbeid – refleksjoner og nyere forskning*. Tapir Akademiske. pp. 37- 69.

Marthinsen, Edgar (2003): *Sosialt arbeid og symbolsk kapital i et senmoderne barnevern*. Rapport nr 9. Barnevernets utviklingssenter i Midt-Norge.

McBeath, G., and Webb, S. (2002): Virtue ethics and social work: Being lucky, realistic, and not doing one's duty. *British Journal of Social Work* 32, pp. 1015-1036.

Minahan, Anne & Pincus, Allen (1973): *Social work practice, model and method*.

Parton, Nigel (1999): Some thoughts on the relationship between theory and practice in and for social work. Theorising Social Work Research Seminar 1, 26.5.1999. What Kinds of Knowledge?

Parton, Nigel (2000): Some thoughts on the relationship between theory and practice in and for social work. *British Journal of Social Work* 30, pp. 449-463.

Parton, Nigel, Thorpe, David H., Wattam, Corinne (1997): *Child protection: risk and the moral order*. Basingstoke: Macmillan.

Perlman, Helen H.(1957): *Social casework, a problem-solving process*. University of Chicago press.

Rawls, John (1999): *En teori om rättvisa*. Daidalos.

Said, Edward (1996): *Representations of the intellectual*. Vintage books.

Schön, Donald (1983): *The reflective practitioner: how professionals think in action*. Basic Books.

Searle, John R. (1997): *Konstruktionen av den sociala verkligheten*. Daidalos.

Socialstyrelsen (2005): På väg mot socialtjänstuniversitetet? – en uppföljning av Socialstyrelsens stöd till strukturer för kunskapsutveckling inom socialtjänsten 2002–2004. Sverige.

Soydan, Haluk (1993): *Det sociala arbetets idehistoria*. Lund: Studentlitteratur.

Taylor, Charles (2007): *A secular age*. Random House.

Tronvoll, Inger M. & Marthinsen, Edgar (2001): *Sosialt arbeid – refleksjoner og nyere forskning*. Tapir Akademiske.

Villadsen, Kaspar (2004): *Det sociale arbejdes genealogi. Om kampen for at gøre fattige og udstadte til frie mennesker*. Hans Reitzels forlag.

Webb Stephen A. (2007): The comfort of strangers: social work, modernity and late Victorian England Part I. *European Journal of Social Work* 10 (1) pp. 39-54.

Webb Stephen A (2007): The comfort of strangers: social work, modernity and late Victorian England Part II. *European Journal of Social Work* 10 (2) pp. 193-207.

Notes

1   Said, Edward (1996): *Representations of the intellectual.* Vintage books.

2   http://midwales.com/peopleplaces/rowen/

3   This is based on a review of the first 100 major theses in Norway (1975-2000) and the first 15 doctorate works in Norway.

4   FORSA, foreningen for forskning i sosialt arbeid, the Association for Research in Social Work, has been established in all Nordic countries during the last two decades.

5   the development used here as an example counts primarily for Norway (Marthinsen og Tronvoll 2000).

6   International Association of Schools and Social Work

7   International Association of Social Work

8   Exeter centre of excellence and SCIE were established during the 1990s funded by public investments under Tony Blair.

9   Speaking mostly of Norway here

10 Sheldon 1978. p.18

11 Quote from a lecture by a rep. of the Norwegian Bureau of Statistics.

2

Research orientation
and expertise in social work:
Challenges for social work education
Synnöve Karvinen-Niinikoski

Introduction

At the doorstep of the emerging knowledge-society, research- and learning-mindedness have become central goals for social work education in developing knowledge-based social and welfare services. Getting social workers and social care staff to use research knowledge in their day-to-day work is a key aspect of the drive to modernize social care (Fisher 2002). There are national and governmental programmes for promoting knowledge- and evidence-based services and developing a knowledge base for social care and providing best practice guides (Thyer & Kazi 2004). All this is connected to reforms of the welfare state throughout Europe. At the same time this is accompanied by a fundamental review of university education according to the Bologna model which is raising debates about the role of research and research education in higher education. Additionally, the debates on our understanding about expertise and the processes of producing it put the role of research and knowledge production at the centre of professional education (Hakkarainen et al. 2004, 41-53, 193-202).

In social work education two main strands emerge in the debate about professional expertise and competencies. The competence-based and the creative, reflective approach both draw heavily on research and scientific expertise, when claiming for qualifications of the professional social worker (see e.g. Lymbery 2003). The focus of this chapter is to discuss (from the Finnish context) the implications of the strong research emphasis in social work education, when examined from the angle of the changing understanding of expertise. The role of research in educating future professionals for social care and human services is also central in regard to the new European frame for higher education. The aim of this paper is thus

27

to discuss how the changing understanding of expertise challenges and calls for research-orientation and researcher training in social work education.

The changing relationships of expertise, learning and knowledge production

Expertise is a helpful and, in the social and learning sciences, a widely discussed concept in pondering over the questions about what kind of future social work professionals should be trained today (Hakkarainen et al. 2004; Karvinen-Niinikoski 2004). By definition expertise sounds quite traditional and it has long since been a goal of vocational and professional education like social work (Eraut 1995). Expertise can simply be defined as 'high-level knowledge and skills by which the expert can manage the complex problems and processes of his/her field with the minimal risk of mistaking' (Saaristo 2000, 32). Additionally, the discourse on the development of expertise from novice to experienced expert is well known for social work education (Fook et al. 2000) striving at educating qualified professionals.

The traditional professional expertise based on institutional stability, monopolized academic knowledge and hierarchical professional positions can no longer exercise its jurisdiction. Instead, there is a change process of such depth as to cause crises of professional expertise (Eräsaari 2003). In the field of social welfare this is partly due to the re-construction of institutions of the welfare state and regimes, but is also due to our changing understanding of knowledge and knowledge creation and learning. In the latest research on expertise, the learning and knowledge re-constructed understanding of expertise (Hakkarainen et al. 2004; Eräsaari 2003) has become a concept that is helpful in seeing what kind of new relationships are emerging in the production of knowledge and how these change the core competencies and positions of future professionals.

According to a Finnish group of researchers on expertise and learning (Hakkarainen et al. 2004, 8-15), three different metaphors of learning can be found: the individual acquisition model, the participation model and the knowledge creation model. Traditionally expertise is based on ideas of competencies based on individual abilities and dispositions and the concept of expertise refers to a wellorganised body of domain-specific knowledge usable in effectively solving complex problems in a stable context. The educational and learning model implied in this can be called the acquisition metaphor. According to this model, learning is a process of transmitting knowledge to an individual learner. Another approach would be the participation model. This model emphasises the role of social communities in the development of expertise and learning as an interactive process of participating in various cultural practices and shared learning activities, rather than a simple process of individual knowledge formation. Knowledge here is rather seen as an aspect of participation in cultural practice than existing either in a world of its own or in individual minds. Neither of these metaphors, however, appears to address the processes of deliberately creating and advancing knowledge, which would be essential for modern society. A third way, a knowledge-creation metaphor, is therefore needed. According to this metaphor, learning is seen as 'analogous to innovative processes of inquiry where new ideas, tools and practices are created, and the initial knowledge is either substantially enriched or significantly transformed during the processes' (Hakkarainen et al. 2004, 12). The issue is about encouraging formation of new knowledge and innovations rather than adaptation to the existing culture or assimilation of current knowledge. This kind of learning can be seen as a collaborative effort and individual initiative embedded in fertile collaborative practice is the basis for an innovative community. The production and education of experts within this approach require a combination and simultaneous adoption of all the three metaphors of learning at the levels of individual, community and organisation. Knowledge and expertise are also understood to be in a new way reflexive and contextual by their nature very much due to contingency and ambiguity in the emerging knowledge society. There is a shift from acquisition and transmission of knowledge to construction and invention of knowledge, towards innovative knowledge production (Nowotny 2000).

A central theme within these discourses is the search for models of collaborative and innovative knowledge production and learning allowing the search for alternative methods of action and innovation. Many of these models will include moments for research, critical reflection, studying, experimentation and evaluation following the same cyclical ideas that can be found in the Kolbian (Kolb 1984) model of experiential learning or the ideas of expansive learning (Engeström 1992; 2005). What is emerging is a new understanding of expertise as networked expertise. Networked expertise is a dynamic, knowledge creative and innovative expertise and refers to 'higher-level cognitive competencies that arise, in appropriate environments, from sustained collaborative efforts to solve problems and build knowledge together' (Hakkarainen et al. 2004, 9). Social work expertise by no means consists of only cognitive elements, but includes and integrates formal theoretical (factual and conceptual), practical and experiential (procedural knowledge and skills, tacit and intuitive) and self-regulative (meta-cognitive and reflective) elements (Tynjälä 2004, 176). Ideas of expertise and expansive and transformative learning have been central in developing social work education (e.g. Yellolly & Henkel 1995; Gould & Taylor 1996).

In social work, this shift toward constructive, reflexive and innovative networked expertise matches the urge to cope with the ever-changing complexity that has to be dealt with even in the everyday practices of the profession (Karvinen-Niinikoski 2004). At the same time, however, there are hardening demands for the profession to show a kind of more traditional professional expertise according to the model of evidence-based practices, searching for the best scientific evidence of good practices and effectiveness of the services delivered (Fisher 2002; Thyer & Kazi 2004). Despite these partly opposite trends in the development of expertise, one can consider that the need for research-oriented practice becomes ever more obvious, especially when the task of producing knowledge and social reports from the everyday life of citizens is added to the workload of social workers (Hussi 2005; Närhi 2004).

Research-oriented social work as a professional ideal for Finnish social work education and practice

The concepts of research-oriented, researching-practice and practitioners as researchers have been central to the Finnish debate on social work education since the 1980s. The agreement that the qualifications for a competent social worker should be at Masters degree level has led to a strong emphasis on the production of researchoriented practitioners and on establishing a field of social work research and methodological development in Finland. Much of this research-oriented ethos stems from the old professionalistic interests of making social work an academic profession, but also to a large extent from the vision of social work expertise as knowledgecreative and reflective and heavily practice and context related. Social work education in Finland currently follows these ideals, providing the qualified professional social worker with a Masters degree in social work including researcher education. This is the basic degree for social workers in Finland and Finnish qualified social workers are thus also entitled to scientific post-graduate education for the doctoral degree (Satka & Karvinen 1999).

Concern about social workers' lack of research-mindedness, in other words their low individual adoption and interest in and 'lazy' use of research-based knowledge and their lack of ongoing attempts to keep abreast of up-to-date research findings and professional knowledge which has been reported in the UK and Sweden (Bergmark & Lundström 2002), is however familiar also in Finland (Mäntysaari 1999). Besides the so-called 'culture of silence' (Mutka 1998; Satka & Karvinen 1999) there are many reasons discussed in the latest social work research (e.g. Osmond & O'Connor 2004) about why social workers express difficulties in claiming their professional expertise. The concern about a lack of research-mindedness can also be considered to be lying behind national government-funded programmes for knowledge- based social services in Scandinavia and the UK [e.g. the establishment of the Social Care Institute of Excellence (SCIE) in the UK or the Institute of Evidencebased Social Work Practice (IMS) in Sweden]. In these programmes one of the main goals is to produce a solid and evidence-based knowledge base for social care and to create organisational structures for the dissemination and use of this knowledge in decision-making as well as in professional practices (Fisher 2002). One can conclude that at the same time as the traditional expertise is being questioned by recent research (Hakkarainen et al. 2004) there seems to be an ongoing and deep-rooted political process of modernising services, management and education in the social field according to neo-professional revival of the traditional dream of individual professional expertise and technical rationality. These are, however, quickly altering debates and at the moment there is emerging, e.g. in SCIE, a policy of inclusive systematic knowledge reviews, where the aim is to incorporate all kinds of studies and different kinds of knowledge in a dialogue with a wide range of stakeholders for a democratic knowledge production for underpinning evidence-based social welfare (Fisher 2005).

The urge towards research-based or knowledge-based services and professional practices carries with it many professional and managerial interests and could be called a kind of neo-professionalism under the wings of new-managerialism (Parton 2004). The grounds for the importance of research-orientation in social work education can, however, also be found in the processes of generating reflexive expertise and producing new and innovative knowledge in our changing world (Fook 2004). Research-mindedness is a concept used by SCIE in the British approaches for knowledge-based services and concerns very much the dissemination and use of research-based knowledge in decision-making and professional practice by individuals even though the organisational and cultural aspects are recognised (Walter et al. 2004). Another concept brought into this debate about developing social care and social work practices is learning-mindedness (Martinsen 2004, 299), which refers to the ideas of learning organisations and learning working cultures in developing social work expertise. This vision comes very close to the participation perspective (Hakkarainen et al. 2004) discussed above. The third, the Finnish version, that could be called practice-research-mindedness, implies the ideal of a researching-practitioner and practice research and innovative knowledge production (Karvinen-Niinikoski 2005).

Anyway, the great challenge and difficulty in social work is to cope with uncertainty and continuous change, the urge to interpret and create understanding according to the different and particular living situations of people and to find optional contextual and reflective ways and methods in solving and combating social problems. What is needed is a kind of new expertise that steps out from the traditional hierarchical expert positions into different negotiating contexts where the people and their networks are given a voice of expertise in their own life in finding solutions for the problems to be solved.

New understanding of expertise and knowledge and changing paradigms for knowledge production

According to recent research about the so-called post-modern knowledge society and research in learning and research in professional expertise (e.g. Bereiter & Scardamalia 1993; Eräsaari 2003; Hakkarainen et al. 2004; Saaristo 2000; Karvinen 1999; Tynjälä et al. 1997) it can be concluded that our understanding of knowledge and knowledge generation is changing as well as the relationship of knowledge and knowing reflected in the concept of expertise. The position of scientists and professionals as experts and knowledge creators is re-constructed in relation to the expertise contained in the personal experience of both practitioners and citizens, the users and providers of human services in our case. The new ideas of expertise and knowledge emphasise new kinds of negotiations, co-operational and networking environments in the processes of learning and of knowledge production. Expertise and knowledge are understood as more open and dialogical and even conditional for negotiations. They are seen to be context-dependent (Nowotny 2000), the context being an important source for generation and validation of knowledge. Additionally, the knowledge of street level professionals and the lay-expertise of service-users are seen as necessary parts in the dialogue.

There is a need for new kinds of mechanisms of innovative knowledge production, forums for the dialogue in promoting knowledge creation and an epistemic pluralism (e.g. Nonaka et al. 2000; Nowotny et al. 2004). All this sounds familiar from the angle of social work and could be called reflexive expertise. Reflexive expertise can be regarded as a kind of orientation process relating experience to powerful meanings and calling also for an epistemological standpoint in contextual and experiential factors of knowledge generation without excluding forms of counter-expertise or lay experience (Eräsaari 2003). This involvement in social life and appropriation within everyday life itself is a basic and traditional element in social work, but a new feature of 'expert knowledge' in general (Fook et al. 2000). Reflexivity can be considered as one of the core qualifications of future social workers and it connotes anchorage in researching skills, as reflexivity calls for (re)conceptualisation and creativity in professional practices where the issue is about dealing with something the does not even exist, yet, but has to be constructed, designed and learned (e.g. Engeström 1992). Instead of traditional knowledge development, gradual accumulation of knowledge or constant epistemological revolutions we now have to look for spatial arrangements and transformations in the relationships between these arrangements (Eräsaari 2003). This is a challenge for social work education in creating forums for learning and knowledge creation and production and learning.

Open expertise and paradigm shifts in knowledge production in social work

When looking at the developments in expertise and knowledge production there seem to be many parallel processes going on in social work practice and education. They reflect the changes and challenges in professional practices. A paradigm shift or emergence of several parallel and changing paradigms for knowledge production and for understanding of expertise in social work can be recognised, as described in Figure 1.

The pools in looking at the changes and development in expertise and knowledge production are open and closed expertise, the vertical pools in the figure. Open expertise recognises uncertainty and instead of claiming

instituionalized
closed expertise

| academic traditions; monopol. knowledge & professionalised technical rationlity | emerging new structures and forms; EBP; knowledge management; reflective practice |
| professional traditions; pragmatic and experiential knowledge; practice | critical reflection & partnership in knowing; critical practice -research and researcher orientation |

established/ traditional knowledge production

emerging knowledge production

reflexive, open expertise

Figure 1 Paradigms for knowledge production and expertise: towards critical practice research and researcher orientation in social work (compiled by Lymbery, 2003, p. 112).

to be the only one to possess proper knowledge and professional skills, it will be open to questioning, communication and even to polemics as well as having a willingness to negotiate and reconstruct expertise according to the different contexts of action. The context (the space for communication) is left open (to allow for communication) (Eräsaari 2003). Closed expertise, as opposed to open, is a severe and unconditional strategy, ethos or mentality, which creates a strong link between core knowledge and specific advice or recommendations. This form of expertise prevails in the administrative traditions and may be even strengthening in social work through managerialist ideas of knowledge and evidence-based practices. In its very essence social work, however, inclines towards open expertise, for example, through being client-centred. On the horizontal level there are pools of traditional and emerging knowledge production. In social work there is a long tradition of practice development and teaching based on practice-knowledge and experience and aiming at critical professionality. Both the institutionalisation and academisation of social work professions have brought with them strong elements of knowledge production and research for strengthening social work expertise. Today the evidence-based movement promotes strongly a kind of neo-professionalism, which in many cases may be quite opposite to the developments and demands of reflexive expertise seen in the ideas of contextual and critical practices. Instead of hierarchical expertise to find the best solution there is the search for establishing arenas, if not agoras, for knowing in partnership and establishing contextual and creative knowledge-production. However, instead of provoking dualisms of old and new, the idea of looking at the different traditions and paradigms obviously with different ideas of expertise is to describe the dynamic forces of creating social work expertise for today and for the future (Karvinen-Niinikoski 2005).

Developing social work expertise and knowledge production: The importance of researcher education

The process of knowledge production has received new emphases in the generation of expertise. There is a shift from the acquisition of knowledge towards reflective knowledge building and innovations. The understanding and qualifications of this new kind of expertise call for conscious epistemological and methodological approaches discussed and learned in researcher education aimed at knowledge production in social work as an essential part of professional training (Karvinen 1999). Contextual practice is an emerging concept in social work in response to these changes in understanding expertise (Fook 2002, 142- 147; Healy 2003; Yliruka 2005). Practice-research is an emerging concept for describing the new relationships of knowing and knowledge creation the building of professional expertise and the discipline of social work (Shaw 2005; Satka et al. 2005). Practice-research includes, aside from the traditional understanding of adaptive-research, an idea of a research field with special epistemological and methodological approaches and a specific and innovative culture for knowledge creation following the ideals of open and networking expertise with a close practice-relationship. It also includes practitioners as researchers and knowledge producers of their own practice and of them developing a critical relationship to it.

The very essence of expertise within a rapidly transforming society tends to be the capability of continuously expanding one's current competencies. It is very dynamic by its nature. This implies a progressive problem-solving as a basic element of expertise. This means that an actor will continuously address more challenging problems, deepen his or her knowledge, and function at the edge of his or her competence as accumulation of experience decreases the cognitive processing load. This kind of expertise relying on progressive problem solving can be called dynamic expertise (Hakkarainen et al. 2004, 35- 41). Dynamic expertise not only parallels the research process to a great extent, but also calls for researcher-orientation as a basic element.

Expertise as progressive problem-solving will have to integrate the processes of knowledge generation from all three different perspectives: expertise as knowledge acquisition for the individual expert, expertise as social-cultural processes of knowing, and expertise as generating new knowledge and overcoming the old solutions and achieving innovations. What is important both in developing the professional practices and educating future social work practitioners is to create structures that support and integrate all these elements. It is an issue of creating a joint developmental culture for practice, research, learning and developmental work.

Research-mindedness in social work education: Educating reflexive experts

Research-mindedness sounds like a good fit as a goal in social work education. Especially at the Masters level of study according to the Bologna model, the concept needs to be extended towards the reflexive and progressive expertise discussed in this paper. In reflexive expertise there is an inclination toward knowledge creation and also an understanding of expertise not only as an individual stance studied and gained within university degree studies, but as a shared and dynamic one gained in networking and knowledge creative communities of practice, where practice and research meet in a creative dialogue of developing social work. This kind of practiceresearch-mindedness is a goal in the Finnish developmental work for social work education (Satka et al. 2005) aiming at reflexive expertise. Though there is a long tradition of researcher education in social work there is still a long way to go in order to create structures for integrating research into practice, in order to educate reflective practitioners with practice-research-mindedness.

In Finnish social work education there is an on-going renewal process, not only due to the Bologna process but due to the efforts in integrating practice, teaching and research in a developmental way in order to promote the social work profession and education as progressive forces in promoting social-welfare services to meet citizens' needs. There is experience over two decades in establishing university-based teaching and researching units for this integrative work. The latest development has been the establishment of a nationwide network of centres for excellence and expertise in the field of social welfare and social work. This process has been strongly supported by governmental funding and a national project and programme, Social Work 2015, for promoting social work development. In these processes practice-research-mindedness is one line to be supported along with other, more administrative goals. Important steps in the field of social work education have been the establishment of social work as an autonomous university discipline. Education for reflexive expertise is important in the five advanced level specialist social worker programmes called professionallicenciate degrees. The specialisation is provided in the following areas: children and youth, marginalisation processes, community work, rehabilitation and empowerment,

and service management and leadership. In these programmes the idea of reflexive expertise is central, as the aim is to give experienced social workers the task to construct and create special social work expertise on the basis of their own practical experience and expertise gained in their working lives. Doctoral programmes for social workers, which are provided both at the national level and by each of the six universities responsible for social work, also emphasise the importance of reflexive relation to social work practice. Also at ground level professional education there are creative integrative efforts for bringing teaching, research and researcher training closer to practice, for example Helsinki University has established, together with Helsinki and other cities in the Helsinki metropolitan area, teaching and researching units and clinics for social work (for example, Heikki Waris-instituet and Matilda Wrede-clinic; Praksis-unit). The aim is to create a joint developmental culture with practice institutions, structures for creative knowledge production and arenas for co-operative learning. Also providing opportunities for practising social workers and students to run research on their own work and social work practice is important. The idea of reflexive and developmental expertise is also central in the efforts of establishing a network of trained practice-teachers who are provided with a central role in creating the structures and practices for learning and teaching in reflexive practice (Karvinen-Niinikoski 2005; Yliruka 2005).

Conclusion

I have stated that research and researcher education provide some specific opportunities in developing social work expertise and in innovative knowledge production in the field. It is the dialogical dynamics in different kinds of knowledge and differentiating contexts for the generation of knowledge and expertise that make the understanding of research and the need for researcher education necessary in the education of future social work professionals. Seeing expertise as a dynamic and progressive problem-solving process and as an issue of knowledge creation (Hakkarainen et al. 2004, 39; 194) also opens up new ways of combining practice development and social work education. The emphasis is on knowledge creation and innovations, which are by no means territories for outside experts, but for a kind of knowledge-creating community for learning and knowledge management (Nonaka et al. 2000), where the knowledge creation and production in the every-day professional practices are integrated into research-based knowledge production.

This is also part of the Finnish ideal for social work education, the researcherorientation, the practice-research-mindedness, which could be used for describing a professional who is trained for and given opportunities for taking a role of a researcher as an integrated part of professional practices. The issue is not only about individual expertise but also about co-operative aspects of expert-communities and actually something that goes beyond these. One basic, underlying problem is the one that is so difficult to go beyond. It is the problem of integrating research and professional practice. A challenge for social work education is to produce for the future knowledge-active and creative professionals capable of innovative knowledge production. The problem with this idea has been the prevailing tradition of understanding expertise as individual knowledge acquisition. The late efforts at Helsinki University in establishing a new kind of teaching and researching cooperation with the practice field in the context of social work education and the developmental work for the discipline of social work is strongly looking forwards towards the developing ideas of networked and dynamic expertise and practiceresearch. By integrating researcher and practitioner education in the field of practiceresearch, social work education might be able to develop a curriculum for meeting the needs for flexibility in the emerging European knowledge-society.

References

Bereiter, C. & Scardamalia, M. (1993): *Surpassing Ourselves: An Inquiry into the Nature and Implications of Expertise*. Chicago: Open Court

Bergmark, A. & Lundström, T. (2002): Education, practice and research: knowledge and attitudes toknowledge, *Social Work Education* 21 (3) pp. 359- 373

Engeström, Y. (1992): *Interactive expertise. Studies in distributed working intelligence*, Research Bulletin, vol. 83, Department of Education, University of Helsinki, Helsinki: Yliopistopaino

Engeström, Y. (2005): *Developmental Work Research. Expanding Activity Theory in Practice*. International Cultural-historical Human Sciences 12, Berlin: Lehmans Media

Eräsaari, R. (2003): Open-context expertise. In *Yearbook 2003 of the Institute for Advanced Studies on Science, Technology and Society, Tecnik- und Wissenschaftsforschung* [Science and Technology Studies] A. Bamme, G. Gertzinger & B. Wieser (eds), Vol. 41, Profil, München-Wien, pp. 31- 65

Eraut, M. (1995): *Developing Professional Knowledge and Competence*. London: Falmer

Fisher, M. (2002): The social care institute for excellence: the role of a national institute in developing knowledge and practice in social care, *Social Work and Social Sciences Review* 10 (2) pp. 36- 64

Fisher, M. (2005): *Knowledge Production for Social Welfare: Enhancing the Evidence Base*, forthcoming

Fook, J. (2000): Deconstructing and reconstructing professional expertise. In B. Fawcett (ed.) Practice and Research in Social Work. *Postmodern Feminist Perspective*. pp. 104- 119

Fook, J. (2002): *Social Work: Critical Theory and Practice*. London: Sage

Fook, J. (2004): What professionals need from research. Beyond evidence-based practice, In D. Smith (ed.) *Social Work and Evidence-based Practice*. Research Highlights in Social Work 45, London: Jessica Kingsley. pp. 29- 46

Fook, J., Ryan, M. & Hawkins, L (2000): *Professional Expertise. Practice, Theory and Education for Working in Uncertainty*, London: Whiting & Birch

Gould, N. & Taylor, I. (eds) (1996): *Reflective Learning for Social Work*. Aldershot: Arena

Hakkarainen, K., Palonen, T., Paavola, S. & Lehtinen, E. (2004) *Communities of Networked Expertise. Professional and Educational Perspectives*, Sitra's (The Finnish National Fund for Research and Development) Publication Series, no. 257, Oxford: Elsevier Ltd

Healy, K. (2003): *Participatory Knowledge Creation in Social Work: Recognising*

Diversity, Promoting Collaboration, Nordic Conference of Schools of Social Work, SSKH, Helsinki

Hussi, T. (2005): Sosiaalinen raportointi kokemustiedon käsitteellistäjänä, In M. Satka, S. Karvinen-Niinikoski, M. Nylund & S. Hoikkala (eds) *,Sosiaalityön käytäntötutkimus* Helsinki: Palmenia-Kustannus. pp. 144- 158

Karvinen, S. (1999): The methodological tensions in Finnish social work research, In S. Karvinen, T. Pösö & M.Satka (eds) *Reconstructing Social Work Research. Finnish Methodological Adaptations* , SoPhi, University of Jyväskylä, Jyväskylä. pp. 277- 303

Karvinen-Niinikoski, S. (2004): Social work supervision: contributing to innovative knowledge production and open expertise, In N. Gould & M. Baldwin (eds) *Social Work, Critical Reflection and the Learning Organisation*, Aldershot: Ashgate,. pp. 23- 39

Karvinen-Niinikoski, S. (2005): Sosiaalityön opetus, tutkimus ja kehittyvä asiantuntijuus, In M. Satka, S. Karvinen-Niinikoski, M. Nylund & S.Hoikkala (eds) *Sosiaalityön käytäntötutkimus* Helsinki: Palmenia-Kustannus. pp. 73- 96

Kolb, D. A. (1984): *Experiential Learning. Experience as the Source of Learning and Development*, Englewood Cliffs, NJ: Prentice Hall

Lymbery, M. (2003): Negotiating contradictions between competence and creativity in social work education, *Journal of Social Work* 3(1) pp. 99- 117

Mäntysaari, M. (1999): Sosiaalityön tutkimuksen suuntaamisesta. Sosiaalityön tietoperusta. *Janus* 4 (7) pp. 355- 366

Martinsen, E. (2004): "Evidensbasert" praksis og ideologi. Nordisk sosialt arbeid , vol. 24, pp 290- 302

Mutka, U. (1998): *Sosiaalityön neljäs käänne. Asiantuntijuuden mahdollisuudet vahvan hyvinvointivaltion jälkeen*, SoPhi, Jyväskylä

Närhi, K. (2004): The Eco-social Approach in Social Work and the Challenges to the Expertise of Social Work , *University* of Jyväskylä, Jyväskylä Studies in Education, Psychology and Social Research 243

Nonaka, I., Toyama, R. & Konno, N. (2000): SECI, Ba and leadership: a unified model of dynamic knowledge creation, *Long Range Planning* ,vol. 33, pp. 5- 34

Nowotny, H. (2000): Transgressive competence. The narrative of expertise, *European Journal of Social Theory* 3 (1) pp. 5- 21

Nowotny, H., Scott, P. & Gibbons, M. (2004): *Re-thinking Science. Knowledge and the Public in the Age of Uncertainty*, Cambridge: Politi Press

Osmond, J. & O'Connor, I. (2004): Formalizing the unformalized: practitioners' communication of knowledge in practice. *British Journal of Social Work*, vol. 34, pp. 677- 692

Parton, N. (2004): Post-theories for practice: challenging the dogmas. In L. Davies & P. Leonard (eds) *Social Work in a Corporate Era. Practice of Power and Resistance.* Aldershot: Ashgate. pp. 31- 44

Saaristo, K. (2000): *Avoin asiantuntijuus. Ymparistokysymys ja monimuotoinen ekspertiisi [Open Expertise. The Environmental Question and Multiple Expertise],* Research Center for Contemporary Culture, University of Jyvaskylä

Satka, M. & Karvinen, S. (1999): The contemporary reconstruction of Finnish social work expertise. *European Journal of Social Work* 2 (2) pp. 119- 129

Satka, M., Karvinen-Niinikoski, S., Nylund, M. & Hoikkala, S. (2005): Mitä on sosiaalityön käytäntötutkimus? ['What is practice-research in social work?'], In M. Satka, S. Karvinen-Niinikoski, M. Nylund & S. Hoikkala (eds) *Sosiaalityön käytäntötutkimus.* Helsinki: Palmenia- Kustannus. pp. 9- 19

Shaw, I. (2005): *Critical social science and practice research. British Journal of Social Work,* forthcoming

Thyer, B. & Kazi, M. A. F. (eds) (2004): *International Perspectives on Evidence-based Practice in Social Work ,* Venture Press, Birmingham

Tynjälä, P. (2004): Asiantuntijuus ja työkulttuurit opettajan ammatissa. Kasvatus 35 (2) pp. 174- 190

Tynjälä, P., Nuutinen, A., Eteläpelto, A., Kirjonen, J.i & Remes, P. (1997): The acquisition of professional expertise - a challenge for educational research. *Scandinavian Journal of Educational Research* 41 (3- 4) pp. 475- 494

Walter, I., Nutley, S., Perry-Smith, J., McNeisch, D. & Frost, S. (2004): Improving the use of research in social care practice. *Knowledge Review 7,* Social Care Institute of Excellence. Available at www.scie.org.uk/publications/knowledgereviews/kr07.pdf

Webb, S. A. (2001): Some considerations on the validity of evidence-based practice in social work. *British Journal of Social Work* 31 (1) pp. 57- 59

Yellolly, M. & Henkel, M. (eds) (1995): *Learning and Teaching in Social Work. Towards Reflective Practice.* London: Jessica Kingsley

Yliruka, L. (2005): Sosiaalityön itsearviointi kontekstuaalisena käytäntönä. In Sosiaalityön käytäntötutkimus M. Satka, S. Karvinen-Niinikoski, M. Nylund & S. Hoikkala (eds) Palmenia-Kustannus, Helsinki, pp. 124- 143

Acknowledgement

This chapter was first published in *European Journal of Social Work* Vol. 8, No. 3, September 2005, pp. 259-271.

3
Knowledge production and social work: Forming knowledge production

Tove Rasmussen

Introduction

Not only new knowledge but also knowledge production itself has become an important issue in social work. Knowledge in social work has been discussed with respect to its reliability and utility (for example, evidence-based social work), whether it is situated, tacit or reflexive, and as professional knowledge under pressure, but increasingly the question of knowledge production itself has become an issue. An important aspect of practice research is that it represents a challenge to the dominant institutionalization of knowledge production. In this respect, the aim of practice research is to claim legitimacy for certain types of knowledge and to develop processes to produce them.

This is a challenge in a knowledge or information society (Bell 1974) which is characterized by several new tendencies in the governing and production of knowledge. Practice research may be an answer to the scepticism about, and criticisms of, (traditional) expert knowledge in late modernity (Giddens 2000) or in the risk society (Beck 1992). If we consider practice research as a particular form of knowledge production and 'implementation', three perspectives will help us understand the development of such knowledge: the epistemology, sociology of knowledge and conceptualization of professions. Using different theories and research results, the aim here is to use a different perspective to sketch the point of departure, prerequisites and possible dilemmas for practice research rather than to present any kind of fully developed theory in the area.

From knowledge to knowledge production

Society is changing ever more rapidly, challenging many of the hitherto known 'ways of thinking' and categories used in everyday life, as well as in the social sciences.

> In my view it simply has become too difficult not to be a constructivist. Regardless of the field of social science one focuses on, the most noticeable thing is change, and changes often touch upon or challenge fundamental values, raising questions about the constituent character of what we see. (Åkerstrøm Andersen 1999, 9)[1]

Not only are we witnessing change and frequent suggestions (or demands) to use new concepts but also there are clear signs that knowledge has gained another role in society. The simple, rational (but now also naïve) picture of neutral knowledge, that it is *first* produced and *later* used in different areas, is increasingly being replaced by an almost opposite logic. Now, when a new agenda, way of branding or strategy is decided, there is a demand for knowledge to support the decisions.

> Within government ... discursive institutions have been established in order to develop scientific discourses and to diagnose the condition of society, with the intention of controlling the political agenda, defining the framework for negotiation and installing a sense of responsibility in organisations, political parties and individuals. (Åkerstrøm Andersen 1999, 11)

Constructivist perspectives are one way of dealing with the 'hidden premises' of knowledge production. Instead of using the 'new language' and concepts as points of departure in research, research can be used to reveal the creation of these new perspectives, concepts and agendas, or in other words to de-ontologize the creations.

The so-called 'epistemological turn', which has had a widespread influence in English language discussions of social work (Healy 2000; Howe 1994; Leonard 1994; Parton 1995; Parton & O'Byrne 2000; Pease & Fook 1999) (Leonard 1994)[2] can be seen (as suggested above) as a necessarily scientific answer to important changes in the knowledge society. Although some of the premises of 'postmodernism' can be debated, there is no doubt that this development in scientific research has brought new perspectives on social work to the field, as well as generating new knowledge.

When we recognize that one of the premises of the social sciences must be the idea that societal phenomena are inseparable from our subjective conceptions of them (leaving no 'neutral place' for the scientist), the question of knowledge – everyday knowledge as well as scientific knowledge – takes on new meaning. It becomes relevant to pose questions about different types of knowledge, such as practice knowledge, which can be seen as simply different from scientific knowledge rather than inferior to it. It becomes important to work not only with the concepts and categories used in social work practice but also with those used in science. We should not assume that science possesses the only 'true' concepts, theories and categories.[3] We should also be willing to question the concept of expertise, which has often been conceptualized in traditional science as a form of scientific knowledge rather than as a 'way of thinking' that is useful to practitioners (Karvinen-Niinikoski 2005; Satka & Karvinen 1999; Schön 2001).

The epistemological turn, read as excluding naïve realist and universal perspectives, can also be seen as one of the prerequisites for practice research, or at least practice research in its newly relevant incarnation. This does not mean that practice research should be restricted to one (for example, purely constructivist) scientific perspective but only that in addition to producing scientific knowledge (which is presumed to be useful for social work), practice research can also question how knowledge is produced and used. If social science cannot deliver universal (or just relatively stable and transnational) knowledge about dominant social problems (and the best ways to solve them),[4] or even produce common reliable concepts and categories, the obvious answer is to produce knowledge in the context where it will be used. We must also consider how different forms of knowledge can be combined or brought into a fruitful interplay. If it is not possible to define the different problems that social workers encounter or to determine relevant measures, then the question of how social phenomena are conceptualized becomes as important as the phenomena themselves, and it becomes important in turn to consider how different conceptions of social phenomena are developed in relation to practice research.

These types of questions and discussions, and the growing strategic attitude towards knowledge production in different fields of society, clearly point to the need for other types of knowledge production, such as those generated in practice research.

The institutional aspect of (scientific) knowledge production

Knowledge production can be discussed in terms of the sociology of knowledge.[5] From this perspective, it becomes important to analyse the institutionalization of knowledge production. The dominant form of institutionalization expresses the normal conceptions of what constitutes different types of knowledge, possible hierarchies of knowledge, and the formal procedures and institutions needed to produce, for example, scientific knowledge.

If practice research represents a challenge to the dominant institutionalization of knowledge production, we must examine the opportunities and difficulties this presents. Social institutions are not easily changed, but there are changes taking place in the relationship between knowledge production in the scientific and practical fields, and practice research is a part of those changes.

Gibbons and colleagues claim that the 'modes' or regimes of knowledge production have changed (Gibbons et al. 1994). The traditional institutionalization of knowledge production at universities or other scientific institutions is called 'Mode 1'. In this regime, knowledge is produced in traditional scientific hierarchies, organized in disciplines, and secured by peer reviews. Cognition and 'true' knowledge are the products. The emerging type of knowledge production, which tries to produce knowledge that is useful or relevant to actors outside the university, is called 'Mode 2'. It includes people from different fields (both inside and outside scientific institutions), tends to be transdisciplinary, and is organized in non-hierarchical networks. Rather than peer-reviewed products published in scientific journals, the products are evaluated on their usefulness in the context for which they are produced.

According to Gibbons et al. Mode 2 is a growing form of knowledge production that exists alongside the traditional Mode 1 form of knowledge production. Mode 2 represents a new way of organizing the interplay between science and society (Table 1).

A closer look at Mode 1 in relation to knowledge in social work is depicted in figure 1 overleaf.

The one-way arrow reflects how reliable knowledge is thought to be produced, and following the premises, it is only when practice in social work is based on implemented scientific knowledge that one can speak of knowledge-based (or traditional) professional work.

Table 1
Modes of knowledge production

	Mode 1	Mode 2
Orientation	Cognition	Usefulness, application
Formal organization	Universities,	Co-operation between scientific institutes different types of organizations, universities, companies, public sector, etc.
Organizational type	Scientific hierarchies	Networks
Knowledge	True	Reflexive
Output and quality control	Scientific journals, peer review	Networks, usefulness

It is questionable how closely this model reflects the reality of social work,[6] but it still represents the widespread and officially supported[7] conception of how knowledge in the field of social work is created and used. Some of the problems in the very long (and often unfruitful) discussion of the relation between theory and practice, could be attributed to this model (and to the epistemological turn noted previously): if the modelling of a situation is inconsistent with the way things are perceived to work, it will tend to produce a lack of understanding and/or inconsistencies in central concepts.

It seems obvious that the development of scientific knowledge production in social work could be fruitfully supplemented with knowledge production that follows the principles of Mode 2. Practice research is better characterized as this type of knowledge production. Mode 2 provides a much better framework for the central issues in practice research, because it more directly addresses the problems and needs of practitioners in the field. When practitioners form networks, they can develop the perspectives, concepts and categories that are relevant to their needs. The question of 'implementing' research results would drastically change under this regime, because the 'users' are also co-producers. By generating knowledge gained from different positions and perspectives, such research would be reflexive and well grounded in specific practices rather than presuming to produce the one right answer to address one pre-described category of problems or methods.

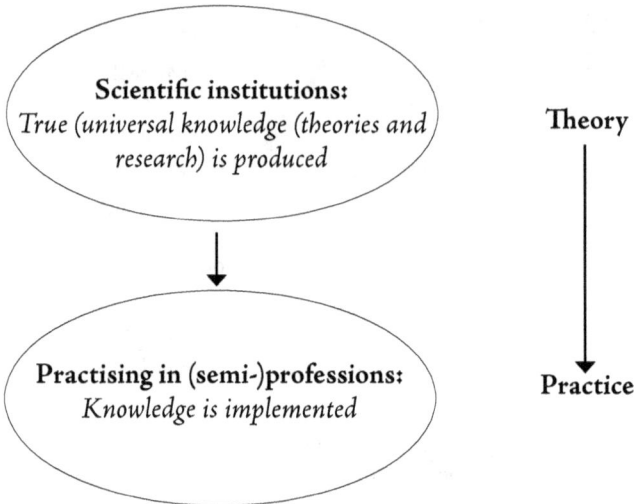

Figure 1

In its most radical form, the premises of practice research can be expressed in figure 2.

The process of knowledge production cannot be seen as restricted to the scientific field. Knowledge production (which involves the use of different perspectives or 'theories' and reflection) occurs not only in scientific fields but also in the practice of social work and in the daily life of the citizen as well, albeit with different premises and goals in different institutional settings. Practice research can be seen as a set of processes that organize and qualify knowledge production across different institutional settings.

However, there are still major dilemmas in using 'new modes' of knowledge production. Both inside and outside of science, institutionalized modes of knowledge production are deeply connected to the judgements of actors (including decision-makers) from different fields who define, for example, what is or is not scientific. The question is not just about making the most rational and justified choice about how to produce the most 'useful' knowledge. The 'status' of the knowledge that is produced can itself be important for the development of future knowledge production.

If Perlizzione is right, when he claims, that radical uncertainty or the epistemological turn on the one side replaced the modern image of knowledge as able to produce one description by, for example, shared concept and standardized ways of combining and analyzing facts – and on the other *preserved* that 'modernity has given science the status as the

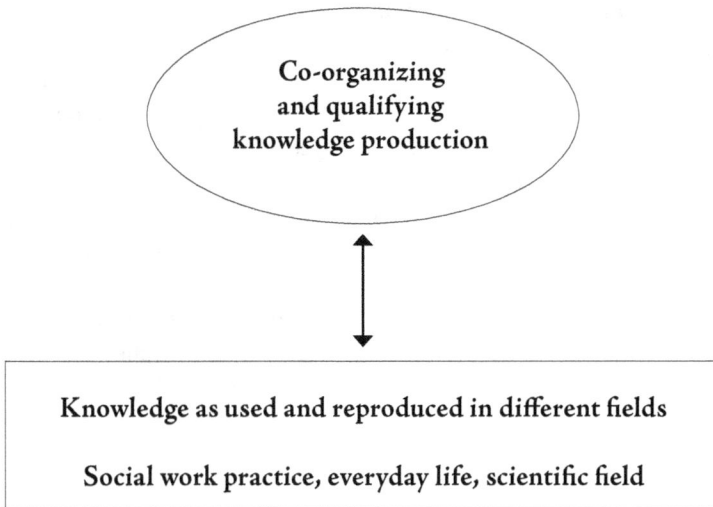

```
┌──────────────────────────────────┐
│          Co-organizing            │
│          and qualifying           │
│       knowledge production        │
└──────────────────────────────────┘

                  ↕

┌────────────────────────────────────────────────┐
│  Knowledge as used and reproduced in different fields │
│                                                    │
│  Social work practice, everyday life, scientific field │
└────────────────────────────────────────────────┘
```

Figure 2

only truly public knowledge' (Pellizzoni 2003), the distinction between scientific and other types of knowledge cannot be ignored in practice research.

Is it possible to preserve the status of the scientific part of knowledge production in Mode 2 when some of the hitherto important premises, procedures and institutions are questioned in the process of organizing and qualifying knowledge? Research shows that there might be difficulties.

With respect to Mode 2, some have questioned whether the description of the historical movement from Mode 1 to Mode 2 is adequate.[9] If it is not, one cannot expect ongoing changes in the criteria used to value the status of research (Pestre 2003).

Within science, researchers have identified problems in the status or symbolic capital (Albert 2003; Bourdieu 1996) of Mode 2 research, and questioned whether a trend towards strengthening Mode 2 types of knowledge production is valid. There may well be a return to Mode 1 approaches, even though there is pressure from 'epistemological turn' in its narrow and procedure prescribing sense, critics regarding its 'ritualistic mode of rationality' (Starbuck 2006), where the accepted methods and questions are often preferred (and supported by research organizations) over attempts to answer important new research questions. Despite these criticisms, symbolic capital in scientific fields still tends to hinge on Mode 1 knowledge production, which can be published in prestigious peer-reviewed journals.[10] New systems of evaluating research by counting published output may reinforce this tendency (depending on the exact form of system), even if unintentionally. Mode 2 research, then, may be regarded (and perhaps also formally measured) as 'low-grade' research (low symbolic capital), which may make it difficult to finance projects, recruit researchers and fill positions. There is, however, no direct connection between symbolic capital in scientific fields and symbolic capital in other fields, such as outside institutions, which can be partners in research and financing.

Outside of science, and in the relationship between scientific and other fields (for example, the political), Mode 2 research approaches also have problems related to the traditional institutionalization of knowledge production. Discussions of, and political support for, evidence-based professional work might be taken as an illustration.

Evidence based research in social work has grown and gained considerable acceptance in political systems in Nordic Countries (see, for example, the specific type of evidence-based research advocated by the Nordic Campbell Center.[11])As a form of knowledge production, evidence-based research in social work has characteristics of both Mode 1 and Mode 2 regimes. It is similar to Mode 2 research approaches because it aims to produce useful and socially relevant information, and because it emphasizes networking with politicians, leaders in the field and other professionals.[12] However, evidence based-knowledge production is also similar to Mode 1 research approaches in their most traditional form, because it:

- claims to be scientific *because* specific methods, procedures and peer review activities, are used,
- claims to produce universal knowledge, and
- uses the traditional model for application or implementation (as described above).

This type of evidence-based research follows the principles and methods of the natural sciences and in so doing draws on the prestige (or symbolic capital) of traditional natural science research.[13] Judged from a social science perspective, this kind of evidence-based knowledge has serious problems. Claims for universal knowledge about social conditions and processes have been heavily criticized in the sociological literature[14] and by the epistemological turn, both directly and indirectly (Krogstrup 2003; Pawson 2006)[15].

Despite these criticisms, from outside of science, the evidence-based researchers' claims to scientific rigor – RCT and meta reviews – may well be the most convincing argument they make for the value of the knowledge they produce.

Practice research, of course, will have to deal with these types of problems. The problem of the status of knowledge could raise considerations about how practice research is organized – how its processes and parts relate to the dominant forms of institutional research. However, it could also suggest the need for further discussion of the distinction between scientific knowledge and other types of valuable knowledge.

Professionalism and knowledge production in social work (practice)

For practice research, the conditions for and the framework of knowledge produced in practical social work is an important issue. As discussed with respect to scientific knowledge, knowledge derived from social work practice is gained in a particular societal context, and it should not be regarded as authentic knowledge. One of the important concepts connected to knowledge in social work practice is professionalism (or profession), which implies close connections to scientifically produced knowledge. To understand practice research in this area better, I shall examine current changes in the conditions for knowledge production in social work and its interplay with professionalism.

The traditional understanding of professions has been increasingly challenged in the last two to three decades (Evetts 2003; 2006; Gleeson & Knights 2006; Pfadenhauer 2006; Quicke 2000) This is most clearly reflected in interplay with changes in the welfare state, but it can also be seen in wider societal developments. Changes in the institutionalization of knowledge production have been less emphasized.

If we examine social work, we can see that knowledge is formed by different social processes (Philp 1979). Politics in the welfare state as well as common norms and ways to justify decisions in the modern society, form a framework for practice in social work. From this perspective, knowledge production at universities, in educational settings and in social work practice (as well as in practice research) is only part of the broader societal processes that form and reform social work.

In the traditional conceptualization of professionalism, knowledge is one of the core elements in most understandings of professions. Evetts, for example, regards 'profession as a generic group of occupations based on knowledge both technical and tacit' (Evetts 2003).

At the same time, though, professionalism is very intimately connected to the societal institutionalization and regulation of knowledge (and power). The Parsons-based school has identified professionalism as a normative value system in which professionals are seen as playing an important stabilizing role in society. In contrast, the Weber-inspired[16] understanding of professionalism regards it as an ideology that emphasizes self-interest, status and income (Evetts 2003; Hjort 2005). It has primarily been in writings from the Parsons-based school that the oft-mentioned characteristics of professional groups has been developed. It has been argued

> that professional work required a long and expensive education and training in order to acquire the necessary knowledge and expertise; professionals were autonomous and performed a public service; were guided in their decision-making by a professional ethic or code of conduct; they were in special relations of trust with clients as well as with managers/employers, and were altruistic and motivated by universalistic values. (Evetts 2006, 516)

The traditional (universal) welfare state and its organization has often been seen as an important framework for social work because it provides the subject of focus – the social problems, beneficiaries, means-based solutions (involving values and norms) to develop criteria of deservingness, and so on. Considering the welfare state in light of professional groups and knowledge production, another perspective becomes important. The specific organizational setting of the (traditional) welfare state can be described as a combination of bureaucracies and professions (Clarke & Newmann 1997; Freidson 2001). This specific organizational setting might be so common that it is (still) regarded as orthodox, and it forms the basis for how professionalism is understood. Co-existing bureaucratic and professional 'jurisdictions' and ways of doing things have properly always been competing (in this setting), but they also complement each other. Bureaucrats must accept at least a minimum of professional autonomy if the decisions made are to be seen as legitimately knowledge based or informed. Professionals, in turn, must accept at least a minimum of bureaucratic regulation if the decisions made are to be legal (Weber 1982).

Changes in professionalism are reflected in a wider societal context. It has been argued that professions have increasingly encountered problems with trust and legitimacy because of the loss of both cognitive and normative superiority in postmodern societies characterized by individualization and pluralization (Pfadenhauer 2006). The system and the client have lost confidence in the 'mono-occupational functional system' (Pfadenhauer 2006), and individualization and pluralization (which underlie the loss of universal truth in modernism) do not leave room for shared normative grounds.

An example of how 'shared normative grounds' have been lost in the Danish universal welfare state can perhaps be found as early as discussions in the 1980s about living conditions. We saw a movement away from seeking good living conditions for all to arguments for differential living conditions, determined according to different life-modes, and later, according to different individual lifestyles.[17] The loss of the cognitive and normative superiority of professions is illustrated by both politically oriented and research-oriented criticisms of social work. However, it is very difficult to separate various types of criticism from political agendas aimed at reforming the welfare state.

The relationship between changing views of professions and changes in the welfare states can also be illustrated by New Public Management and movements towards the management-oriented regime (Clarke & Newmann 1997), post-bureaucratic organizations (Svensson 2006), and the audit society (Costea & Crump 2008; Gleeson & Knights 2006) or neoliberal society (Sewpaul & Hölscher 2004).

In the last two decades, the Nordic welfare states (or societies) have been described as being significantly influenced by New Public Management.[18] In the public sector, well-known keywords such as privatization, (semi-) marketization, competition, output orientation, economic incentives as core regulation, contracting, low trust, professional leadership and free choice (as well as different models for governing contracts aimed at securing quality control)[19] have become orthodox, and they have collectively changed the 'logic' of the bureaucratic–professional regime seen hitherto.

In Nordic Welfare societies, the change in social work seems much more related to changes in the institutional framework for the regulation and processing of knowledge, services, and service providers (and receivers) than to changes in different policy areas.[20] Rather than change through traditional socio-political discussions, changes in the welfare states have taken place through depoliticized changes in discourses and regulations inside the public sector. Social work, as well as knowledge production in practical social work, is now being shaped in dramatically different political and institutional settings. The challenge facing professionals is profound.

As a result of changes in the public sector in the last few decades, the changes in professionalism have often been regarded as a kind of 'deprofessionalization', or even the dissolution of professions (Clarke & Newmann 1997; Svensson 2006).

> We use the term deprofessionalization to refer, first, to the fragmentation and routinization of social work and the concomitant loss of opportunities for exercise of creativity, reflexivity and discretion in the direct practice. (Healy & Meagher 2004)

Deprofessionalization is also understood here to be comprehensive – not only are less qualified staff being hired to do social work but also highly qualified professionals are working in positions where their knowledge and abilities are largely underutilized. Deprofessionalization also involves fragmentation, insecurity and uncertainty, as one's autonomy decreases and the demands for accountability increase (Gleeson & Knights 2006). Indeed, demands for accountability have replaced the trust people once gave to professionals. Examples of eroding autonomy under deprofessionalization include having to use set criteria for outputs rather than professional judgement, the standardization of decision-making, the use of 'global' procedures and regulations to guide work, and the implementation of evidence-based concepts that must be followed very closely.

In Denmark, professions have not only new organizational forms and partners but also new discourses and types of apparently non-political demands to contend with: output measures, demands for declarations or fully developed concepts for social work interventions (e.g. MST), demands to follow different kinds of procedures, and so on. Often, these demands are instituted under the guise of quality management,[21] and mandatory, bureaucratically decided methods in different areas of social work must be followed. Such demands, which contradict traditional political government, indirectly (but nevertheless, quite effectively) set norms for what constitutes valuable knowledge and interventions in social work. They also promote (sometimes as unintended consequences[22]) a development towards specific types of knowledge.

Parton reflects on these type of processes in relation to their impact on the knowledge in use. On the basis of the increasing influence of new information and communication technologies in British social work, he describes a change, where narrative-based ways of thinking and operating are replaced by data-based ways of thinking and operating.

> ... social workers are becoming, primarily, information processors. Not only can 'the subject' of social work knowledge be seen as being in the process of transformation into a series of discrete categories but also the 'social' nature of the work is disappearing. (Parton 2008)

Parton's description seems recognizable in the Nordic context as well, because the demands for knowledge (or data to monitor social work) have increased dramatically,[23] and the time spent in client contact has decreased to a minimum. The types of 'information' or 'data' collected in Nordic social work are, to a large extent, the same in nature as those described by Parton. They are the data that are readily processed in information and communication technologies, such as discrete dates and other indicators needed for outputs, service standards, etc.

In a more comprehensive public sector context, professional regulation in social work can be seen as being (partly) replaced by managerial regulation. The goals, framework, loyalty and identity of social work change from being derived by the profession to being mandated by (specific) management-driven private or public units, which are in competition with each other (Clarke & Newmann 1997) This can be seen as the unmaking of the profession.

This totally changed environment for social work professionals may change to a degree, where there is no empirical evidence to support the traditional conception of social work professionalism. Professionalism, however, may already have turned into something else. Paradoxically (but perhaps in line with increasing managerial regulation), it can be shown that since about the mid 1990s, the concept of professionalism has become attractive for different vocational groups as well as for some 'social systems' and states (Evetts 2003; Hanlon 1998). A new discourse about professionalism seems to have emerged, one in which professionalism is constructed more from 'above' or from outside the profession. In this discourse, professionalism is defined in company mission statements, recruitment campaigns, policy procedures and manuals, and in market slogans appealing to customers – or more generally speaking, 'as discourses of occupational change and social control' (Evetts 2003; 2006) Professionalism is used here, in line with the Parsons school, to reflect positive values, including trust. The autonomy of the profession at an organizational level,24 though, is not implied in this discourse.

In a knowledge production context, the insight that social work practice tends to become fragmented, routinized, and insecure, with knowledge tending to be more informational rather than creative, is important. However, the most important insight may be that the knowledge process in social work is increasingly governed from outside in ways that do not seem to support quality social work in the eyes of the profession. On the contrary, a picture of ever-worsening social work performed under ever-worsening conditions is emerging. This dark situation becomes still bleaker if we take a broader societal perspective and see that client confidence in the professions has been lost.

The dominant perspective on knowledge in the discussion of change in professionalism has been that of traditional professionalism. The cognitive- and expertise-oriented aspects of professionalism have been underdeveloped in this discussion. In other contexts, researchers have suggested that we need to change our understanding of expertise (Karvinen-Niinikoski 2005; Schön 2001). A new formulation of this aspect of professionalism, from the inside, may address some of the needs of the present situation.

In the following section, I shall try to sketch the changing understanding of expertise, which has been proposed elsewhere.

Knowledge production: Combining different perspectives

If we examine trends in knowledge production, at least two interconnected developments seem to characterize the current situation.

- The change in the role of the profession suggests a weaker *link* to the education of professionals and to (independent) scientific research in the area of the profession, and consequently, to the strengthening of bureaucratic and market-based knowledge production.
- Governmental changes in the types and forms of knowledge required to do social work change the form of knowledge production in practical social work – for example, management or 'systems' demands for the gathering of certain types of information, or their instructions for categories to use or procedures to follow, or restrictions on access to (and analysis of) information from models in other disciplines or professions – in short, the more governed knowledge or information

handling is in the social work practice, the more likely it is that the types of knowledge/information the social workers gather will change.[25] This change, along with new methods, procedures and categories of service users, etc., will likely also affect social workers' 'ways of thinking' and handling knowledge/information.

With respect to the change in the role of the profession, we have already seen that social workers have previously relied heavily on scientific research (depending on how closely we believe professionalism is connected to the logic of Mode 1 knowledge production, which was important in the historic forming of the professions). Svensson suggests the strongest possible connection between Mode 1 logic and professional knowledge.

> Professional knowledge is usually regarded as formal possession of credentials in a certain discipline not connected with practice or qualification at work. (Svensson 2006, p.585)

Parallel to newer discussions of expertise, he contrasts assertive knowledge (declarative knowledge, knowing what) with tacit knowledge, which is identified as the ability to recognize, to judge, to assess or to see patterns, and categorized as experimental knowledge (Svensson 2006).

Philp characterizes social work knowledge in the following way.

> One can characterise social work as straddling a split between internal subjective states, such as pain, want, suffering, love and hate, and objective characteristics, in that they are awarded statuses, such as old age, crime, debt, handicap, illness and madness. The knowledge produced under social work's regime of truth is one which describes a process whereby these individual states and objective statuses are transformed into a social subject. A subject marked by his capacities for self-determination, responsible citizenship, and general sociability. .... Social work knowledge, then, produces an individual whom we can regard as a subject because he does not have any overpowering objective or narcissistic characteristics. Social work knowledge attempts to demonstrate potential sociability.(Philp 1979, 92)

This is exemplified in the following.

The social worker does not say that the vandal did what he wanted to, for in doing so, the role of the social worker would disappear. What he does, rather, is to allude to the underlying character, the hidden depths, the essential good, the authentic and the unalienated. (Philp 1979, 99)

From this point of view, there is (in principle) no problem in the ongoing process of gathering information, which characterizes the objective status from 'outside', but there may be obstacles to gathering knowledge about the subjective and its transformation to sociability. In fact, the objective status does not qualify as social work knowledge. We can see, then, a possible loss in social work knowledge. It is the loss of a form of knowledge that cannot be compensated by traditional research or the knowledge or information that is processed by management layers in the social work organizations.[26]

If the 'knowledge aspect' of professionalism is emphasized, it seems that social work has never been comfortable with the traditional understanding (and institutionalization) of professionalism. To some degree, of course, this is also the case for other professions (Schön 2001). In social work, it is possible to obtain assertive knowledge about objective statuses, and bases for, and types of, transformation processes; but it does not seem possible to standardize meaningfully or to generalize the recognition processes and assessments that must be performed to distinguish between objective statuses and individual states. Formalizing all processes would imply a dramatic increase in the specificity of objective statuses and possible means for transformation, and it would reduce the citizen to a dysfunctional 'social machine', a picture that does not seem compatible with the social subject as a self-responsible (social) individual. If plurality and individuality have gained in importance, it could be argued that objective statuses must be held in more 'general' or 'abstract' categories, and means of transformation must be more varied and individually chosen.

If social work has been only partly (or poorly) served by traditional Mode 1 and profession-based knowledge, then more than just another type of research (Mode 2) is needed. We need research on objective statuses and individual states as well as new knowledge about various means of transformation that may be applicable in specific types of cases.

Conclusion

There is strong evidence that knowledge production in social work, in practice as well as in the scientific fields, has changed in several dimensions in the last two to three decades (in the Nordic countries, perhaps mostly in the last decade). The knowledge society (as well as the rise of late-modern, postmodern, and neoliberal societies) has been marked by new ways to produce, to govern, to qualify and to use knowledge, as well as widespread questioning of hitherto high-status expert knowledge, and in consequence the professions have been similarly affected..

At the same time, traditional universal welfare states, which (through bureaucratic professional regimes) have relied on the traditional institutionalization of knowledge production, have especially been transformed in this area. Trends in new types of institutionalization appear to have dismantled the traditional understanding of professions. More plainly speaking, one could say that the professions are no longer seen to have important knowledge about their clients, who, in turn, are now to be regarded as citizens who can speak and make decisions for themselves. Professions[27] have also become weaker in their claim to have the best knowledge about the fields in which they work. Managerial, administrative and bureaucratic systems, which formerly were regarded as 'interfering' with core processes in the production of knowledge and the practice of social work, now hold sway.

In part, changes in the public sector can be seen as responsible for the critical attitudes towards expertise in late-modern or postmodern society. More generally, changes in the public sector, which are undoubtedly based on chosen ideas of government, governance and management (and which properly will be changed in the following decades), will necessarily be seen as providing new answers to deeper societal changes. The situation seems to rule out a defense of the traditional core criteria of professions (expert knowledge based on education and traditional research) as realistic criteria for future social work.

Practice research can be regarded as one of the new(er) possible answers to create (a new) professionalism in social work. Despite changes in the public sector and the new relationship between social workers and those they serve, it seems unlikely that the central processes in social work (such as social transformation processes) have become superfluous. Practice research could, as suggested in the model described earlier, be a co-qualifying knowledge production process at the centre of social work expertise.

There are, however, several challenges in conducting practice research. It can be seen as having little status in scientific research fields. Conversely, it may be regarded as competing with the bureaucratic or managerial governing of knowledge production (or an activity that should be controlled by the bureaucracy). While it may be easier to follow the dominant institutional pathways, that may not be the most fruitful approach.

References

Åkerstrøm Andersen, Niels (1999): *Diskursive analysestrategier*, København: Nyt fra Samfundsvidenskaberne.

Åkerstrøm Andersen, N. (2006). *Borgerens kontraktliggørelse*. Kbh.: Hans Reitzel.

Albert, M. (2003). Universities and the market economy: The differential impact on knowledge.

Ansbøl, R. (2008). *Økonomisk styring, prioritering og planlægning i kommunerne: Introduktion til mål- og kontraktstyring, planlægningsværktøjer og metoder samt udfordringer i kommunerne* (6. udgave ed.): Frederiksberg: Danmarks Forvaltningshøjskole.

Beck, U. (1992): *Risk society: Towards a new modernity* (Reprinted ed.). London: Sage.

Bell, D. (1974): *The coming of post-industrial society : A venture in social forecasting.* London: Heinemann.

Berger, P. L., & Luckmann, T. (1971): *The social construction of reality: A treatise in the sociology of knowledge.* Harmondsworth, Middlesex: Penguin Books.

Bourdieu, P. (1996): *Symbolsk makt: Artikler i utvalg.* Oslo: Pax.

Busch, T. (2007): *Modernisering av offentlig sektor: Utfordringer, metoder og dilemmaer* (2. utgave ed.). Oslo: Universitetsforlaget.

Clarke, J., & Newmann, J. (1997): *The managerial state.* London: Sage publications.

Costea, B., & Crump, N. (2008): Managerialism, the therapeutic habitus and the self in contemporary organizing. *Human Relations, 61*(5), 661.

Dahl, G., Nilsson, K., & Sunesson, S. (1986): *Ska forskning vara nyttig?* Stockholm: Socialstyrelsen.

Dahler-Larsen, P. (2008): *Kvalitetens beskaffenhed* (1. udg. ed.). Odense: Syddansk Universitetsforlag.

Esmark, A., Bagge Laustsen, C., & Åkerstrøm Andersen, N. (2005a): *Poststrukturalistiske analysestrategier.* Frederiksberg: Roskilde Universitetsforlag.

Esmark, A., Bagge Laustsen, C., & Åkerstrøm Andersen, N. (2005b):

Socialkonstruktivistiske analysestrategier. Frederiksberg: Roskilde Universitetsforlag.

Evetts, J. (2003): The sociological analysis of professionalism: Occupational change in the modern world. *International Sociology, 18*, 395.

Evetts, J. (2006): Introduction: Trust and professionalism: Challenges and occupational changes. *Current Sociology, 54*, 515.

Freidson, E. (2001): *Professionalism - the third logic*. Cambridge, UK: Polity Press.

Gibbons, M., Limoges, C., Nowotny, H., Schwartzman, S., Scott, P., & Trow, M. (1994): *New production of knowledge. the dynamics of science and research in contemporary societies*. London: Sage.

Giddens, A. (2000): *Modernitetens konsekvenser*. Kbh.: Hans Reitzel.

Gleeson, D., & Knights, D. (2006): Challinging dualism: Public professionalism in 'troubled' times. *Sociology, 40* (2), 277.

Greve, C., & Ejersbo, N. (2008): *Moderniseringen af den offentlige sektor* (2. ed. ed.). Kbh.: Børsen.

Hanlon, G. (1998): Professionalism as enterprise: Service class politics and the redefinition of professionalism. *Sociology, 32*, 43.

Healy, K. (2000): *Social work practices: Contemporary perspectives on change*. Thousand Oaks, Calif.: Sage.

Healy, K., & Meagher, G. (2004): The reprofessionalization of social work: Collaporative approaches for achieving professional recognition. *British Journal of Social Work, 34*(2), 243.

Hjort, K. (2005): *Professionaliseringen i den offentlige sektor* (1. ed. ed.). Frederiksberg: Roskilde Universitetsforlag.

Højrup, T. (1983): *Det glemte folk: Livsformer og centraldirigering*. [S.l.]: Institut for europæisk Folkelivsforskning.

Howe, D. (1994): Modernity, postmodernity and social work. *British Journal of Social Work, 24*, 513.

Karvinen-Niinikoski, S. (2005): Research orientation and expertise in social work - challenges for social work education. *European Journal of Social Work, 8*, 259.

Krogstrup, H. K. (2003): *Evalueringsmodeller: Evaluering på det sociale område*. Kbh.: Systime.

Leonard, P. (1994): Knowledge/ power and postmodernism. *Canadian Social Work Review, 11*(1), 11.

Mannheim, K. (1968): *Ideology and utopia. an introduction to the sociology of knowledge*. London.

Martinez-Brawley, E. (1999): Social work, postmodernism and higher education. *Social Work, 42*(3), 333.

Merton, R. K. (1968): *Social theory and social structure*. New York, NY: The Free Press.

Mouritsen, J. (1997): *Tællelighedens regime: Synlighed, ansvarlighed og økonomistyring gennem mål og rammer i statslige institutioner* (1. udgave ed.). Kbh.: Jurist- og Økonomforbundet.

Nilsson, K., & Sunesson, S. (1988): *Konflikt, kontroll, expertis: Att använda social forskning*. Lund: Arkiv.

Olsson, E. (1993): 'Naiv teori' i socialt behandlingsarbete. *Nordisk Sosialt Arbeid, 2*.

Parton, N. (1995): The nature of social work under conditions og (post) modernity. *Social Work and Social Sciences Review, 5*(2), 93.

Parton, N. (2008): Changes in the form of knowledge in social work: From the 'Social' to the 'Informational' *British Journal of Social Work, 38*, 253.

Parton, N., & O'Byrne, P. (2000): *Constructive social work : Towards a new practice*. Basingstoke: Macmillan Press.

Pawson, R. (2006): *Evidence-based policy: A realist perspective*. London: Sage Publications Ltd.

Pease, B., & Fook, J. (1999): *Transforming social work practice: Postmodern critical perspectives*. London: Routledge.

Peile, C., & McCouat, M. (1997): The rise of relativism: The future of theory and knowledge development in social work . *British Journal of Social Work, 27*(3), 343.

Pellizzoni, L. (2003): Knowledge, uncertainty and the transformation of the public sphere. *European Journal of Social Theory, 6*, 327.

Pestre, D. (2003): Regimes of knowledge production in society: Towards a more political and social reading. *Minerva, 41*(3), 245-261.

Pfadenhauer, M. (2006): Crisis or decline? problems of legitimation and loss of trust in modern professionalism. *Current Sociology, 54*(4), 565.

Philp, M. (1979): Notes on the form of knowledge in social work. *The Sociological Review, 27*(1)

Quicke, J. (2000): A new professionalism for a collaborative culture of organizational learning in contemporary society. *Educational Management Administration & Leadership, 28*(3), 299.

Rasmussen, T. (2002): 'Levekår, livsformer og livsstil'. In G. Niklasson (Ed.), *Socialfag for pædagoger* (1.th ed.,). København: Frydenlund.

Satka, M., & Karvinen, S. (1999): The contemporary reconstruction of finnish social work expertise. *European Journal of Social Work, 2*(2), 119.

Schön, D. A. (2001): *Den reflekterende praktiker. Hvordan professionelle tænker når de arbejder*. Århus: Klim.

Sewpaul, V., & Hölscher, D. (2004): *Social work in times of neoliberalism: A postmodern discourse* (1. ed. ed.). Pretoria: Van Schaik.

Starbuck, W. H. (2006): *The production of knowledge: The challenge of social science research*. Oxford: Oxford University Press.

Svensson, L. G. (2006): New professionalism, trust and competence: Some conceptual remarks and empirical data. *Current Sociology,* (54), 579.

Weber, M. (1982): *Makt og byråkrati: Essays om poltikk og klasse, samfunnsforskning og verdier* (4. ed. ed.). Oslo: Gyldendal norsk forlag.

Notes

1   See also the translation: Åkerstrøm Andersen (2003) *Discursive analytical strategies – Understanding Foucault, Koselleck, Laclau, Luhmann,* Policy Press, Bristol.

2   The 'epistemological turn' referred to with a variety of concepts as ecological-, feminist-, poststructuralist-,or postmodernist perspectives, linguistic turn or constructivism (Peile & MCCouat, 1997).

3   For example, Bourdieu uses the expression 'scholastic' to criticize how concepts and categories are often developed from a non-practical or scholastic position but do not make sense in practical situations.

4   'In some behavioural sciences, including social work, finding the Holy Grail of scientific knowledge has led to disappointment. Universal truths about human conditions have not helped to solve individual problems but have become the 'metanarrative of coercion'(Howe, 1994), a situation that is contrary to the essence of social work (Martinez-Brawley, 1999)

5   The traditional sociology of knowledge (Berger & Luckmann, 1971; Mannheim, 1968; Merton, 1968), and newer representatives, such as Bourdieu and Foucault.

6   See note 3 and, for example,(Dahl, Nilsson, & Sunesson, 1986; Nilsson & Sunesson, 1988; Olsson, 1993).

7   Referring to the role different institutions play in training social workers (in the different Nordic countries, this education may occur inside or outside the university). In this model, the political institutions are absent – they are discussed elsewhere.

8   Instead of seeing theory-driven, evidence-based knowledge as clearly distinguishable from practice, the constructivist position emphasizes theories as context based, expressing chosen perspectives on the research field (see for example Esmark, Bagge Laustsen & Åkerstrøm Andersen 2005a; Esmark, Bagge Laustsen & Åkerstrøm Andersen 2005b)

9   'Mode 1 cannot be accepted as an accurate characterization of the knowledge economy in the West since the sixteenth century' (Pestre 2003)

10   Starbuck shows that the system of reviewing has major weaknesses.

Empirical research shows that there tends to be little agreement when reviewers assess the quality of articles for publication in scientific journals.

11 The Nordic Campbell Center was established in 2002 (now named SFI-Campbell), and has received substantial governmental support, see 'Evaluering af Nordisk Campbell Center' (Evaluation of the Nordic Campbell Centre), juni 2007: 6

12 See, for example, programmes in the Nordic Campbell Center.

13 Bourdieu maintains that the natural sciences have the greatest prestige among the different disciplines or research areas.

14 Use of the traditional scientific positivistic ideal of science has been criticized heavily – for example, by Habermas, Bourdieu, Foucault, Luhmann, etc. – and can be seen as a very naïve, unfruitful and insufficient position in social science.

15 From the perspective of evaluation research, it is a paradox, that the evidence-based research, which is based upon the classical effect–evaluation model, can be 're-established', without having solved any of the severe problems, this model has been criticised for. Among these, the 'black-box' problem can be mentioned (e.g.(Krogstrup, 2003)

16 M. S. Larson's *The rise of professionalism* (1977, Berkeley: University of California Press), and A. Abbot's *The system of professions: An essay on the division of expert labour* (1988, Chicago: University of Chicago Press) are seen as main contributions.

17 Thomas Højrup's theory about life-modes became an opportunity to discuss the extent to which needs (and norms and values) are common (Højrup, 1983). See also Rasmussen, 2002).

18 Changes in the public sector have, in different frameworks, been described by several scholars, e.g. (Ansbøl, 2008; Busch, 2007; Greve & Ejersbo, 2008; Mouritsen, 1997)

19 This has been a common 'instrument' for some years, which also implies a certain way of looking at, and handling, organizations, e.g. EFQM, CAF, KVIK, http://www.fm.dk/Arbejdsomraader/Offentlig%20modernisering/Kvalitet%20og%20styring/Styring%20af%20statslige%20institutioner.aspx (051009)

20 In contrast to the UK, for example, where the Thatcher Government highly politicized the welfare state and the public sector, changes in the Nordic Welfare States could be described as depoliticized.

21 For example, Dahler-Larsen has described the mechanisms of qualitative management as implying typification, interpolation, temporalization, quantification, etc. (Dahler-Larsen, 2008)

22 Control, for example, in the form of output measures (which always measure what it is possible to measure instead of what the original idea was) has the

well-known tendency to replace the original idea or goal, and further to neglect initiatives as well as knowledge about what cannot be measured.

23   In the Danish Association of Social Workers, there is a current discussion of the bureaucratization of social work, because increasingly large parts of the work they do are for administrative purposes. For example, in social work dealing with child care, only 14% of the social workers' time is spent in contact with clients (*http://www.socialrdg.dk/index.dsp?page=8844*) d. 21-11-08.

24   The discourses can imply a disciplinary mechanism, where discourse of professionalism is used as an appealing way to govern 'professional conduct at a distance' (Fournier 1999, cited in Evetts 2006).

25   It is not possible just to handle new information demands in addition to previous practice demands.

26   It can be discussed, whether some of the bases for Philp's understanding of social work knowledge are changed. It is evident that new demands are being made of the client in the transformation to sociability (e.g., to take responsibility for his/her own change and changeability), and this might involve decreased demands on the social worker's knowledge about the subjective individual. For example, Åkerstrøm Andersen (2004; 2006) has identified one of the new 'techniques' in social work, the 'social contract'. The 'social contract' is made between the public authorities and the 'client' regarding the client's hitherto private sphere, and it determines how he orshe needs to change or develop.

27   Professions here include scientific social work.

4
Theorizing practice research in social work

Lars Uggerhøj

Introduction

Practice research is an emerging approach within social work research. The basic foundation of practice research is building theory from practice (not only from academia). The approach is based on a combination of research methodology, field research and practical experience.

It is impossible to examine and initiate a research process solely from a researcher's point of view, because he or she – as well as social work – is always under the influence of the political and institutional context that frames the phenomenon or the issue in focus. In the words of Gredig and Sommerfeld:

> If we want scientific knowledge, and especially empirical evidence, to play an effective role in professional action, then we have to focus on the contexts where the processes of generating knowledge for action actually take shape, that is, on the organizations engaged in social work. (Gredig and Sommerfeld 2008:296).

Nevertheless, an ideal of research is to conduct independent 'in-context' research that – from a neutral position and with no pressure from outside – can study any problem at any time.

Valid criticism may be made of the possibility and desirability of this position. Why should researchers be able to adopt a position untouched by tendencies and trends, and why should they distance themselves from the results of such research? These questions raise an interesting and important discussion topic, one that is necessary in all research at all times.

This discussion is, however, not elaborated further in this chapter. For further elaboration, please read Edgar Marthinsen' chapter on this issue.

My starting point is that research closely connected to, and under the influence of, practice, with the aim of improving such practice, is of the same high quality as research on the social distance between researcher and the subject. The interface between practice and research, and the degree to which these processes mutually interfere, are even more important than in other research processes. I do not intend to limit this discussion to a certain degree of distance from the phenomenon investigated. Distance can be both useful and necessary in the research process.

This chapter will focus on practice research, and is consequently concerned with the possibilities of collaboration where influence is exerted in two directions – both from practice to research and from research to practice. That is to say, it focuses on research and practice in social work.

A theoretical and methodological approach to practice research in social work

As argued throughout this chapter, social work research, practice and education are very well suited to practice research. To elaborate and define practice research in social work, it is necessary to consider definitions of connected approaches and theory.

A natural connection that widens the understanding of practice research is what the Danish researcher Bent Flyvbjerg refers to as 'the science of the concrete' (Flyvbjerg 1991), or what I would call 'actual science'. This is bottom-up knowledge production, or a field of research oriented towards subjects more than objects. To restore social science to its rightful place in contemporary society, Flyvbjerg suggests that researchers should return to classical traditions of social inquiry and reorient practice towards what he defines as 'phronetic social science' (Flyvbjerg 2001). For Aristotle, the highest of three intellectual virtues was *phronesis*, where judgements and decisions were based on values, and as such quite distinct from *episteme* (analytical) and *techne* (technical) knowledge (Flyvbjerg 2001:55–60). Flyvbjerg defines the science of the concrete, or actual science, as pragmatic, variable, context-dependent and praxis-oriented science (Flyvbjerg 2001:57). It operates via practical rationality based on judgement and experience (Flyvbjerg 2001:58), in which some key elements are:

+ *getting close to reality* (the research is conducted close to the phenomenon or the group studied and is subject to reactions from the surroundings, and remains close during the phases of data analysis, feedback and publication of results),

+ *emphasizing little things* (the focus is on minutiae, where research studies the major in the minor and where small questions often lead to big answers);

+ *looking at practice before discourse* (discourse analysis is disciplined by analysis of practice, and research focuses on practical activities and knowledge in everyday situations);

+ *studying concrete cases and contexts* (research methodically builds on case studies, because practical rationality is best understood through cases; practices are studied in their proper contexts);

+ *joining agency and structure* (focus is on both actor and structural level; actors and their practices are analysed in relation to structures, and structures in terms of agency); and finally

+ *dialoguing with a polyphony of voices* (the research is dialogical and includes itself in a polyphony of voices, with no voice claiming final authority) (Flyvbjerg 2001:132–139).

According to Flyvbjerg, theory has a minor position and context a major one in phronetic social science. Flyvbjerg does not criticize rules, logic, signs and rationality – in fact, he states that it would be equally problematic if these elements were marginalized by the concrete. However, he criticizes the dominance of these phenomena to the exclusion of more context- and practice-based phenomena (Flyvbjerg 1991:46, Flyvbjerg 2001:49). As the above-mentioned key elements suggest, Flyvbjerg emphasizes that dialogue has a central position in actual science – dialogue with those who are studied, with other researchers, and with decision-makers as well as with other central actors in the field. From this position, research cannot provide straight and simple answers as often seen in more traditional research processes. He stresses that 'no one is experienced enough or wise enough to give complete answers' (Flyvbjerg 2001:61). The task of phronetic social science is not to provide simple answers or statements but

> to clarify and deliberate about the problems and risks we face and to outline how things may be done differently, in full knowledge that we cannot find ultimate answers to these questions (Flyvbjerg 2001:140).

Flyvbjerg is not emphasizing actual science or phronetic social science on behalf of natural science but stressing that society needs not only natural science but also phronetic-oriented social science to fully investigate developments and processes in modern societies. He argues that both natural and social sciences have their own strengths and weaknesses, depending on subject matter, and that social scientists therefore need to reflect much more on these differences, making it possible to capitalize or build on their strengths, rather than to mimic vainly their natural science counterparts. He puts it this way: 'Where natural sciences are weakest, social science is strong' (Flyvbjerg 2001:53), and:

> Just as social sciences have not contributed much to explanatory and predictive theory, neither have the natural sciences contributed to reflexive analysis and discussion of values and interests, which is the prerequisite for an enlightened political, economic, and cultural development in any society, and which is at the core of phronesis (Flyvbjerg 2001:3).

From this position, practice research may very well be a way to transform phronetic social science into everyday practice. Phronetic social science could very well constitute both a theoretical and a methodological framework for practice research in social work.

Another natural element of practice research is the connection with mode 2 knowledge production. While mode 1 knowledge production is defined as building upon traditional research approaches guided only by academic norms, mode 2 knowledge production is characterized by application-oriented research where both frameworks and findings are discussed and evaluated by a number of partners—including laymen—in public spheres (Kristiansson 2006).

> Mode 2 knowledge production takes place in an interaction between many actors, each and every one of whom represents different interests and contributes a variety of competences and attitudes. It is characterized by a relatively flat network- and collaboration-oriented structure marked by organizational flexibility, and shows no sign of becoming institutionalized in conventional patterns. (Kristiansson 2006:18 - my translation)

The number of researchers will expand from a few privileged people to a mixed group in the production of knowledge.

> Other actors once dismissed as mere 'disseminators', 'brokers' or 'users' of research results, are now more actively involved in their 'production'. (Nowotny, Scott & Gibbons 2001:89)

In this way, mode 2 research must be bottom-up rather than top-down in orientation (Nowotny, Scott & Gibbons 2001:113).

The reason why mode 2 knowledge production and research has attracted interest, according to Kristiansson, is the increasing attention to research and its influence on society. This attention has created increasing interest in research into both political and social issues, and in solutions and understanding based on different disciplines instead of a single discipline. As summarized by Gibbons et al., 'Mode 2 knowledge is created in broader transdisciplinary social and economic contexts' (Gibbons et al. 1994:1).

According to Kristiansson, there are a variety of interests within mode 2 knowledge production and research that constitute different expectations of, and demands on, knowledge, development, research design, and findings. Different interests in practice research are discussed below in this chapter. Instead of solving possible conflicts among different stakeholders, mode 2 acts within and together with them. That is, collaboration and partnership extend from the very beginning to the very end. In this way, knowledge production

> arises in the light of a specific logic which participants must develop in common to be able to act together and towards the problem (Kristiansson 2006:19 - my translation)

In this way, mode 2 is a clash between traditional research evaluated solely by peers and that evaluated both by peers and – as Kristiansson puts it – by a crowd of assorted partners with different agendas. To develop mode 2 knowledge production, all partners must accept ongoing reflection on differences.

Kristiansson also emphasizes that mode 2 is characterized by a new type of knowledge especially connected to practice. Like phronetic research, mode 2 research challenges traditional understanding of knowledge production.

> Mode 2 research is, in brief, characterized by its focus on solving problems in specific contexts of practice. In this way, research is controlled by specific tasks, not by the free choice of the researchers. Mode 2 research is application oriented, and oriented more towards generating solutions than towards generating new knowledge. (Rasmussen, Kruse & Holm 2007:124 - my translation)

As Rasmussen, Kruse and Holm put it later, mode 2 research is only valid if individuals or groups of people in the specific practice concerned find the results applicable and useful.

As the descriptions and definitions of phronetic social science and mode 2 knowledge production suggest, there seem to be several movements in the same direction in modern society towards more context-based, dialogue-oriented and partnership-focused research and knowledge production. Practice research in social work is closely connected to, and based on, this orientation and – as the rest of this chapter will show – translates abstract and theoretical concepts into more concrete definitions and practice.

Needs and possibilities for practice research – in practice

Throughout the past 10 years, practice has been confronted with increasing demands to reveal outcomes of public support (Osborne 2002, Heinrich 2002). Buzz words such as documentation, effect and evidence-based practice have become part of everyday social work – both to help politicians and administrative leaders manage growing economic problems and simply to acquire further knowledge about the results of social workers doing social work: what works for who under which conditions. This is stated in the core values of the Department of Social Services in the municipality of Aalborg, Denmark: *Assessment of Coherence between Effort and Results are Common Evaluation Principles* (my translation) (Kjærsdam 2009). This political and administrative focus has put research in the centre of developing and defining social work. This focus has led not only to interest in managing budgets in social work but also to an interest in more knowledge-based – not only experienced-based – development of both social work and social workers. This is to produce new knowledge and learning strategies on a scientific foundation and in close collaboration with local needs. Thus the demand to reveal outcomes of public support and the modern growth of complexity and uncertainty in society (Nowotny, Scott & Gibbons 2001:47) support the development of new kinds of knowledge production in practice.

Another point of the 'new' knowledge production is that it is based not only on more general and large-scale research but also on locally based research and/or evaluation. These kinds of research project are intended to bolster learning processes in which managers and social workers become partners in research instead of only consumers of it. As a manager in the municipality of Aalborg, Denmark, remarked:

> Findings from research and evaluation must be discussed with employees with reference to the learning process and to continuing development, and: the need for evidence-based knowledge has to be ensured in a collaboration process with partners with relevant research competence. (Kjærsdam 2009 - my translation)

The learning – or collaboration – process involves not only discussing research findings but also respecting partners throughout the research process, and, in areas where research has been dominating and exclusive for many years: the process of producing research questions. As a manager in the municipality of Aalborg stated sharply: 'We want independence concerning description of research-relevant areas' (Kjærsdam 2009 - my translation).

The development and expressed needs within practice strongly indicate a growing need both for a transparent outcome of public support, and for advancing knowledge-based learning processes in a close collaboration with education and science based research. Development in Denmark has shown that although some municipalities build up small research departments, they need 'outsiders' to evaluate public support. It is also clear that outside research partners must be open minded towards allowing practitioners and service users to join the research process – from producing research questions, through data collection and analysis, to the information obtained and the transformation of findings into new methods in social work.

Needs and possibilities for practice research – in research

A Danish example further illustrates why researchers find practice research interesting. For researchers, the need to include this type of research is based on an understanding that the institutional context – the framework for social work – is essential to studies and investigations in social work (see Flyvbjerg earlier in this chapter). Naturally, the framework of a meeting – for example, between clients and a department of social services – is not an inconsequential matter, and thus the results of initiatives launched by authorities are uncertain. At the same time, research initiatives including practice will potentially influence studies, evaluations and research applicable to practice. Through critical research into the field of social work, the focus of the Danish research network 'Social Work Research Group' (FoSo) at Aalborg University is to enable service users and marginalized citizens to take control over their own lives. This kind of research includes user-centered and/or practitioner-inclined approaches to social work practice and study of the institutional structures that contextualize those practices. More specifically, FoSo aims to enable researchers:

- to explore the perspectives of social work practitioners and service users or marginalized persons in relation to social issues;
- to explore how social work practitioners and service users or marginalized persons respond creatively to their social locations, that is, to explore their own agency in welfare processes;
- to explore the social construction of social problems and the implications of these processes for social work practice and the enablement of service users and marginalized persons;
- to study the institutional structures contextualizing and shaping social work practice (including, for example, law, regulative structures, welfare systems and organizational structures);
- to promote strategies by which social workers and service users or marginalized persons can assist service users/marginalized persons to take more control over their own lives; and
- to develop theory from practice, to develop research methods, to promote the use of theory in social work practice and to develop social work methods. (http://www.socsci.aau.dk/foso/eng-index.htm 2006)

With these goals, researchers within the network have difficulty in following traditional paths in science, because knowledge derived from, and understood only by, practice must be unfolded and discussed among researchers, practitioners and service users. It is impossible to understand practice knowledge from a neutral and distant position. One could say that it is impossible for researchers in social work to produce much necessary knowledge unless they collaborate closely with practice and practitioners.

Nordic examples of practice research

During the past decade, (practice) research projects concerning the development of social work services have been launched in all the Nordic countries. These research projects have been connected very closely to the above-mentioned needs in practice or in the development of social work practice. Although many of these projects and processes may not have been called practice research from the beginning – in fact they may have had many different names, such as development of knowledge, evaluation, trying new forms of social work, collaboration between social work, education and research – all have, through these processes, become closer to what above is called practice research, mode 2, the science of the concrete, actual science or phronetic social science.

In Sweden, the Swedish Ministry of Social Affairs established the Centre for Evaluation of Social Services research unit (Centrum för utvädering av socialt arbete). This resulted in the implementation of the National Support for Knowledge Development programme in the Department of Social Services. The basis of the programme was as follows.

> The linkage between social work based in municipalities and universities/ schools of social work must be developed. This could happen by, for example, creating a better structure for field placements, with benefit for both universities and municipalities. A much better organization of basic education, further training, and advanced education at the schools of social work must be developed. The link between practice and education and between practice and research constitutes the basis of the knowledge production in the Department of Social Services. A learning field placement must build a structure with continuous collaboration between the Department of Social Services, education and research. (Socialstyrelsen 2005:15–16 - my translation)

To promote collaboration among universities, institutions and municipalities, the Swedish programme established structures that promoted ways of working across organizational boundaries that placed knowledge-based practice at the centre of interest. A number of initiatives – for example, research sequences – were developed, and special practice-oriented seminars and education, practice centres for student work, and combinations of research/practice positions were organized.

In Finland, the approach was influenced by the economic downturn in the 1980s and 1990s. In this period, social work development and social work research took place in the municipalities. The economic crises prompted local authorities to focus on basic social work initiatives, not development or research. At the end of the 1990s, new collaborative initiatives were launched to connect municipalities and regions in consortia that simultaneously created new possibilities to establish research in social work as well as to establish stronger connections among practice, research and development initiatives. Furthermore, a new and stronger government-sponsored collaboration between practice and universities in which all municipalities participated was launched. The result was the establishment of centres of excellence of social welfare and development units. According to an evaluation of the processes and the result, the above-mentioned centres and development units are today the central development actors in the field of social work, since they have created a natural base and meeting point for education, research and practice. The evaluation also shows that it is necessary to focus on permanent financial support instead of temporary project-based support if researchers and educators are to become permanent members of the network (Lähteinen 2005).

In 2006, Norway established the so-called 'College University and Department of Social Services' (the HUSK project). The initiative was undertaken by the Norwegian parliament (Stortinget), which advanced the following argument:

> Several attempts to develop competence within the Department of Social Services have been made; for example, in initiatives for drug addicts, homeless people and service users with economic and debt problems. Some have, however, claimed that the divergence among research, education and practice is too big. (st.prp.nr.1 2005-06 p. 240 from the Department of Health and Caring - my translation)

The Norwegian parliament decided that the purpose of the project was:

+ to promote firm and equal structures and arenas for collaboration among research, education and the Department of Social Services;
+ to strengthen practice-based research; and
+ to strengthen knowledge as the foundation of social work practice.

It is imperative for knowledge-based practice in the programme that employees participate in ongoing and process-based development of competence through learning organizations, in which there is room for collective knowledge production. In addition, the Norwegian programme highlights a user perspective in central and local organizations and in the development and implementation of projects within the programme.

In Denmark, a pilot practice research project has been launched. The goal is, over a period of five years, to boost collaboration between research, education and different municipalities, focusing on the development of knowledge-based practice. To establish ongoing and specific relations among practice, research and education, the purpose of the project is to identify activities that:

+ enhance practice qualifications exercised within regional or municipality settings;
+ establish a research-based development of practice;
+ create a platform for research in practice within the field of social work;
+ establish exchange of experiences among specific practice and relevant education;
+ establish relevant training and education within the area of social work; and
+ develop new types of research, education, and practice. (Ebsen and Uggerhøj 2007:3)

As the above-mentioned projects show, over a number of years, there have been various kinds of collaboration between practice and research in social work in the Nordic countries. Despite misconceptions and different historical approaches to social work, it seems that the need and wish to develop practice research in social work is similar.

Barriers to practice research

Despite the presence of comparable social issues, the historical background of research in social work in the Nordic countries varies[1]. As mentioned above, the strongest traditions in social work research can be traced to Sweden. Since the 1970s, Sweden has aimed at promoting social work research, with efforts including the establishment of professorships, PhD programmes and important periodicals like *Socialvetenskaplig Tidsskrift* (*The Journal of Social Science*). In recent years, social work research has also become an increasingly important issue in Finland, prompting Finnish universities to establish PhD courses in social work. In Denmark and Norway, the establishment of topical master's degree programmes, PhD programmes and university courses for social workers, and the establishment of professorships in social work has occurred primarily since the 1990s.

Being a relatively new field in Finland, Norway and Denmark, social work has not yet positioned itself as an independent academic subject. An important factor in the establishment of social work at the Nordic universities was the wish to use research to enhance the qualifications of practice and to support the knowledge production of social-work-related topics (see above, and the first chapter in this volume). This was urgent, and it has produced the unique possibility of establishing research that from the very beginning focused on context rather than just on its own traditions, which only later was able to build bridges between theory and practice. This does not mean, however, that relations between research and practice and the development of research in social work practice are unproblematic. Below, the discussion of conflicting interests will reveal the contrasts.

Qualified practice is built on many related elements. One of the most central elements – although not the only one – is social workers' knowledge about the effects of initiatives and planning in social work. The fulcrum of the research is the elements that create a natural relation between research and knowledge-based practice and regular evaluations of ongoing initiatives. Hence, an identity of interests exists, but it is essential that the distinction between ends and means should be clear in the collaboration between practice and research as well as in the development of practice research. As an introductory note, it must be emphasized that there is an essential difference between a researcher and a person who works in a profession: the researcher views research as a goal in itself, while the practitioner views research as means. To the researcher, research and the research process are the main objectives. The practitioner's goal is to present initiatives and viable solutions to social problems. This does not mean that the interests of research and practice are necessarily different but that researchers and social workers must remember the difference in interests between them. Currently, the desire to involve research in the development of social work and to develop more academic social work education is increasing, as mentioned above.

In the past, there has been great doubt about the usefulness of academic research in social work circles, and I do not deny that it remains today. This doubt, I believe, stems from attempts by researchers to exercise autonomy from practice; that is, to maintain research as an academic field independent of practice. The interest in basing knowledge on academic knowledge in social work has – as mentioned above – created a shift from practice to research. The essential element of this new approach is that different research methods relate to practice and the provision of high-quality social services.

What is practice research?

In discussions of practice research, its essential nature is often unclear. As Pain writes in a literature review of practice research:

> Despite the many years of research into practice (Gibbons 2001) and debate concerning it, there is still a lack of consensus about what practice research includes and what lies outside its boundaries, and there are continuing debates about paradigms and methods, collaboration and ethics (Pain 2008:1).

It seems that two approaches can be characterized. This chapter does not adopt one or the other but includes parts of both in what we understand as practice research in social work. To understand and discuss this, it is, however, first necessary to examine the approaches separately. The first approach defines practice research as research conducted in close collaboration with practice, where it is not crucial who collects data or performs the analysis, although it is under the management of trained researchers and institutions. This approach primarily focuses on the framework, goals and outcomes of the research process. The above-mentioned Nordic projects represent this position.

The second approach defines practice research as research, evaluation and investigation conducted by practitioners. This approach primarily focuses on the roles of the researchers. The Danish research leader Knud Ramian together with a group of English researchers (Ramian 2003) represents this approach.

A third approach, connected to the second, focuses specifically on user participation in research processes. This position includes not only practice research but also all kinds of research activities. Approaches one and two will be examined and discussed below. The discussion about involving users in research processes is important, but it is not specifically connected to practice research. This is a general issue for all kinds of scientific work. Practice research can involve users or can be conducted without them, but it is important to have the discussion and to make a decision concerning user involvement in the research process.

In approach one, the starting point is that it is necessary and desirable that there should be a close – and often locally bound – collaboration between practice and research, with mutual commitment. However, both sides must primarily do 'what they are best at'. It seems that a wish or even ideal to establish an unproblematic collaboration among research, education and practice in social work has developed. The ideal could be considered a strength at first, but in the long run, it endangers both research and practice. It is not possible to establish an unproblematic collaboration but at most to make it less problematic. The desire for, and the ideal of, the unproblematic collaboration entails the risk that research, education and practice will become toothless – they will, to put it bluntly, risk falling to the lowest common denominator. This would in all probability lead to never-ending disagreements or obvious conflicts of interest which would affect all aspects of the discussion. There will always be differences in interests between the two areas. If research and practice are to be valid, it is crucial that these different elements should not be diluted. The struggle between partners and conflict between the two fields is, from their perspective, the best potential for both areas. For example, research must always be entitled to look behind the truth, the self-understanding and ideals in practice and always to focus on grey or perhaps invisible areas in practice. If research must have regard to problems in collaboration caused by unpopular findings, the rationale for the research field will be threatened.

It is difficult to ascertain how collaboration between practice and research in practice may be organized, as it must begin with locally based organizations and issues that probably change from time to time. A recent statement on practice research by a participant at the 'Practice research: developing a new paradigm' conference said:

> Practice research involves curiosity about practice. It is about identifying good and promising ways in which to help people; and it is about challenging troubling practice through the critical examination of practice and the development of new ideas in the light of experience. It recognizes that this is best done by practitioners in partnership with researchers, where the latter have as much, if not more, to learn from practitioners as practitioners have to learn from researchers. It is an inclusive approach to professional knowledge that is concerned with understanding the complexity of practice alongside the commitment to empower, and to realize social justice, through practice. (Salisbury Statement 2009:2–3)

Practice research cannot be research findings planned, conducted and 'delivered' by a researcher to practitioners. The main point is that practice and research develop all collaboration in common because practice research must be in tune with all participants. It also means that collaboration can appear differently and may change in the following ways

1. The research could be planned and discussed by researchers and practitioners but carried out by researchers.
2. The research goals and questions could be set, and they could be discussed throughout the process and be part of a learning process where both researchers and practitioners participate all through it.
3. Research could be part of an ongoing research process in which it is hard to distinguish learning processes and research/examination processes.

This division into three arenas within practice research may be connected to what Ilse Julkunen defines as first-, second- and third-person inquiry in the next article in this issue.

The second approach is based on a definition that is similar or identical to practice research in the first approach. According to Epstein:

> Practice-based research may be defined as the use of research-inspired principles, designs and information gathering techniques within existing forms of practice to answer questions that emerge from practice in ways that will inform practice. (Epstein 2001:17 – my translation)

However, connected to this, it is said that

> practice research ... is a phenomenon that occurs when practitioners commit themselves to something they call research in their own practice while they, at the same time, practice social work. (Ramian 2003:5 – my translation)

This distances this approach from approach one as practitioners are expected to be active researchers. The difference is even more specific when Ramian defines six features in the perception of the phenomenon of practice research (Ramian 2003:5) (my translation).

1. It is conducted by practitioners at work using at least 80% of their working hours as practitioners.
2. The research questions focus on problems connected to everyday practice.
3. Common recognized scientific methods are used.
4. Projects are made feasible.
5. Findings are communicated to other practitioners.
6. The research field is in practice.

With Ramian's six features, it is stated that practice by this definition is the site of the research institution (instead of the university), a view supported by Rehr, who said that practice-based research studies are practitioner led (Rehr 2001). Ramian later underlines that

> the practice researcher adjusts his or her strategy and methods in ways that make it possible to conduct research activities in practice. (Ramian 2003:6)

According to Ramian, (research) practitioners have an interest in, and are dependent on, finding solutions to problems in practice, while traditional researchers are busy meeting the requirements for validity of the research (Ramian 2009). Ramian points out that the short gap between research and practice that occurs when practitioners carry out research increases the possibility of producing knowledge relevant to practice and applying findings to practice. Ramian also points out that findings from practice research are not presented in typical academic journals but rather through media such as conferences and seminars (Ramian 2003).

To highlight the central elements in practice research and to emphasize the importance of the focus on practice, Ramian refers to a study of health care where Reed and Biott stress that practice research:

1. is integrated in practice;
2. is a social process in which peers participate;
3. is valued by all participants in a project;
4. is imbued by development thinking;
5. leads to action and therefore focuses on aspects of practice that the researcher in some ways can control and influence;
6. identifies and studies the impact of social political and historical factors on practice;
7. stimulates discussions on values;
8. is designed to involve all participants;
9. increases professional imagination and the participants' capability to analyse everyday activities;
10. produces knowledge that can be replicated in ways that will interest a larger forum (Reed and Biott 1995).

While Ramian's six features seem to divide the two positions, it is, interesting that Reed and Biott's features on the other hand seem to connect the two approaches, because the latter characteristics could also include approach one and seem to emphasize some aspects of phronetic social science (see above).

According to Ramian, practitioners need not be trained researchers but must be skilled in research to perform research. A collaborative practitioner research network must be established to support the practitioner researchers during the process. Although some focuses are similar, the two approaches appear to diverge at this point, as the first approach requires that the responsibility for research projects will be carried out by trained researchers. Ramian has lately defined his research approach as 'research light' – investigations with a narrow and specific focus that may be completed in 5–10 days by practitioners with few research skills but involved in a 'collaborative practitioner research network' (Ramian 2009). By this Ramian distinguishes 'research light' from what he calls large-scale research as well as longitudinal research and research in depth. These kinds of research, according to Ramian, must be conducted by trained researchers but build on findings from research light (Ramian 2009). At this point, approaches one and two agree, but it is vital to approach one to attach importance to the responsibility of trained researchers for the research process, whether light or heavy.

One problem in the definition of practice research in approach two seems to be that traditional research resembles old-fashioned social or natural science. Harmaakorpi and Mutanen (2008) point out in an argument for more practice-based innovative processes that

> the experts in innovation processes cannot just pour knowledge into the innovation partners and then disappear from the scene. (Harmaakorpi & Mutanen 2008: 88)

This criticism could very well be used to promote approach one as well, because this approach is characterized by innovative collaboration processes from defining research questions to the analysis of data. Both approaches emphasize the differences between research and practice, but while in approach one the differences are seen as natural and inspiring parts of the collaboration and the research process, in approach two they appear to be locked into irreconcilable positions, and researchers are characterized as unwilling to consider the needs and traditions of practice. While Harmaakorpi and Mutanen stress that partners require common interests and intentions determined by practical context, approach one stresses that the partners need to 'do what they are best at' and that no partner can determine what is right: that is, the struggle between the different interests is the strongest potential within the collaboration. For further discussion, see below in this article. Referring to the discussion of modes 1 and 2 above, it seems that approach two locks researchers (for example from universities) into mode 1, making them unable to move towards mode 2, while approach one seems to be understood as mode 2.

To prevent unnecessary conflict between the two positions about the same notion and to maintain the differences, it may be helpful to define them in the following way:

1. Research that focuses on collaboration between practice and research (approach one) is defined as *practice research*;
2. Research that focuses on processes controlled and accomplished by practitioners (approach two) is defined as *practitioner research*;
3. Research that focuses on user participation in the research process (approach three) is defined as *user-controlled research*.

On the above-mentioned basis, this chapter and book focus on approach one and *practice research*, which is defined as:

+ critical and curious research that describes, analyses and develops practice;
+ research based on generally approved academic standards;
+ research built on experience, knowledge and needs within social work practice;
+ research where the responsibility for the research is entrusted to generally approved research institutions;
+ close, binding and locally based collaboration between researchers and practitioners in planning, completing and disseminating the research;
+ research where findings are closely connected to learning processes in practice;
+ participatory and dialogue-based research relevant to developing practice and validating different areas of expertise within the partnership; and
+ research that produces, analyses and describes specific issues in both empirical and theoretical general coherence.

This approach does not exclude practitioners from the research process. On the contrary, practitioners are often included at different levels in the research process and as researchers, but trained researchers still bear responsibility for research quality. The focus is not on the role of the researcher but on the content of the research. It is 'to use the best from both parts' in a respectful collaboration. One could say, with the words from the Salisbury Statement (Salisbury Statement 2009:4), that the foundation of the approach is practice-minded researchers and research-minded practitioners. Or in the words of Epstein and Blumenfield:

> Under the right organizational conditions, with the right kinds of support and consultation and a 'practice-based research' perspective, social work practitioners can actively and enthusiastically engage in research that has implications for their own practice and for practice in other settings. (Epstein and Blumenfield 2001:3)

While both practice and academic wisdom are valued, the point of this chapter is that this approach and definition of practice research is open and inclusive instead of closed and exclusive. It is focused on knowledge production and learning processes in social work practice and research as a whole instead of mainly on processes within chosen practices.

Different interests in practice research

Although I have argued that both practice and research have an interest in collaboration in research processes, this is not tantamount to a total convergence of all areas in the field. On the contrary, as mentioned above in this chapter, it is useful to be aware of contradistinctions that cannot be neutralized, as this would risk establishing collaboration focused on the lowest common denominator. Some of the natural contradistinctions – and consequences thereof – will be discussed below. The basis of the discussion is that the following are stakeholders in practice research:

+ users;
+ social workers;
+ administrative management and organizations;
+ politicians; and
+ researchers.

Users have a natural interest in receiving the best support possible. Although many users hope that their participation in studies of social work may have a more general impact on qualifying, for example, for public support (Uggerhøj 1995), their attention will be on receiving the best researched support for their own individual and specific problems. A study on user experience and pedagogical treatment in a Danish institution that deals with families at risk suggests that users judge the intervention differently according to the severity of their problems (Uggerhøj 2000). Furthermore, the study shows how users and social workers judge the same activity differently. While social workers judge selected interventions positively according to their specific task of observing families in the family home, users judge the same activity negatively according to their need to obtain help and support for their individual problems from professional social workers instead of just being observed (Uggerhøj 2000). The example shows the inherent contradictions in the complex work of a family home. There are contradictions and dilemmas that both social workers and users must live with and accept because they are impossible to solve.

Social workers are bound to a political, organizational and professional context. It is not possible for social workers solely to satisfy their own values or needs expressed by users. The legislation stipulates possibilities and obligations; for example, interventions/economic support for particular problems and demands that may be placed on users to obtain support. Furthermore, the resources and the social worker authority are often covered by legislation. Moreover, the administrative and/or political details of management in social work often influence interpretation and application. At the same time, local authorities, politicians and civil servants interpret the legislation that organizes and structures social work differently in various organizations and municipalities. Finally, social workers' educational background, professional values and ideals influence the way social work is implemented in practice. Professional values and ideals often appear in contradistinction to organizational frameworks and to some extent also to user needs, as mentioned above.

Generally, *administrative management and organizational frameworks* are influenced by politically defined boundaries, local cultures and political traditions. Moreover, the desire of social work management and organizations to 'establish order in chaos' concerning user problems and to appear responsible and rational may conflict with the desires of users and social workers to focus on their individual issues and understanding of the issues. These desires are based on the users' own understanding instead of a rational public understanding. Management needs – together with political requests for more documented and effective social work – often lead to a focus on evidence-based knowledge production and research instead of other research approaches.

Politicians should focus on tools to measure the effects of political decisions and to explain them to citizens. The individual needs of users and descriptions of collaboration processes in social work have less importance, because these are often considered to be the concern of an individual user or included in a particular social worker's professional competence.

Researchers' approaches are influenced by their own research area and needs as well as university management's requirements that they should justify themselves in the academic field. Research areas and academic needs do not always converge with the needs and requirements of social work practice. The demand for publication in peer-reviewed periodicals with detailed and traditional criteria for research, content and article structure may conflict with the needs for information in practice. Furthermore, researchers may be influenced by the specific focus of those who benefit from services – often seen in the economic circumstances of the tender. Finally, the scientific need for distance from the subject of research may appear to conflict with the necessity for practice in proximity. That is, the scientific ideal of objectivity and unwillingness to influence practice conflicts with the need of practitioners to influence and include research in developing practice, which is an interesting and difficult contradiction.

The different stakeholders cannot and must not necessarily combine completely, but it is crucial that practice research constitutes a series of contradistinctions and confluences, which entails dilemmas that both research and practice must address. Dilemmas are not resolved but must be included in the practice research process.

Challenges for research and practice

As mentioned above, actors in social work arenas, such as practitioners, claimants, researchers and users, have different interests. These interests are important to all of them and significant for society as well. They are so important and significant that functioning well depends on the possibility of retaining these different interests. Instead of attempting to balance or reconcile these differences, it is essential to illuminate them if collaboration is to be established. Moreover, in this way, it is possible for the parties involved to gain greater understanding of each other and their respective interests. It is possible to relate this meeting of different interests to other power struggles; for example between management and employees and between users and social workers where awareness and visibility are key issues in establishing respectful collaboration, yet without eliminating natural differences. Research finds itself in the most powerful position and thus has a special obligation to promote awareness of different interests, exactly as the powerful position of social workers with regard to users gives them a special obligation to use it positively in their relationship.

My claim is that researchers have a special position and responsibility to respond to these contradistinctions. It is thus evident that the possibility of a dialectical approach is based on differences and contradistinctions that are crucial to the raison d'être of the two fields and that enable the two areas to challenge each other. From this position, my claim is also that a researcher could or should never become a practitioner, or vice versa. However, this does not mean that efforts should not be made to utilize these differences to inform social work.

My position with regard to change and development in practice research in social work and to collaboration between researchers and practitioners is based on the Marxian process of 'change through the conflict of opposing forces' (The Free Dictionary by Farlex) and not the Hegelian process of 'arriving at the truth by stating a thesis, developing a contradictory antithesis, and combining and resolving them into a coherent synthesis' (The Free Dictionary by Farlex) meaning that contradictions are abolished and new realizations emerge.

As in the introduction of the science of the concrete and phronetic social science, it is, at the same time, important to recall Flyvbjerg's comment that no individual is wise enough to give sufficient answers (Flyvbjerg 2001), meaning that the role of both researchers and practitioners is to advance parts of the answer in an ongoing dialogue about issues in practice and research, and concerning how eventually to resolve these issues. From this point of view, research and practice both possess part of the answer and part of the solution, and thus both researchers and practitioners produce knowledge. Thus, importance is attached to challenges from different interests and at different levels.

As mentioned above, *the challenge from research to practice* is to examine existing truth and common understanding – in the words of Bourdieu: the social worker *doxa* (Bourdieu 1972, Bourdieu 1982) – that is, to establish awareness and elucidate phenomena, actions and considerations to which the practitioners tend to be blind – precisely because they are in practice. From this point of view, it is less challenging simply to describe and measure effects of everyday social work practice. My goal is not to deny that it is interesting to carry out studies on social work and its effects, but such research does not necessarily challenge practice, research and society, as it risks focusing only on insight within practice. Thus, too close a connection and understanding between research and practice is futile and may hinder the emergence of new knowledge.

The challenge from practice to research is to support or provoke research to become more creative in understanding practice built on complexity, and to act flexibly instead of constructing a paradigm suitable for research. It should also challenge research to be aware of elements of power in both social work and research processes. From a practice point of view, research improves the comprehension of everyday problems as well as encouraging more informed solutions to these problems. This approach challenges the scientific tendency to view a phenomenon from an abstract and theoretical position. The theoretical and analytic approach is pivotal in the internal 'science war' in basic research which – frankly speaking – has high status, and practice research, which has low status. Thus, practice will challenge research at its core, as some researchers will look upon this as research being in danger of losing its basis and identity. In spite of declarations of equality , social work is marked by human beings' different reactions to the same problem. Hence, research in social work has to be able to establish studies of this action-oriented field and the built-in differences between research and practice. Social work research must in this way challenge and intervene in dynamic, complex and ever-changing practice, knowledge and context: the ongoing construction of society of which social work is a part.

Practice research in social work is characterized as being capable of simultaneously influencing and being influenced by practice. It is a research field linked especially to practice, and its scope and independence are defined by the breadth of life, and thus it risks lower status within academic society. Research must focus also on actions, not only on findings, and on quantitative aspects, because these have a profound impact on practice. To express this in another way, actions become findings in a research process, while findings become actions in a practice process. In this way, practice research in social work and social work practice must, so to speak, walk hand in hand without becoming lovers. Practice research seems to constitute common ground for both practice and research, where it is possible to challenge both fields. Research must emphasize that knowledge is produced by both research and practice, meaning that research must establish a close partnership with management, social workers and users in the development of research projects, in the data collection process – for example, by including practitioners and users in this process – and in the development of action research and the development of interview methods. The strength of both practice and research in this view is that they address difficult challenges. The danger for both fields is that they may avoid and reject the challenges.

Conclusion

Practice research is necessary in the ongoing development of social work, but it is also a meeting point for different views, interests and needs, where complexity and dilemmas are inherent in the collaboration and challenge of both practice and research. Practice research in social work cannot develop from either practice or research alone but from both together.

Practice research in social work is not a special research method. On the contrary, it is possible and often necessary to use different research methods, as this often strengthens the research. The critical issue is that the selected research methods must answer research questions posed by research and practice in every study. Certain creative research processes – for example action research as will be described in Karin Kildedal's article on action research in local authority practice in the next issue of this journal – will be beneficial in processes of development and those in which participants interact. However, to establish a practice research project, these are not required. As mentioned earlier in this chapter, practice research is, from my point of view, inclusive rather than exclusive.

Trained researchers are responsible for practice research, unlike practitioner research, where the responsibility and execution lie within practice. Practice research involves practitioners and users as researchers and as collaboration partners throughout the research process and does not prevent practitioner research from being part of the process.

It is possible – although not always necessary – to involve users in practice research. If users participate and are responsible for the research process, it should be characterized as user-controlled research.

In practice research, questions are considered important to both practice and research. The aforementioned Danish pilot project in practice research does not only address questions related to actual practice. It is also possible and necessary to focus on research angles that have considerable abstract and theoretical connections. Hence, it is vital in such research projects to raise practice-based evaluations and investigations to a more theoretical level, enabling researchers to answer questions in depth and to develop new theories and/or new methods in social work. It is pivotal that practice research should be connected to specific needs in everyday social work.

It is possible for practice research to integrate analysis and to produce findings that cannot be translated directly to specific changes in practice. In co-operation, practitioners and researchers can easily implement a theoretical study; for example, on the basis of one or more empirical studies. Thus they may obtain types of knowledge other than evaluations, and investigations based on a high degree of transferability will be able to impart this knowledge. As mentioned before, it is pivotal that both practice experience/knowledge and research experience/knowledge should be involved in practice research processes. One of the considerations of research is exactly how to implement theoretical and more abstract analysis that should also be conducted in practice research projects. However, if practice research must be included in knowledge production processes and/or practice, it must become part of processes in practice, not only be part of traditional research processes. Research cannot remain on the sidelines and leave the process once data collection and analyses are complete. Research must be involved in providing information. For example, it must educate practitioners in new social work methods/tools, or in new and different ways of carrying out social work, and it must be involved in turning theoretical and analytical findings into useable tools in everyday social work —essentially being a part of learning processes in practice. Moreover, representatives of practice need to be involved or at least to accept that practical issues must be turned into theoretical issues or propositions, and must be involved in developing methods for practice research. It is necessary for both sides to be open-minded and to learn from each other. Not only will practice learn from research but also research will learn from practice which will inform and develop research and research methods.

Practice research must be part of a learning process. Furthermore, researchers must extend their role to become partners in a developing process. Practitioners must be not only consumers of research but also partners in a learning process. This change of role will make practitioners use findings not merely as results but as part of developing everyday practice and methods. They must commit themselves to a learning process of which research findings are a necessary ingredient.

Although this chapter has sought to define practice research – for example, by discussing the difference between practice research and practitioner research – the aim is not to produce a 'waterproof' understanding. The aim has been rather to present important discussions and contradictions as well as to argue for the necessity of keeping these discussions and contradictions alive. Frankly speaking, discussion of practice research – considering all the different aspects discussed in this chapter – is much more important than a limited definition.

References

Bourdieu, P. (1972): *Outline of a Theory of Practice*, Cambridge: Cambridge University Press

Bourdieu, P. (1982): *The Logic of Practice*, Cambridge: Polity Press

Flyvbjerg, B. (1991): *Rationalitet og magt*, København: Akademisk Forlag

Flyvbjerg, B. (1998): *Rationality and Power: Democracy in Practice*, Chicago: University of Chicago Press

Flyvbjerg, B. (2001): *Making Social Science Matter: Why Social Inquiry Fails and How It Can Succeed Again*, New York: Cambridge University Press

Gibbons, J. (2001): *Effective practice: social work's long history of concerns about outcomes*, Australian Social Work, 54 (3), September 2001, pp. 3–13.

Gibbons, M. et al. (1994): *The New Production of Knowledge*, London: Sage Publications Ltd

Gredig, D. & Sommerfeld, P. (2008): *New Proposals for Generating and Exploiting Solution-oriented Knowledge*, Research on Social Work Practice 18; 292.

Ebsen, F. & Uggerhøj, L. (2007): *Praksisforskning i socialt arbejde*, Unpublished application.

Epstein, I. (2001): *Using Available Clinical Information in Practice-based Research: Mining for Silver While Dreaming of Gold*. In Epstein, I. & Blumenfield, S. (eds.) (2001): 'Clinical Data-mining in Practice-based Research – Social Work in Hospital Settings', New York: The Haworth Social Work Practice Press.

Epstein, I. & Blumenfield, S. (eds.) (2001): *Clinical Data-mining in Practice-based Research—Social Work in Hospital Settings*, New York: The Haworth Social Work Practice Press.

Harmaakorpi, V. & Mutanen, A. (2008): *Knowledge Production in Networked Practice-based Inno-vation Processes – Interrogative Model as a Methodological Approach*, Interdisciplinary Journal of Information, Knowledge and Management, vol 3, 2008.

Heinrich C. J. (2002): *Outcomes-based Performance Management in the Public Sector: Implications for Government Accountability and Effectiveness*, Public Administration Review, Vol. 62, No. 6, pp. 712–725, Journal of Information, Knowledge and Management, 3, 14.

Helse- og Omsorgsdepartementet (2005): *Forsøk med nye samarbeidsformer mellom forskning, ut-danning og praksis i sosialtjenesten: St.prp.nr.1 (2005-06)*, Oslo: Helse- og omsorgsdepartementet.

Hunter, E. & Tsey, K. (2002): *Indigenous health and the contribution of sociology: a review*, Health Sociology Review 11, 1–2, (http://hsr.e-contentmanagement. com/11.1/11-1p79.htm)

Kjærsdam, W. (2009): *Veje til kvalificering af socialt arbejde,* Upubliceret undervisningsmateriale.

Kristiansson, Michael René (2006): *Modus 2 vidensproduktion,* DF Revy nr. 2, februar 2006.

Ljunggren, Synnöve (2005): *Empiri, evidens, empati—Nordiska röster om kunskapsutveckling i so-cialt arbete,* Århus: Nordiska ministerrådet och Nopus, Nord: 2005:5

Lähteinen, M. (2005): *Kunskapsutveckling och kompetensuppbyggande* in Ljunggren, Synnöve (2005) 'Empiri, evidens, empati – Nordiska röster om kunskapsutveckling i socialt arbete', Århus.

Nordiska ministerrådet och Nopus, Nord: 2005:5.

Nowotny, H, Scott, P. & Gibbons, M. (2001): *Re-thinking Science – Knowledge and the Public in an Age of Uncertainty,* Cambridge: Polity Press.

Osborne, S. (2002): *Public Management – A Critical Perspective,* London: Routledge.

Pain, H. (2008): *Practice Research Literature Review,* unpublished draft, University of Southampton.

Ramian, K. (2009): *Evidens på egne præmisser,* Vidensbaseret arbejde 2009, 1. februar 2009 2. årgang.

Ramian, K. (2003): *Praksisforskning som læringsrum,* Uden for Nummer 7/2003.

Rasmussen, J., Kruse, S. & Holm, C. (2007): *Viden om dannelse – Uddannelsesforskning, pædagogik og pædagogisk praksis,* København: Hans Reitzels Forlag.

Reed, J. & Biott, C. (1995): *Evaluating and Developing Practitioner Research. Practice Research in Health Care: This Inside Story,* London: Chapman Hall.

Rehr, H. (2001): *Foreword* in Epstein, I & Blumenfield, S (eds.) (2001) 'Clinical Data-mining in

Practice-based Research – Social Work in Hospital Settings', New York: The Haworth Social Work Practice Press.

Salisbury Statement (2009): *The Salisbury Statement on practice* research, http://www.socsci.soton.ac.uk/spring/salisbury/, University of Southampton.

Socialstyrelsen (2005): *Nationellt stöd för kunskapsutveckling inom socialtjänsten,* Stockholm: Socialstyrelsen.

The Free Dictionary by Farlex http://www.thefreedictionary.com/dialectic

Uggerhøj, L. (2000): *Den indviklede udvikling,* København: Center for Forskning i Socialt Arbejde.

Uggerhøj, L. (1995): *Hjælp eller afhængighed,* Aalborg Universitetsforlag, Aalborg.

Winter, S. (1983): *Effektivitet og produktivitet i den offentlige sektor 1,* Politica, Bind 15, 3.

http://www.socsci.aau.dk/foso/eng-index.htm 2006

Note

1   The Nordic countries consist of Denmark, Finland, Iceland, Norway, Sweden and their associated territories, which include the Faroe Islands, Greenland and Åland. In this chapter, the Nordic countries refer to the following four countries: Denmark, Finland, Norway and Sweden.

5
Critical elements in evaluating and developing practice in social work:
An exploratory overview
Ilse Julkunen

Introduction

In the last decade the emergence of new modes of knowledge production has been much debated. There has been a shift of emphasis from acquisition and transmission of knowledge to construction and production of knowledge. New actors have stepped in and the roles of the researchers are being discussed critically. Also the outcome of research – the usefulness of research with respect to practice development – is a topical agenda. New models of producing knowledge are thus evolving while at the same time welfare communities feel the pressure of demands for legitimation through research and evaluation. Effectiveness, knowledge and management have become central demands and have spread throughout the governance of the welfare state. This is not just a matter of an increasing discourse, but also evaluation practices in different forms. This is where evaluation steps in.

This article explores the practice of doing evaluation in social work through the changed role of the researcher. It highlights the position of the researcher and their chosen perspectives, and critically evaluates what the consequences are for the development of practice. It starts by reflecting on the researcher role and then considers more widely the issue of multiple ownership of the evaluation practice.

Evaluation is a giga-trend cutting through our era (Vedung 2004). In the Nordic countries it was influences by the emergence, from the 1960s, of the evaluation discipline in the USA. Today evaluation is highly pluralistic. It covers a broad landscape and different models have been developed through the decades. There has been a transition from evaluation as academic research to a more participative and dialogue based form of research where evaluators and evaluatees meet. Different approaches exist as do different reasonings. Rajavaara (2007) has analyzed what kinds of rationales exist for effectiveness and their impacts on welfare state activities, using Finnish social policy and social work research as case studies. The study considered debates and empirical research dealing with the effectiveness and quality of social services and social work. Rajavaara claimed that in the 2000s dialogical research and evaluation forms were quite common within the welfare sector; she found the evaluation practice within social work in Finland to belong to the interaction-based style of reasoning. By interaction-based style is meant that the target of knowledge is action-based and the subjects of knowledge are all the actors involved in the process. The perspective is democracy driven, striving towards shared knowledge, development and change. This democracy-driven perspective is grounded partly in a critique of representative democracy and partly in a concern for evaluation as learning (Vedung 2004). The pluralistic dimensions of evaluation with its different justifications and reasonings make it even more important for an evaluator to contemplate which perspective to choose and also the consequencesof their choice. How do we look at practice through the eyes of evaluation? What does the chosen method do the phenomenon? Can pluralism be realized in practice, and what are the changes that different perspectives and methods have brought forth?

After 10 years of being active in evaluation practice and research I wanted to explore the critical elements that I have experienced, which are essentially inherent in evaluation, and examine how they have changed during this time. Divergent views as such certainly belong to scientific development, but how do we look at these disputes? Is there a risk that we see more fractures and divergencies between different approaches? Or, should we look at fractures differently? There have been claims that what seems to be gaping divides between evaluation theories may shrink when the practice is examined (Donaldson & Scriven 2003). This is one aspect of this case study: to elaborate on the making of evaluation. There is an abundance of literature on different methods and approaches but the making of evaluation, the practice itself, is seldom described. And the making is *sui generis*, a mixture of different methods, including diverse standpoints, and aspects of values, emotions and moral judgements.

Another point that I want to make concerns the emergence of the new vision of evaluation, a vision that increasingly recognizes evaluation as an active partner in human service organizations. This new vision, I claim, has meant a very rapid development of new methodologies, and can thus be seen as a forerunner for the application-directed type of research. Ernest House remarked as early as 1986 that 'the practices of evaluation has been substantially transformed by the growth of internal evaluation'. What has made it possible, is the evaluation's strict adherence to practice. Evaluation research has had to deal with practical questions of how practice is being carried out, how it can be studied and evaluated and how the outcomes can be communicated with the practice. This aspect is closely connected to the challenges and practices of practice research.

The third point is one of synthesis, and a critical one. Is there a risk of narrowing down evaluation as a tool for welfare service and as an application-directed type of research? Where does theory step in? And should we stop at pluralism and complexity or are we heading into a new integrative phase, a phase that looks more deeply into the structures and systems involved? A phase – or a paradigm – that is holistic and strives at organized complexity?

But why a personal perspective and why a process approach? I started out in the traditional scientific manner; critically investigating and comparing evaluation methods that were based on different rationales. The problem was that I was not capable of highlighting the complexity and the change in the process. I needed to consider cases and contexts, but foremost the researcher mind. The solution was telling a development story and thus describing both the critical elements in the practice as well as stating where I stand as an evaluator. (cf. Hildrum & Strand 2007; Schwandt 2002) As Thomas Schwandt (2002, 189) has phrased it:

> Evaluator identity is about creating a narrative – a story – of who they are and what they should be as professionals. Telling such a narrative is inescapably to take a moral stance.

Research, evaluation and change

Recently, there has been discussion on the issue of scale and wider influence in both research and evaluation (Reason 2001; Ennals 2005; Gustavsen 1998; Gustavsen 2001; Chen 2005). Questions have been raised about the connectedness between research and a broader impact. What is the scale of our research and how is it connected to change? Peirce claimed in 1990 that

> evaluation is seldom capable of creating radical changes and that an instrumental use of evaluation, or research for that part, is an illusion. The real change actors are the ones who are working within the practice and the best way to understand an idea or action or system is to change it.

Here we can see a clear notion of how evaluation and practice are separate. The evaluator is an external researcher and it remains unclear how the use of evaluation is transferred and how it in fact can be connected to change. What was clear, however, was that Peirce saw the practitioner as the change agent.

But let us explore the connectedness: One way of examining research connectedness is to elucidate the methodology and the different forms of research and clarify the scope of research. Reason and Torbert (2001) have differentiated the scope of research through the division of first-person inquiry, second-person inquiry and third-person inquiry. First-person inquiry refers to the reflective researcher who brings inquiry into everyday practice seeing research as informing the practice and themselves, as perhaps self-appointed change agents. Second-person inquiry is a more co-operated inquiry in which a face-to-face group of co-reseachers engage together in cycles of action and reflection through research. The third-person inquiry goes further than this and tries to contribute to wider movements.

Nonwithstanding, change also happens at the interpersonal level, in people's minds, in attitudes and orientations, and in how we seek to understand each other in different encounters and contexts. These differences can be elucidated via Gadamers' (1989) three ways to encounter situations and people that challenge our expectations and assumptions. Here the encounters with researchers and field practice may serve as a good example. The first approach to encounter is to try to discover the typical behaviour of the other and to make predictions about others on the basis of experience. This is the methodological attitude of the social sciences, the idea of theoretical contemplation of an object of our understanding. In the second type of encounter, the interpreter acknowledges the other as a person, but this understanding is a form of self-relatedness. This can be understood as a form of sympathetic listening in which we interpret others in our own terms and refuse to risk our own prejudgements. The third way of understanding begins with the full acknowledgement that as interpreters we are situated within a tradition. It is only from such a position that an interpreter can experience the other truly as another. Hence, understanding requires an openness to experience, a willingness to engage in a dialogue with that which challenges our self-understanding.

A third dimension in research connectedness is the programme level. Programmes for workplace development have a wide range of goals by which their outcomes can be evaluated. First of all programmes have workplace-level goals that include 'first-degree' goals relating to immediate improvements in actions targeted by the project and 'second-degree' goals relating to the sustainability of outcomes at participating workplaces, which typically requires changes in work practices. Chen (2005) often refers to this as a shift from internal validation to external validation. Thirdly programmes have generative goals that concern ways in which the outcomes and experiences gained at individual workplaces benefit other workplaces, stakeholder groups or the general public. Outcomes and experiences typically cannot be shifted from one context to another *as such* but rather in the form of generative ideas to be reflected on and shaped as required in the new context.

With these three elements I will pursue the journey of research asking: What are the critical elements in knowledge production processes in evaluation practice on a personal level? (how do we look at practice and knowledge), on a methodological level (how do we do the research?); and on a programme level (what are the outcomes of research?). Who are seen as change agents, the researcher and the research community or the practice and how have these changed?

Scientific happenings

Let me first start with a more generic approach. As a researcher I have a long experience of large surveys and quantitative analyses. Quantitatve research is often described as a deductive process with clear questions, hypotheses and tests. In its most rigid form the quantitative researcher is external and does not have any values or feelings. He (and usually it is a he) is a positivist who interprets and relates to the interviewed with a methodological atttitude and contemplation of an object (cf. Gadamer 1989). The research process as such is homogenous and straightforward. There is no risk of misunderstanding. This, at least, is the image of quantitative research. But, as Hammersley (1995; 1992) and also many researchers have pointed out in criticizing this view, the divide between qualitative and quantitative research is arbitrary. Looking at social research methodology in terms of paradigms is really unhelpful. It exaggerates the depth of empirical differences in view among reserachers, and the scale and the impacts of these in the practice of research. Moreover, it gives the impression that these issues can and should be researched simply by a choice among paradigms. The distinctions tend also to obscure the complexity of the problems that face us as researchers. For me it is not a question of either/or but of both/and, which in practice can have many dimensions; by using different methods, but also, by combining different orientations and using qualitative lenses in weaving quantitative data, reading the data both vertically and horisontally.

Quantitative research processes use statistical analyses but the research process as such includes processes that are qualitative. Dialogue exists both with interviewees as well as with the analytical material. Yes, material does speak back. It is a process that starts out by hypotheses but changes on the way, as new questions arise and new hypotheses are formed. Lofland & Lofland (1996) emphasise freedom in the research process and this can and is used also within quantitative research. Reflecting on my position as a researcher and how the research relates to other actors, one can conclude, in contrast to the usual image of quantitative research, that the research was a creative process. The creativity was made possible through the interaction with other researchers but also through encounters with the interviewees. The knowledge achieved through this process was not 'unabashedly aimed at removing uncertainty or redusing diversity' (cf. Schwandt 2002, 198), quite the contrary it tried to set different aspects into question. Still, what was achieved at this point, was merely a change of mind, a critical reflectiveness that opened the forces that shaped my mind as a researcher. It did not though have a wider influence than face-to-face interactions. The research results were presented to the public, as well as to the interviewees, although disseminated mechanically through 'scientific happenings'. This traditional interview research can well serve as an example of a first-person inquiry seeing research as informing the practice and the researcher as the self-appointed change agent.

Interactive evaluation practice

The first evaluation (1997) I was involved in can be characterised as a mixed-method approach with a realistic twist. I was fortunate to be involved in a fairly long-term evaluation process for nearly four years following a development project for young children at risk of exclusion from work and education. From a request for an outcome-oriented and cost-effectiveness evaluation we managed to negotiate a more multidimensional approach, involving different researchers and various methods, focusing on service and user, process and outcome. And combining both surveys, cost-effectiveness studies, process analysis, time analysis and life story interviews. A critical, realistic evaluation can be seen as a challenger to the traditional effectiveness evaluation. The fact that one must know and understand what the results are made up of is emphasized in this approach. In this evaluation process we did not follow the realistic evaluation design to its fullness, trying to grasp the so-called clear box or white box through mechanisms, contexts, modifiers and outcome (Pawson & Tilley 1997). Instead we chose to view the material from different angles and let the different results reflect one another. This form of multidimensional evaluation process is seldom achieved in evaluation practice, but we as researchers chose to use this form of methodology to grasp the complexity of the practice focusing both on process and outcome and both on the practice and the user of the practice (Julkunen et al. 2000).

Table 1
A multidimensional evaluation research process

	Welfare Practice	User
Outcome	Cost-effectiveness	Effects on the life-situation
Process	Monitoring	Subjective experiences

In this reflection we also included the practitioners in the project. It was a co-operative inquiry where we worked together as researchers to better understand aspects of the project world, and also to find ways to act more effectively and search for practical forms of knowledge. The innermost core in evaluation is said to have a strict adherence to practical work: how it is actually carried out, and not how it is described as being carried out. It is a question of getting ones hands dirty, of digging into the real practice. At a personal level we as researchers encountered many obstacles, skepticism and fear at first, even criticism. Eventually, we succeeded in setting a dialogue with the project personnel and the process itself was developmental. It was a continuous developmental communicative interchange through which the project members and we as researchers gained more insight in the logic of the project.

What was our role as evaluators? As evaluators we came to serve as interpreters, helping the practitioners to better understand the logic of the project. We described and explained and were not engaged with normative criticism- at least how we felt it to be. Sue White (2001) talks about auto-ethnography and refers to the necessity to translate back and forth of experience-near and experience-distant concepts. In generating auto-ethnographic work, researchers attempt to more fully realize the ideal of reflexivity, which is the idea that the researcher needs to be aware of his or her role as a researcher. This was not an easy process. We had difficulties in finding the right platform for the discussion; should we just present the results or involve the practitioners in evaluating the results and how should we go about doing it? We started off rather traditionally, presenting the results and at the same time evaluating how the results were perceived. We listened sympathetically, understanding the claims of the practitioners, but it was from the standpoint of us as outside researchers.

> At first we felt a mutual insecurity in what was behind the spoken words. It took a while to find the right meeting rituales and relevant subjects to discuss. After a while trust between us increased and we came to know each other's manners. (Julkunen et al. 2000, 176)

We achieved then a mutual understanding, but we were not involved in a common framework or process. We were the experts and this led to a process where our expertise was in even greater demand. One may claim that the practitioners saw themselves as change agents, but up to a point, they became dependent on us as experts. A different approach was surely needed.

From interactive evaluation to inclusive learning

The following turn in the realistic twist emerged from our being engaged in a development project that we had together with practitioners at the welfare office (2003). As a case it consisted of an application of realistic thinking, and was designed and performed as a single case evaluation. A key question was to find answers to why a certain intervention had an effect. It was a struggle to understand what the results are made up of, and through this to try to develop future practice. By analyzing – and creating – the documentation we can find out what the practice consists of, what interventions and processes there are, and what their consequences are for the users. It is an approach that is based on consideration of each individual case and on professional evaluation of these circumstances. Theoretically it is based on realism and it is required to have some understanding of the underlying thoughts of the philosophy of science on which realism is based.

> We started out by trying to clarify for ourselves the realistic concepts and thinking. The process was both challenging and complicated. Starting required outside guidance and counseling as well as analyzing the evaluation mode and getting it more in touch with practical work. (Högnabba et al. 2005).

The three-year development project consisted of workshops, consultations, seminars, together researching, and together dwellings: in Thomas Schwandt's words (2007)

a mode of engagement with the world in which the familiar things around us are non-deliberately and effortlessly co-opted into our current activity to form an extension of our being and doing

Here, the learning dimension came into place. It was clear that in order to get more far-reaching results in practice, we needed to place emphasis on learning. We wanted to develop a tool to assist practitioners to make sense of the practice, and for this development work needed support of theories and movement between empirical observations and theories. From a practitioner perspective this may be a shift from street-level bureaucrats to street-level intellectuals (Marthinsen in this issue). This is well illuminated by a practitioner in the report that followed the project :

> *We were able to make use of the realistic approach in the experiment in many ways. The use of the concepts of realistic evaluation helped to analyze the reality in a new way. For instance, we learned to think, analyze and theorize the mechanisms underlying a phenomenon. The realistic approach is made clearer also in other ways by the role of theory in the research: especially the dialogue between empiric results and theories becomes easier to manage.*

Nevertheless:

> In the use of different research methods and verification of outcome, the same difficulties and problems were encountered as in other approaches. (Högnabba et al. 2005, 123)

The realistic evaluation method did not as such survive as a pragmatical tool, but what did survive was the theory, a research-mindedness, and, I claim, a change in thinking about practice. The practitioners learned to think, act and analyse the practice in a new way. This became a more far-reaching result. Program theory (Chen 2005) seemed then successful as a conceptual mirror or map (cf. Connolly 2006). The process was created in dialogical forums, and was practice based, where both academic and stakeholder theories intertwine. It included a rather large group of people, with the urge to learn together. As researchers we were positioned merely as facilitators, but failed to systematically evaluate the process.

This case exemplifies a democracy-driven approach and serves as an example of the second person inquiry where we as researchers are engaged together in cycles of action and reflection. Reflecting on it is also a question of being engaged in elucidating work models not as static products, but as generative metaphors which may lead to new ideas and images of how to change social systems.

From group interaction to wider influence

The wider influence in evaluation has been triggered by developing evaluation models (Seppänen-Järvelä et al. 2006). Developing evaluation, particularly the deliberative democracy approach, is gaining ground in the evaluation practice. It is a procedure that promotes not only more profoundly informed views on the service but also empowers citizens.

In this example of the evaluation process the user dimension also enters. User involvement has been argued from a direct-democracy and deliberative-democracy case (Vedung 2004). The deliberative feature engenders a discursive, reasoning, discussing, learning–through–dialogue encounter, which may educate clients to become better citizens in general: 'the consumer as citizen rather than the consumer as customer' (Jenkins & Gray 1992, 296).

In early 2000s I became aquainted with the user-oriented BIKVAmodel, a democratic and development oriented evaluation model that was originally developed in Denmark (Krogstrup 1996; 1997; 2004). This model has been developed in response to growing demands for involving the users in evaluations in the mid-1990s. The object of the model is, through including users in evaluations, to secure correlation between the users' perception of problems and the public services, and hence between the users' perception of problems and the social work at different levels in the organization. A unifying element in this model is the change process which gives meaning and direction to the evaluation. The idea is, that the users hold important knowledge that can contribute to goal-direct the services of the public sector. The evaluation process is bottom-up, oriented toward learning, and is expected to contribute to methodological development. The evaluation starts with focus groups of users where the problems that the users find relevant are discussed, but front stage staff (employees in direct contact with the users), managers, and politicians are also included. Hence, the users are assigned a key role in this model as triggers for learning. Through this dialogue public organizations receive knowledge on how to develop practice. Dialogic and improvement approaches are embedded in the model, which can thus be seen as one way of revitalizing praxis and the moral-political life of society (Schwandt 2001). But how to implement it in practice and avoiding the expert trap?

The fourth example is a teaching and learning process (2005) where we applied peer working methods and explored the user-oriented evaluation method together with practitioners who wanted to learn the method and pilot it in practice. We created a one year peer working group following the different steps in the evaluation process and sharing the experiences (Hänninen et al. 2006). Our interest and aim was to experiment how the method fit into developing welfare practices in a Finnish context and test whether the method could function as an internal evaluation, and furthermore, through the pilots lead to the creation of structures for user involvement. In so doing we included several communities of practice (Wenger 1998) – in fact over two years altogether 23 different practices, where the participants within and across these communities of practice were connected by a set of relationships and a set of shared experience. Our sessions formed a common set of boundary objects, such as mutual development goals and shared project plans (cf. Hildrum & Liavåg Strand 2007). This may be characterised as an open environment where practice developed at different levels, at the learning forums where practitioners and researchers (or we as teachers) met, at the practical environment where users and practitioners met, and at a personal level where the thinking developed.

In peer learning the process is built on support from each other, so there is constant change between the roles being supported and giving support. Support cannot be ordered but favourable conditions can be built up (Hyväri 2005.) Peer learning is also an emotional, social and dynamic process. Learning always involves emotions, without which learning is claimed not to be possible. Emotions and factional knowledge is intertwined and learning by doing and actively testing is involved in skills. It comes more close to the forms of auto-ethnographic work embracing personal thoughts, feelings, stories, and observations as a way of understanding the social context we were studying.

Susanne Hyväri (2005) concludes, that for peer learning to be successful a common space is needed, where experiences can be shared. This also requires a set of shared rules. In peer learning specific elements are the build blocks. In our setting we built on the learning processes that have been analysed in pedagogy. For instance, Hakkarainen (2001) talks about research oriented learning which has the common denominator of shared knowledge. Still, we had a rather broad and open approach, a process that did not just focus on shared knowledge about the methodology but also about the practice. What changed, or did anything change? The intention was to monitor the process and the process ended with a common publication where the practitioners critically assessed the process in their own practice. We found difficulties associated with the practitioner's location within the organization and about the tensions between practitioner's own experiences of user dilemmas and bringing them into the process. These triggered discussions on using the user evaluation model as an internal evaluation. The practice insight is however essential with regard to changes in structures.

> The model strengthened and concretisized the various dimensions of user involvement. Before we had approached the issue problem-orientedly and did not succeed in getting the users involved. The evaluation process gave courage and understanding in that evaluation can bridge the spoken languages of the service providers and service receivers. The authencity of the user voice is preserved in this deliberative process. (Hirsikoski 2007, 28)

The role of the evaluator was also elaborated by the practitioners:

> The evaluator is not the one who changes things, he gives the welfare workers and the leaders possibilities, space and tools for making use of the users

experiences and responses. One could see the evaluator as an active coach during the process. (Högnabba & Paananen 2007, 26)

Learning is much about solving problems and conflicts. Practice may need forms of understanding that are in themselves practical. This was manifested in the peer working process we had. Problems, successes and stories were brought into the group and based on the common ground in which they participated and to which they contributed. It was the practitioners and the developers who set the agenda through their questions, uncertainties and descriptions of how the different steps have been taken. Through these deliberations the different practice communities could reflect their practice. How can we describe our role? Perhaps as development-oriented supervisors, or auto-ethnographic researchers, with the aim of highlighting the theoretical and analytical aspects in the process as well as allowing for innovative processes. A clear structure, but also space for creativity, the direct support and the interaction with other professionals made this a pleasant experience, as one participant phrased it. It was a joint action within which the dialogue between the theoretical and the more practical processes are conducted (cf. Shotter 1999).

Burbules (1993) and Mönkkönen (2007) highlight the concept of dialogue as a process of communication which is directed toward new discovery and new knowledge. Dialogue is in itself not a goal but a process that supports many other goals. Schwandt (2002) discusses Burbules further and argues that dialogue is both a practice that helps us achieve phronesis (practical-moral-knowledge) and a regulative ideal that points us towards the tasks that we need to undertake. As a practice, it is not eristic but constitutes a conversational interaction directed intentionally towards learning. It is not aimed at changing other people but at affecting change in and by participants in the dialogue.

> The process was exciting, respectful and participatory. I believe that systematically fulfilled the evaluation process creates cyclically something new. This, on the other side, helps to understand the meaning of the common responsibility we have: the culture of pride increases. (Thomasén 2007, 40).

The user-oriented evaluation model contributed thus to wider movements, to levels not just in practice but in thinking and eventually at the policy level. The learning process we developed built a new balance of understanding where the second-person, dialogic processes are primary elements that may cause third person systems conditions. This kind of evaluation practice is reframed as dialogical interpretive encounters. It is not the evaluator nor the practitioner that is aimed at in solving a problem, but to understand it. This kind of reasoning involves incoporating the complexity of the situation and making sense of it. According to Gadamer (1981) this kind of reasoning contributes to a broadening of our horizon and our human experiences. This new understanding also transformed and consolidated future strategies in practice. In many of the practice environments structures for better user involvement were developed.

The changed roles and processes in evaluation practice

Evaluation research is applied research intended to exploit new knowledge in solving practical problems and developing the activity. These case studies brought forward in this article show all that the production of knowledge in social work and welfare settings must be seen as a continuum. It needs as well to be grounded in the individual nature of the people involved and their life situations. Professional social workers have often been disappointed in studies presenting average results or evaluation studies based on extensive material where the expected results vanish and disappears.

Evaluation research has had to deal with practical questions of how practice is being carried out, how it can be studied and evaluated and how the outcomes can be communicated with the practice. This aspect is closely connected to the challenges of practice research. What are then these new modes of organizing and completing evaluation practice? In Table 2, I have summarized the different elements inherent in the cases described by disseminating five dimensions: 1) research interest, 2) methodology, 3) apprehention of knowledge, 4) knowledge outcome of research, 5) dissemination process and 6) role of researcher.

There is an ongoing discussion about the evolution of science and society. Much of this discussion has been critisized to be abstract. Tove Rasmussen in this issue discussed the different modes of knowledge with reference to what can be called evidence in social work. The focus in this chapter is on evaluation, with an attempt to highlight the critical elements in the development of evaluation practices through using cases from practice. The cases described in this chapter are not validly comparable but are chosen to highlight both practice and research. It draws attention both to the role of researcher, and the knowledge production and dissemination process.

The first mode is characterised by a traditional research design with the researcher who brings inquiry into practice seeing research as informing the practice and researchers as self-appointed change agents. The validity of the research is assured through scientific peer evaluation. The second mode is a more co-operated inquiry in which a group of researchers and practitioners engage together in cycles of action and reflection through research. Here the practitioner is seen as the change agent and an integration of a reflective mode is seen as essential. The validity is tested inside the practice incorporating dialogues with involved actors. The third mode is a more open and extensive process with multi-dismensional networking and encounters at the interfaces of various operating contexts. Evaluation is seen as an active partner in the process of knowledge and validity is repeatedly tested not only inside the practice but outside the community involving different networks. This can be described as co-evolution of science and society with reference to Helga Nowotny (2006).

Karvinen- Niinikoski (2005) stresses that the shift towards open expertise has increased the significance of interaction. Expertise is not a matter of individual professionals being able to store information and knowledge within themselves but the communication and construction of knowledge, and the development of creative models rests on a sense of community. The researcher role has much expanded from the self-appointed expert to a reflexive and dialogical researcher where the analysis of data involves interpretation on the part of the researcher. However, rather than a portrait of the Other (person, group, culture), the difference is that the researcher is also obliged to construct a portrait of the self. In generating cooperative evaluation researchers attempt to realize the ideal of reflexivity and embrace also personal thoughts, stories and observations as a way of understanding the context. This is much the opposite of a hypothesis driven, (post)positivist research.

The importance of knowledge dissemination was recognised as early as the 1960's and 1970's. These problematics are still a central element of practice development. Since the 1980's the orientation of discussion has been away from structural towards generative approaches and more recently the focus of research has been on how to find solutions to the problems of work and organisations (Gustavsen 1985). The notion of how a change in practices takes place becomes visible through ways of dissemination. Arnkil (2006) compares different concepts of knowledge dissemination and various development strategies, identifying rational planning, learning organisation, and an everyday 'complex response' model each of which impact on development efforts and concepts.

Table 2
Critical elements in evaluation practice

	Traditional evaluation research	Co-operative practice evaluation	Co-evolutive practice evaluation
Research interest	Hierarchical, first person inquiries	Interactive, second person inquiries	Interactive, third person inquiries
Methodology	Surveys and interviews Analysis of data material	Multimethods Single case studies Analysis involves reflective interpretations	Ethnographic and multidimensional evaluation Analysis involves narration of the researcher role
Knowledge apprehention and positioning	High level of expertise Knowledge develops through research	Postmodern expertise Knowledge develops in interaction with practice	Postmodern expertise Knowledge emerges and develops in communication in, at and between different levels
Knowledge outcome	Descriptions, normative judgements New knowledge	Deliberation Dialogue within research Dialogue with practitioners Reflective knowledge	Deliberation and learning New understanding

Table 2
Critical elements in evaluation practice (continued)

Dissemination process	Knowledge transition as a linear process Certain knowledge Quality assessment through scientific peer evaluation	Knowledge production processes Reflexivity Learning from surprises and mistakes - simultaneous learning and development Quality assessment through dialogue	Knowledge production and knowledge development Reflexivity Peer learning, methodological development and developmental evaluation Quality assurance tested through the process of extension
Role of researcher	Researcher as the change agent Research informs practice Internal validation	Practitioner as the change agent Reflections through evaluation Internal validation	Co-evolutive agency Peer learning, evaluation as an active partner External validation

What are then these different modes of organizing evaluation practice and what are the characteristics of the new modes of practice evaluation? Shaw (2006) has argued that following elements are involved: 1) direct concern with the outcome of research, 2) researchers as both subjects and objects, 3) overlap between the production and appropriation of knowledge, 4) personal stakes and objectives, and 5) research process that is one of identity formation.

A new generation of evaluators is said to explore how to engage in a kind of evaluation practice that is at once descriptive and normative, that incorporates the moral and political dimensions of everyday life into the activity of defining social problems and evaluating social programmes as solutions to those problems, and that regards evaluation as a form of social self understanding or interpretation in the traditions of public philosophy (Schwandt 2002, 124; 191). It is a question both of narrating the role of the researcher and of being an active partner both in science and society. A new conceptualization of evaluation is interested in recovering a sense of making and participating rather than just seeing and finding. And to be able to learn from practice, evaluation needs to develop social relationships in open environments.

References

Alasoini, T., Korhonen, S-M., Lahtonen M., Ramstad E., Rouhiainen N., Suominen K. (2006): *Tuntosarveja ja tulkkeja. Oppimisverkostot työelämän kehittämistoiminnan uutena muotona.* Helsinki: Tykes raportteja 50.

Arnkil, R. (2006): Hyvien käytäntöjen levittäminen EU:n kehittämisstrategiana. In Seppänen-Järvelä, R. & Karjalainen, V. (eds) *Kehittämistyön risteyksiä.* Stakes: Helsinki.

Burbules, N. (1993): *Dialogue in Teaching. Theory and Practice.* New York: Teachers College Press.

Chen, H. (2005): *Practical Program Evaluation. Assess and Improve Program Planning, Implementation and Effectiveness.* Thousand Oaks, CA: Sage.

Connolly W.E. (2006): Political Science & Ideology. Atherton Press.

Dahlberg, M., Vedung, E. (2001): *Demokrati och brukarutvärdering.* (Democracy and user evaluation) Lund: Studentlitteratur.

Donaldson, S.I., Scriven M. (2003): *Evaluating Social Programs and problems: Visions for the New Millenium.*

Ennals R. (2005): *Rapid restructuring of European working life – likely health effects and options for preventive action.* Paper presented at the Anglo-Swedish High Level Seminar on Promoting Occupational and Public Health, Stockholm, October 2005.

Fook, J. (2002): *Social work. Critical theory and practice.* London: Sage Publications.

Gadamer H-G. (1981): *Reason in the age of Science.* Cambridge: MA: MIT Press.

Gadamer, H-G. (1989): *Truth and Method.* New York: Continuum.

Gustavsen, B. (1985): Workplace Reform and Democratic Dialogue. *Economic and Industrial Democracy,* 6 (4) pp. 461-479.

Gustavsen, B. (1996): Action research, democratic dialogue and the issue of 'critical mass' in Change. *Qualitative Inquiry* 2 (1) pp. 90-103.

Gustavsen, B. (1998): From experiments to Network Building: trend in use of research for reconstructing working life. *Human Relations* 1 (3) pp. 431-448.

Gustavsen, Björn, Finne, Håkan & Oscarsson, B. (2001): *Creating Connectedness. The role of social research in innovation policy.* Amsterdam: John Benjamins.

Hakkarainen, K. (2001): Aikuisten oppiminen verkossa. In Sallila, P. & Kalli, P. (eds), *Verkot ja teknologia aikuisopiskelun tukena.* Aikuiskasvatuksen 42. vuosikirja (pp. 16-52). Jyväskylä: Gummerus.

Hammersley, M. (1992): Deconstructing the qualitative-quantitative divide. In Brannen J (ed.) *Mixing Methods: qualitative and quantitative research,* Aldershot: Avebury.

Hammersley, M. (1995): *The Politics of Social Research.* London: Routledge.

Hildrum, J., Liavåg Strand G.L. (2007): *Overcoming challenges in Writing about Action Research. The Promise of the Development Story.* Springer Netherlands.

Hirsikoski R. (2007) In Hänninen Kaija, Julkunen Ilse, Högnabba Stina, Thomassén Tarya (eds) (2006) *Asiakkaat oppimisen käynnistäjinä.* Stakes: Helsinki.

Hänninen K., Julkunen I., Högnabba S. & Thomassén, T. (2006): *Asiakkaat oppimisen käynnistäjinä.* Stakes: Helsinki.

Högnabba, S., Julkunen, I., Kainulainen, S., Korteniemi, P., Lindqvist T., Peitola, P. (2005): Steps into Realistic Evaluation in Social Work in Finland. In Peter Sommerfeld (ed.) *Evidence-Based Social Work - Towards a New Professionalism?* Bern: Peter Lang.

Högnabba, S. & Paananen, T. (2007): In Hänninen Kaija, Julkunen Ilse, Högnabba Stina, Thomassén Tarya (eds) (2006) *Asiakkaat oppimisen käynnistäjinä.* Stakes: Helsinki.

Jackson, M.C. (2005): *Systems thinking. Creative holism for managers.* West Sussex: John Wiley & Sons Ltd.

Jenkins, B. & Grey A.(1992): *Codes of Accountability in the new public sector.*

Julkunen, I., Strandell, H., Kangas, H. (eds) (2000): Kunnon elämä...Olisi hyvä jossain. SSKH Skrifter 12/2000.

Karvinen-Niinikoski, S. (2005): Research orientation and expertise in social work /challenges for social work education. *European Journal of Social Work,* 8 (3) pp. 259-271.

Krogstrup, H. (2004): User Evaluation in Practice. In Julkunen, I. (ed.) *Perspectives, models and methods in evaluating the welfare sector - a Nordic approach.* FinSoc Working Papers 4/2004.

Krogstrup, H. (1996): Brugerinddragelse i kvalitetsvurdering af sociale indsatsområder. (User involvement in quality assessment within the social sector) *Nordisk Socialt arbejde* 2/1996. Scandinavian University Press, pp. 114-129.

Krogstrup, H. (1997): User Participation in Quality Assessment. *Evaluation,* 3 (2) pp. 205-224. Sage Publications.

Lofland, J., Lofland L. (1995): *Analyzing Social Settings: A Guide to Qualitative Observation and Analysis.* Wadsworth: Belmont.

Mönkkönen, K. (2007): *Vuorovaikutus. Dialoginen asiakastyö.* Helsinki:Edita.

Pawson, R. & Tilley, N. (1997): *Realistic Evaluation.* London: Sage.

Rajavaara , M. (2007): *Vaikuttavuusyhteiskunta. Sosiaalisten olojen arvostelusta vaikutusten todentamiseen.* Helsinki: Kansaneläkelaitos.

Reason, P., Torbert W. (2001): *Toward a transformational science: a further look at the scientific merits of action research.*

Schwandt, Thomas (2002): *Evaluation practice reconsidered.* Peter Lang Publishing.

Seppänen-Järvelä, R., Karjalainen V. (eds) (2006): Kehittämistyön risteyksiä. Stakes: Helsinki.

Shaw, Ian (2006): Practitioner Evaluation at Work. *American Journal of Evaluation* 27 (1) pp. 44-63.

Shotter, John, Gustavsen Björn (1999): *The role of dialogue conferences in the development of learning regions: Doing from within our lives together what we cannot do apart.* Stockholm: Centre for Advanced Studies in Leadership, Stockholm, School of Economics.

Shotter, John (1999): Must we work out how to act jointly? *Theory and Psychology* 9, pp. 129-133.

Shotter, John (2004): *Goethe and the refiguring of intellectual inquiry: from aboutness-thinking to withness-thinking in everyday life.* University of New Hampshire.

Svensson, Lennart, Göran Brolin, Per-Erik Ellström, Örjen Widegren (2002): *Interaktiv forskning - för utveckling av teori och praktik.* Stockholm: Vetenskaplig skriftserie för Arbetslivsinstitutet.

Thomasén T (2007): In Hänninen Kaija, Julkunen Ilse, Högnabba Stina, Thomassén Tarya (eds) (2006) *Asiakkaat oppimisen käynnistäjinä.* Stakes: Helsinki.

Vedung, Evert (2004): *Utvärderingens bölja*. Stakes: Helsinki.

Wenger, E. (1998): *Communities of Practice. Learning as a Social System.*

White, S. (2001): Auto-ethnography as reflexive inquiry: the research act as self-surveillance In *Qualitative social work research: method and content.* Sage, London.

Wittgenstein, L. (1980): *Culture and Value.* Oxford: Blackwell.

6

The Mirror method: A structure supporting expertise in social welfare services

Laura Yliruka

Introduction

Social work requires time for thought, and space for analysing the experiences arising from one's own work alongside colleagues. While the ability to act is an imperative, social workers should also be allowed to stop and take the time to analyse their experiences in order to learn from them. Trust in one's own professional skills, understanding and experience are necessary, but so too is the courage to acknowledge that one person cannot know everything. Rather, a worker should seek 'mirrors' for themselves and the work community, enabling learning from everyone's own work. Given that social workers must deal with difficult cases and shortcomings in the social welfare system, they must be supported, 'nurtured' and protected in order to prevent any erosion of their working ability. It is therefore vital to find new ways of supporting the work conducted by workers and the work community.

This chapter reviews the self and peer evaluation method Mirror (*Kuvastin* in Finnish) and its use in social work teams as a practice supporting client work and workers' well-being at work and also as a structure providing space for thought. The focus is both on the immediate consequences resulting from the method's application and its long-term consequences outside the Mirror user team. Current evidence on methods and practices contributing to the development of an individual's or a community's expertise is scarce (see, however, Vataja 2008). Although this chapter is mainly method-oriented, it also considers challenges regarding evaluation, reflectiveness and knowledge generation in social work and discusses their link to well-being at work. These themes are looked at within the framework of science and technology studies (Latour 1987; Koivisto 2007).

The key idea of Mirror, a reflective self and peer evaluation method originally developed by a group of social workers in adult services (Mannerström et al. 2005), is to support evaluative ways of working within a social work team and encourage the development of collective expertise. Although a 'light' method, Mirror improves the systematic approach to work. The method is used for analysing team work and supporting learning at work and thus coping at work. The process goes beyond the boundary between the individual and the collective.

The Mirror method was first piloted in 2005, in three social work teams in adult services, co-ordinated by the Finnish Evaluation of Social Services Group (FinSoc) operating under the National Research and Development Centre for Welfare and Health (STAKES). While it seemed that the method could be adopted independently, the first pilot phase showed that its dissemination would in fact require interaction. The first pilot phase led to the creation of the Mirror handbook (Yliruka 2006). Moreover, further piloting and development of the Mirror method was conducted under the sub-project 'Working conditions in social services', funded by the Ministry of Social Affairs and Health. The sub-project's objective was to enable the larger-scale adoption of Mirror. This pilot phase aimed at adapting the model to various operating environments and evaluating its effectiveness.

Further piloting was initiated in stages in January–June 2006. The objective of the related *development* was to:

1. create structures enabling social workers' collective learning and to include continuous evaluation in their basic working methods;
2. enhance the method's usability during the process;
3. improve the method so that social workers could themselves help other professionals who want to begin its use; and
4. extend the method to sectors other than adult social work.

The objective of *research* was to examine the consequences resulting from the adoption of Mirror in work communities.

Based on the findings of this research, this chapter analyses the kinds of work communities and the conditions under which the Mirror method is likely to function successfully; to what extent the method was anchored as a permanent operating structure within the participating social welfare organisations; and how the social work communities benefited from using the method.

Basis of the Mirror method

The Mirror method originated from a desire to harness tacit knowledge for developing self-evaluation methods in social work (Yliruka 2000). The original developmental context for the method was a municipal social services office, where social workers worked with adult clients, with about 100 clients per social worker. Social work was delivered mainly through benefit provision. Social workers worked 'behind closed doors': there was considerable professional autonomy, but little professional discussion within the organisation. Weekly case meetings were focused on questions about living allowances and administrative issues. Social workers were interested in doing social work more holistically, and, when the social services department reorganised the living allowance work, the time and possibility to develop social work was found. There was a professional interest in developing an evaluation method that could be used in work settings. The central aim was to develop a continuous evaluation method and 'learning through living'.

The theoretical basis of Mirror includes the ideas of Ian Shaw (1999) on reflective evaluation, which emphasises two interlinked statements:

1. knowledge arises from action and exists for action; and
2. knowledge is tested in real-life situations.

The motivation for this development derived from the urge to improve social work from the professional perspective and to identify how best to generate practice-based social work evidence in order to respond to the effectiveness requirements set for it (for example, Macdonald 2000). In the method's research and development process, theoretical support was sought from debates on expertise (for example Hakkarainen 2000; 2003; 2004; Saaristo 2000; Nowotny 2000; Fook 2002; Parton & O'Byrne 2000; Bereiter & Scardamalia 1993; Tynjälä 1997) and from theories of knowledge formation and learning communities (for example, Nonaka & Takeuchi 1995; Wenger 1998; Hakkarainen 2003). Structuring the method was closely related to the research project 'The Tricky Social Work' of Helsinki University, concerning social welfare expertise (see, for

Figure 1 Mirror supporting client work.

The situations where Mirror has been found useful

Figure 2 Social worker's knowledge base.

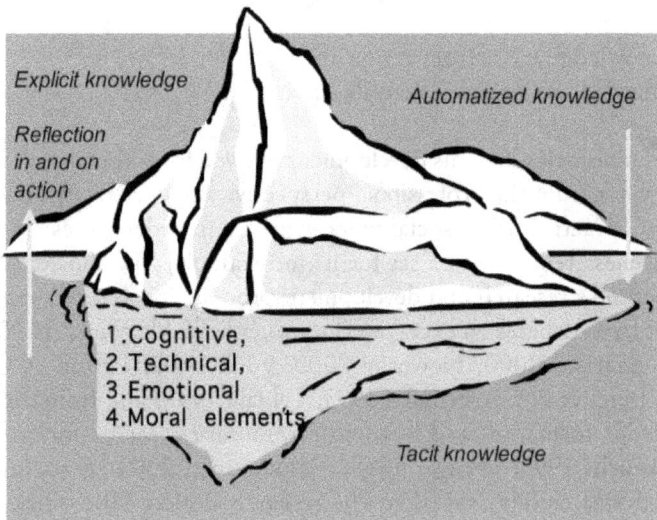

example, Karvinen-Niinikoski et al. 2005).

The Mirror method involves the use of forms designed to support the documentation of one's own work and self evaluation, common peer evaluation meetings, follow-up of the work's progress, and the concluding assumptions of effectiveness. Themes included in the forms are open, rather than based on indicators. The objective of such open themes is to activate the social worker to analyse social work. *Mirror is designed to be used in parallel with the evaluation of social work process conducted together with the client.* The reflective self and peer evaluation process of Mirror consists of four steps:

1. self evaluation of the social worker's own work and preparation for the peer evaluation meeting;
2. peer evaluation discussion within the social work team and the assessment of further work;
3. follow-up in formative or summative evaluation meetings
4. drawing conclusions: team's conclusions on the boundary conditions for social work and on specific themes requiring monitoring or improvement.

Step 1

The method's Step 1, self evaluation by the social worker of his/her own work, uses the Mirror Hall self evaluation form. Step 2 peer evaluation discussion is built on the Internal Mirror of Peer Evaluation form. The structure for Step 3 peer evaluation discussions is provided by the Rear View Mirror and Internal Mirror of Formative Evaluation forms. Finally, Step 4 involves common knowledge creation, and is supported by the Prism form. Steps 3 and 4 take place during the same peer meeting.

In Step 1, a social worker begins the Mirror process by selecting the client case[1] which is to be analysed through self evaluation and for which he/she desires peer group support. *The essential object of scrutiny is the social worker's own way of conducting client work.* Then, the worker reviews the information related to the case and prepares a free format description of the client's situation to serve as material for the peer evaluation. Other material can also be used, such as notes, plans and other client work documents. At this stage, self evaluation is guided by the Mirror Hall form. The name of the form, Mirror Hall, refers to reviewing one's own work from various angles in a certain context. Mirror seeks to inspire the social worker to express his/her own operational theory and articulate tacit knowledge as far as possible (Polanyi 1983; Yliruka 2000) and in a holistic manner: the relationship between goals and means and the factors that affect one's work – both personal and professional (cognitive, technical, emotional and moral elements) (figure 2) and contextual, structural factors, edge conditions. The idea is to reveal thinking and assumptions which are usually not written into the official records.

When using the Mirror Hall self evaluation form, the worker reviews:

+ any opportunities and obstacles for change in the client's life situation;
+ established internal and external factors;
+ resources and risks;
+ social work targets;
+ working method choices;
+ assumed impacts on working methods;
+ the worker's experience on interaction with the client;
+ their expertise-orientation in the client relationship;
+ their role as a social worker in the client relationship;
+ assumptions on how the situation may be influenced by factors related to self (gender, values, attitudes), previous experiences or the current situation of the client relationship under review or structural factors facilitating or hindering client work (such as the service system, established social work practices, legislation and resources)

The worker also evaluates the influence of context on the client relationship and professional concern for the client's situation on a scale from 1 to 4. Finally, the opportunities to utilise one's own professional competences in the client case are evaluated.

Step 2

Step 2 involves a peer evaluation meeting in which the social worker explains the themes he/she has entered into the self evaluation form, while the other listens without interrupting. The evaluating peers are encouraged to participate in an internal dialogue (Bakhtin 1982) using the Internal Mirror form. While listening, the peers jot down questions, thoughts and feelings, work-related suggestions and tips on related reading. The form is designed to steer the peers towards providing positive genuine feedback for the worker whose work is being evaluated. In the peer evaluation discussion, each peer has a turn to speak. The themes included in the Mirror Hall form are considered and subjected to an evaluative debate. All work-related suggestions are collected by the self-evaluating worker for further processing.

Step 3

Step 3 comprises common formative evaluation meetings for monitoring how the client case has progressed since the first peer evaluation: Which work-related suggestions were or were not implemented? Have there been any changes in the worker's interpretation of the client situation or working possibilities? Additionally, the worker assesses what he/she has learned during the process, using the Rear View Mirror form as a support tool.

Step 4

Step 4 is the concluding part. The team will draw their common conclusions on the boundary conditions for conducting social work and on specific themes requiring follow-up or improvement. The team will also make effectiveness assumptions. The Prism form is the support tool for this step.

The method's second pilot phase applied the principles of a 'slow' process ('HIDAS' in Finnish) developed by Kari Pääskynen (2004). A 'slow' process is:

1. personal (something more for oneself, evaluation work supports the worker's own work, peer evaluations increase the team's expertise);
2. target-oriented (focusing on the essential rather than superficial dabbling);
3. open (each member of the community shares their knowledge and experiences; open review of work prevents remaining hidebound by one's own views);

4. dialogic (creative operating culture allows collective thinking); and
5. valuing tacit knowledge (identifying the core of one's own thinking and action, reviewing and verbalising one's own routines).

Mirror in the pain spot of client work

Mirror is particularly used for analysing and evaluating client work situations involving factors which are burdening or worrying the worker. The worker has indeed recognised that this particular client case causes concerns for him/her, its processing may have become prolonged or have stagnated or there may be problems in initiating the work. A literature review of international research concerning working conditions in social welfare (Meltti & Kara 2009) indicates that clients requiring intense work efforts may negatively influence workers' job satisfaction (Gimbel et al. 2002). On the other hand, enabling a change in a client's life has been found to be a strong individual driver of job satisfaction and motivation (Carpenter 1999). In this light, it is very important to achieve a clearer understanding of the types of situations which may cause the worker to feel incapable of enabling change in client's life situation. The basic elements of client work includes commitment and continuity. It is crucial to prevent the worker from losing hope in client work should the client's situation fail to progress as planned, or if the client does not commit to co-operation. The work conducted should be considered in its context: Which means are used in the work? What are the worker's decision-making powers? What limitations, boundary conditions to or opportunities for overcoming the limitations exist in the case in hand? This approach is called contextual social work, and its aim is to provide social workers with a meaningful manner of conducting social work (Fook 2002: 140–144; Yliruka 2005).

Development environment

The development project was co-ordinated by the Finnish Evaluation of Social Services Group, FinSoc (operating under the National Research and Development Centre for Welfare and Health, STAKES). The project included ten social work teams from various social welfare sectors. Eligible teams were sought through a nationally published advertisement at the beginning of 2006. While the selected workers' backgrounds were heterogeneous in terms of education and experience, an interest in obtaining a common vision of their work was common to everyone (Haapamäki & Yliruka 2006; Säiläkivi 2007).

The teams participating in the Mirror development project came from the Greater Helsinki area. This area is characterised by a complex operating environment, a dispersed service sector, a high staff turnover posing challenges to the formation of functioning and co-operative relationships, and the fact that some people remain outside the services (Sosiaalibarometri 2007). Owing to a complex operating environment, a larger city is often better equipped to use Mirror, since social welfare teams often already exist in city organisations, whereas, in smaller localities, a peer group might be harder to find. Among the interested teams, six functioned in child protection and one specialised in family care. Adult social work was represented by two adult social work teams operating in social welfare offices and one team functioning in the Probation Service. Moreover, one team was engaged in youth work within emergency social services, while another represented school social work. Eight of the participating teams existed already, while three had been formed specifically for the Mirror work. The project also included monitoring of the unsupervised adoption of Mirror by a gerontological social work development project in the Greater Helsinki area.

The method was proposed to the teams as a basic structure for their own work, but two of the teams defined the use of the method for promoting inter-team dialogue on social work. Training, tutorial assistance and network meetings were arranged for all participating teams at two month intervals, involving a total of four sessions. In order to support the teams, a virtual working forum was set up on Sosiaaliportti, a Finnish website dedicated to social welfare professionals. Each team was steered towards defining its own objectives according to which it would proceed within the general pilot process.

The teams had various expectations. Some related to the adoption of Mirror as a method, such as its ease of use or targeting, finding space for it and the method's outcomes (thorough consideration of one's own working methods, enhancing the methodical nature of one's work, understanding the client processes). Other expectations concerned the team's functioning (increasing the ability to listen, sharing knowledge, learning from the others' personal working methodas, the team's enhanced ability to support an individual worker, integrity of work) or, in the case of two teams, inter-team learning.

Team-specific tutorial assistance for adopting the method was arranged for all teams. The researcher visited all work communities, guiding the teams in implementing the method. In these meetings, discussions were held on the method's suitability as an evaluative model for the type of client work carried out by the team and, on the other hand, agreements were made on the kind of material each team would be providing for research purposes. Each work community was given electronic forms related to the method, a presentation slide show and material for assembling a Mirror folder. Mirror handbooks were also provided. The teams began Mirror work at different times. While nine teams had commenced by May 2006, the tenth team adopted the method in September 2007. The research data was collected until May 2008.

The whole research data included data on forms from the Mirror meetings, group work material from network meetings, video and audio tape material, final team evaluation forms or recorded discussions, the researcher's study journal and two work community surveys, one conducted before the method's adoption (Haapamäki & Yliruka 2006) (n=87) and the other at the end of the development project in the spring of 2007 (n=44) (Säiläkivi 2007). One of the work community survey's targets was to provide an understanding of the work community as a socio-material network – of its expert practices and orientations, working culture and support structures. Another target was to test the essential elements determined for the Mirror method (Yliruka 2006). These elements define the basic requirements for a socio-material network in order for Mirror to generate the expected outcomes (Koivisto 2007). The analysis has been made by using quantitative methods in the survey data, and interpretative approach in analysing the data as a whole.

Given that the researcher had been among the method's original developers, a reflective development and evaluation approach was important. The researcher had an interest – one shared with the teams – in testing the method and redeveloping it to provide genuine support for work communities. In the evaluation, reliability was sought by separating the development phase and the data analysis phase, and by utilising diversified data, which was also subjected to an analysis by an external researcher. Research authorisations were applied for in the participating teams' cities.

Dissemination of Mirror

Human activity and interaction are mediated processes (Latour 1987; Koivisto 2007). Social work teams can be examined as a formation of socio-material relationships consisting of human and non-human factors such as workers, methods, tools, principles, rules, laws, norms and conventional habits. A team's activity can be seen as a continuous achievement: the team renews its existence through its actions. Methods represent but one factor in team activity (Latour 1987; Koivisto 2007). Consequently, the results or consequences of the Mirror method cannot be explained from only one point of view. The Mirror method as such is an artefact, a crystallization of the essential elements of client work defined during the development work on the basis of negotiations, actions and the creation of meanings (Wenger 1998, 55). It is important to understand that when another work community adopts the method, it needs to reconstruct this hybrid within its context. In other words, the method's minimum requirements must be ensured in the operating environment.

The Mirror development project was primarily a method-based one (Alasoini 2007), but it also sought to implement the principles of the open innovation environment. Instead of attempting to create a ready-made and binding method, the project set out to produce a method which could be adapted according to the operating environment's requirements and which would be open for development and to various actors' ideas. This is a realistic starting point with regard to disseminating the method, since a method will transform once it is transferred to a new operating environment. In addition, the project set out to see how certain core elements of the method would function in various environments. The usability of the method's structure was questioned: Was it essential to separate listening and discussion? Were the selected self evaluation themes meaningful? Would all teams consider documentation as important? Would documentation and follow-up meetings bring further insight to social work processes? Would the structure be seen as supporting or limiting the reflective working process? Furthermore, the project also sought to test the requirements determined as being critical for the method adaptation (Yliruka 2006).

In order to obtain answers for these questions during the project, initial team meetings included a rough assessment of the method's suitability to the working environment. The teams were encouraged to take a critical attitude towards the method. If the method seemed to require changes, this was possible. Network process was also utilised for the method's further development alongside the dissemination. Respecting the idea of open innovation, the method's guidelines and related forms were made freely available during the project through an online environment at the Sosiaaliportti website, subject to registration with the Mirror group.

Findings

In the following, I will explore findings from the Mirror pilot project. I will discuss the aspects of structures produced by the method, the method's further development and its transfer to different social work sectors. The transfer is examined through the consequences of the method adoption in the social work teams (interaction and knowledge creation, learning, well-being) and discussed in relation to the minimum requirements or critical elements of the method.

Peer evaluations were held by the teams every two to three weeks. During the project, all participating teams succeeded in integrating Mirror work as part of their operating structures. The usability of the method was enhanced through editing the forms, on the basis of feedback. However, using the forms in printed versions turned out to be relatively laborious. With regard to the method's further development and the implementation of the project's so-called first-degree changes, it appeared that a method-based network is not necessarily a very effective model (Alasoini 2007, 17), where the aim is primarily the method's dissemination rather than its development. The project did, however, succeed in improving the method based on experiences shared in network meetings and on the researcher's team visits. Furthermore, the teams themselves conducted the changes they considered necessary.

The most tangible development results achieved during the project were related to forms. Two new forms, the Internal Mirror for formative evaluation and the Prism form, were created and the form used in peer evaluation was amended. Although the Prism form was issued during the course of the project, there was not much time for testing its use. In the follow-up survey (3/2008), only one team reported having used the Prism form. According to the team's feedback form:

> *The Prism has helped our Mirror team members to clarify the contents of social work and the field of operation, to understand that workers may have various approaches and working methods. Using the form has entailed a common*

learning process, in which we jointly focus on the contents of social work. Through client cases, we have considered structural means of influencing frequent social work phenomena, such as the increased use of substances by older women (from individual to general level). (P1)

Mirror as a permanent work practice

According to a follow-up survey conducted in March 2008[2], four teams out of ten had adopted Mirror as a permanent work practice. The teams' final self-evaluations preindicated their adoption of the method. It was common to the communities in which the method was rooted that they had achieved at least one team-set target for the Mirror work. At its best, anchoring a method means that it is no longer seen as a project but part of everyday work which the superior can also include in his/her management strategy.

It has not even crossed my mind that this is just some project that we are conducting right now ... (KL3)

Yes, it is a natural part of my own work. Since we agreed that we want to retain this among our team's working methods and to make room and time for it in our schedules next autumn, this aspect has also been strengthened. (KL4)

Within four teams, the method was rooted on a conditional basis. One user team had been transformed due to an organisational reform and another due to team structure reform. This meant that the two teams which had originally joined the Mirror project were dissolved, and the method was transferred by individual workers to two new teams. Two other participating teams announced that they were taking a break and expressed their desire to simplify or adapt the method before continuing its use. These adaptation needs related to the incorporaton of ethical questions and a child's perspective on the forms. A supervisor in one of these teams reported having preliminary agreed with another social work team in the same sector on developing the method further. In total, the method was more or less rooted in a total of eight work communities.

Two teams announced that they would stop using the method. Workers from one of these teams revealed that their superior had failed to commit to the method to begin with, and a regular structure for the Mirror work had never been created. The other team stated that they did not consider

Figure 3 The positive cycle of well-being mediated by Mirror.

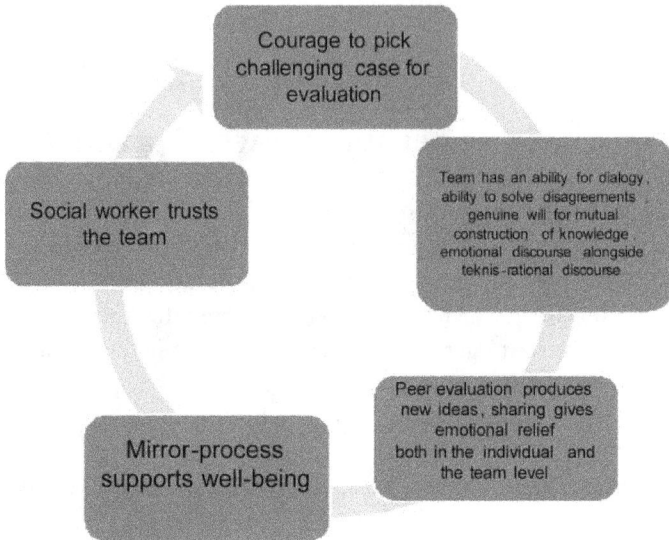

Courage to pick challenging case for evaluation

Team has an ability for dialogy, ability to solve disagreements, genuine will for mutual construction of knowledge, emotional discourse alongside teknis-rational discourse

Social worker trusts the team

Peer evaluation produces new ideas, sharing gives emotional relief both in the individual and the team level

Mirror-process supports well-being

the method suitable for the type of short-term social work they conducted, and they had neither the desire nor sufficient support to adapt the method.

The Mirror's high adaptibility

The project reinforced the belief that Mirror is largely suitable for various social work sectors. The Mirror work functions both in settled work communities and those in transition. In work communities in transition, the use of Mirror is often limited to Steps 1 and 2, self and peer evaluations, since transition often entails personnel changes or restructuring consequences for client work, such as interruptions in client work processes. In such situations, Mirror may function as a structure bringing clarity to chaos. Furthermore, the method has proven useful in the orientation of new workers.

Dialogism and monologism in teams

With respect to analysing one's own work, team support was considered important. The participating teams were categorised based on two extremes: the 'dialogic team' at one end and the 'monologic team' at the other. The rest of the teams can be placed in between and most teams were clearly located *closer to the dialogic type*.

Successful Mirror work requires mutual trust between team members and an interest in common knowledge building. This forms the essence of dialogism (Bakhtin 1982; Mönkkönen 2001). Dialogism is a concept embedded in the interaction section in the Mirror Hall form and it can also be used for analysing interaction within the Mirror user team. Dialogism can be defined as a mutual relationship influencing both or all parties involved (Mönkkönen 2002, 53–56). The characteristics of dialogue-oriented interaction include awareness, interaction under both parties' terms, dialogic reflection (vs. self reflection) and responsible power (vs. denying the existence of power) (Mönkkönen 2002; Järvinen 2007, 16). According to Etienne Wenger (1998), learning in a community of practice – such as a work community in the social welfare sector – involves learning by doing, generating meanings, the formation of identity and participation in the community. Thus, working in one's own social work team not only involves knowledge building carried out together, but also co-construction which affects the members' expertise, identity, knowledge and skills.

In some teams, Mirror seemed to support dialogism. Due to the common processing of cognitive, emotional and practical issues, the workers reported a reduction of anxiety related to client work (cf. Ruch 2005, 115). The 'dialogic team' reported that its members' well-being at work had increased during the process (fig 3). According to Matti Kuittinen (2007), team work may indeed increase job satisfaction, motivation and well-being at work since it satisfies the individual's primary psychological needs, that is to say, social needs, autonomy and competence. In particular, the 'dialogic team' was characterised by the presence of emotional discourse and the ability to process conflicts as a team. Such conflicts were related either to the nature of the case under review or to team activity. This team added its own emotion-related themes to the method's forms. Originally, emotions were included as a theme only in the Hand Mirror reaction forms which were to be filled in for research purposes. This type of activity in a team is an indication of trust between its members. Based on the team-specific work community survey, this team's strengths included trust in the work community even before using the method. This observation was reconfirmed when the same survey was repeated later. The 'dialogic team' also managed to fade the method's structure into the background in the sense that it by no means constrained discussion. On the other hand, the team reported that no major requirements for flexibility had emerged. The Mirror structure supported the team's workflow by freeing members from having to debate the process steps or format, enabling them to concentrate on the core of the issue at hand. Mirror method's peer evaluation structure produces fruitful dialogue, since it does not attempt to predetermine certain attitudes on issues as being desirable (cf. Seikkula & Arnkil 2005, 15) or to limit options.

... and the thinking now enabled goes so deep, the supporting questions provided a lead in the kinds of issues which would not normally emerge in ordinary client work meetings. (KL7)

The work community survey of the 'dialogic team' indicated that work had become more methodical, while targets had grown more distinct and meetings more meaningful. Moreover, opportunities for influencing internal decision-making had improved remarkably, trust in collegial support had increased further, and the sense of solidarity had been reinforced.

By contrast, in the 'monologic team' joint knowledge building was less frequent. Not all team members trusted in the ability of others to produce practicable ideas and solutions, and this affected the whole team's work. In the Mirror peer evaluation discussions (Step 2), various work orientations did emerge but addresses remained monologic. Discussions occurred between those who employed similar work methods, but to a lesser extent among those who represented different types of work orientations. In fact, various perspectives existed merely side by side (cf. Järvinen 2007, 154). One's own working method was expressed but genuine input from others was not expected. It was even considered impossible that others might comprehend one's own client relationship. In the 'monologic team', the utility of the Mirror peer work remained more modest or derived mainly from the insights the workers had obtained from conducting their self evaluation (Step 1). If a peer evaluation discussion is monologic, the worker presents his/her self evaluation form to the team and indicates by tone of voice, expressions or non-verbal communication that no input from other team members is expected. Referring to Kuittinen (2007), it may be that the worker perceives the evaluation as a threat to individual autonomy or competence and sees the method as leading to a herd mentality, rather than resulting in increased collective expertise.

A monologic peer evaluation quickly covers the themes on the self evaluation form, but does not dwell on them. Bypassing the themes may also be due to peers considering that the worker's issues are complete in themselves, true and acceptable or that they should be rejected forthwith. Once issues are deemed complete, there is no room for an evaluative discussion or reflection. When monologism is respectful it does not cause problems to the relationships between team members but hinders joint knowledge building (step 4). If the causes underlying monologism include power struggles, mistrust of the team or supervisor or other phenomena complicating group dynamics, such monologism can become a negative, frustrating and paralysing cycle. Such sessions can also plausibly undermine well-being at work. The work community survey results of the 'monologic team' (Haapamäki & Yliruka 2006) predicted that the method would function poorly within the team. Improving team support and the working atmosphere was defined as a challenge for the work community.

It is possible that, for a 'monologic team', Mirror is not a suitable working method or that more support should be provided alongside it, such as using an external facilitator or supervisor. It should be noted, however, that dialogism and monologism may alternate within a single team depending on various factors. As a consequence, a team cannot be associated with pure dialogism or monologism. Arnkil & Seikkula (2005, 11) state that dialogism is a way of thinking and acting which can be fostered through methods promoting collective thinking and being heard. While Mirror is designed to support a reflective and dialogic team approach, it cannot guarantee dialogism by itself.

The evidence indicates that it is possible to progress from monologism towards dialogism by firmly adhering to those Mirror elements which support dialogism[8]. Improving the quality of dialogism is possible in teams where the essential elements (such as trust) are at a sound basic level. In such circumstances, the method can deepen discussion and promote joint knowledge creation. Dialogism in itself is, however, a quality which needs to be practised.

What kinds of situations were examined with Mirror in various sectors?

For the pilot social work teams working in adult social work and in the Probation Service, the study revealed that client cases deemed difficult and thus selected as Mirror issues involved 'interim-distance client relationships' which caused mental pressure for the worker. If a worker's work is 'interim-distance', he/she is attempting to involve the client in 'close-distance' work' but the client clearly rejects at least some aspects of the co-operation relationship. The worker often attempts to attract the client to 'close-distance' work by using various means or by creating external structures for it, using a variety of 'baits' (Järvinen 2007, 109). By contrast, Mirror issues in child welfare services, school social work and family care mainly included problems in inter-professional work or seeking help in analysing a multi-faceted case and finding an appropriate working method.

The method created clarity in pressured social work

At first, the team representing gerontological social work development was anxious that the method would prove too laborious. In the beginning, the team reported the need for both rapid meetings for discussing several acute client cases at a time and, on the other hand, in-depth meetings for focusing on one client case using a worker's self-evaluation. Free-form description of client work had been used instead of the Mirror Hall. In these cases, discussion remained brief or confusing, or as the gerontological social work team put it: 'poor preparation and an unorganised structure in meetings lead to chaos' (Kaisla 2006). It can thus be concluded that a defined structure supports the organisation of communal activity and sharing acquired experiences (cf. Hakkarainen 2000, 91).

After testing both rapid and in-depth Mirror meetings gerontological social work team considered Mirror-based meetings more important and, as the method became more established, the need for the rapid acute meetings reduced (Kaisla 2006; Liikanen & Kaisla 2007). Indeed, the method, which seemed laborious at first sight, became *a structure providing clarity and reducing the need for acute-type meetings.* Thereby, Mirror brought organisational clarity (Ruch 2005) to client work and rendered it more comfortable for the workers. Several other teams ended up using Mirror once or twice a month, in the context of team meetings on current issues.

Essential elements

The essential elements required of the adopting network for the use of Mirror were specified in the pilot phase. In order for Mirror to generate the expected outcomes, consideration should be given to these elements before using the method. The work community survey was used to illustrate the status of essential elements within the work community. Although the questions did not directly address the essential elements, such an application was possible based on the answers. Based on the first piloting, essential elements included: the capacity to discern the operating environment as multi-dimensional; interest in oral and written reflection; and the ability to provide constructive feedback and dialogic skills (Yliruka 2006, 39–43).

The initial status of essential elements according to the team was then compared with the team-specific Mirror process flow and outcomes. Internal relationships in the team were found to play a critical role. Based on the project, further essential elements were defined as follows: producing knowledge and learning from work as an acknowledged part of social work; social work being understood both as individual and collective work; the immediate supervisor committing to using the method as a tool for developmental management (Rasanen 2008) and doing so consciously; the client's overall situation being used as a starting point for the work; the existence of a peer group; dedicated time reserved for peer evaluation; the predictability of peer evaluation schedules; and the use of the method forms in the process.

Mirror as support for the team's expertise: Working on the various levels of reflection

The project regarded self-directive and reflective activity as the basis for dynamic and network-based expertise. Network-based and dynamic expertise (Hakkarainen et al. 2004) refers to a type of expertise which creates knowledge and competences in innovative ways and requires the presence of common and functioning interaction structures in work communities to support the construction of knowledge. Dynamic expertise sets out to develop each member's individual competences and to go beyond the prevailing operating practices in its network- and community-based processes of creative problem-solving.

Mirror, in its essence, is an analysing and structuring tool for social work meetings. It can also be characterised as a 'slow' method which creates room for itself in the hectic social work environment, generating its impacts in small steps. Workers in all teams stated that, at its best, the working method produced in-depth discussion on social work and its boundary conditions. Teams with long-term client relationships – a condition set for the method's application – considered that monitoring progress in client work was meaningful.

Mirror work conducted in the teams has been analysed, on one hand, based on reflective question types (reflective questions of level 1, 2 and 3) presented in peer evaluation meetings and, on the other hand, through the learning results produced during the process.

Continuing Raeithel's (1983) ideas, Yrjö Engeström has proposed meanings for the various levels of reflection:

+ Questions of reflection type 1 relate to the individual's work: How will I proceed in this task? Is my method the right one and effective? Could my method be better and more effective? What am I actually learning and what do I remember?
+ Questions of type 2 are outward-looking and refer to the common task: What is the essence of this task, why is it like this: what is its aim? What approaches might be considered for this task? Could the task be formulated and defined in a wiser way?
+ Questions of type 3 combine levels 1 and 2 and review the work's object by going beyond the individual and the community boundaries: What is the essence of our common activity, what within it creates problems and what are we trying to achieve? In which direction do we want to modify or develop our activity? How can we organise our co-operation in the wisest way possible? (Engeström 2004, 97–98.)

Based on a compilation of returned Mirror Hall data made in December 2006, of 25 reasons for cases, 16 represented reflection level 1, 6 represented level 2 and 3 reasons indicated level 3 reflection.

Since Mirror focuses on burdensome situations which are causes for concern, the Mirror work was mainly constructed through individual workers' concerns. Frequently, the reason for subjecting a case to peer evaluation as stated on the Mirror Hall form implied that the worker desired confirmation and support, particularly in improving his/her own way of working. This represents reflection type 1. If the reason for self evaluation was defined from the view point of an individual social worker, Mirror guided to use reflection levels 2 and 3 for evaluating the case. Structural themes on the Mirror Hall form guided individuals to look outwards – the worker was steered towards considering his/her work in the light of its limiting and contributing factors. Thus, the Mirror process triggers the whole social work team to think about the level 3 reflective question: What is this common activity and where are we heading for ?

The worker's and the client's targets were kept separate in Mirror Hall form in order to ensure an analysis of the worker's own activity. In some cases, workers had difficulties in separating the client's targets from their own work targets. This indicates that the worker had determined his/her work targets in an expert-oriented way, suggesting it was solely for the client – rather than the worker too – to modify his or her activity.

Reasons representing level 2 reflection in the Mirror Hall data included the following issues: How two activity types in a single organisation might join forces in order to support the client? In terms of the case under evaluation and the effectiveness of the methods used, what is the significance of network or pair work conducted at the office? In one case, a worker desired that other team members would express their opinions on the client's situation, in order to predict future risks or other items which should be addressed.

Level 3 reflection was implied in stated Mirror reasons relating to the acknowledgement of various cultural backgrounds of families in child welfare services, an operational problem within the organisation revealed by a client case and providing support for immigrant children at school.

What was learned from the Mirror process?

Learning results can be analysed, for instance as first- and second-degree results or as generative results (Alasoini 2007, 8). First-degree learning results refer to changes from the participant's point of view, which can be achieved immediately through work. Second-degree results refer to permanent changes, such as a participant's improved reflective ability and competences. Generative results, by contrast, designate work results which

Figure 4 Mirror's importance for social work teams.

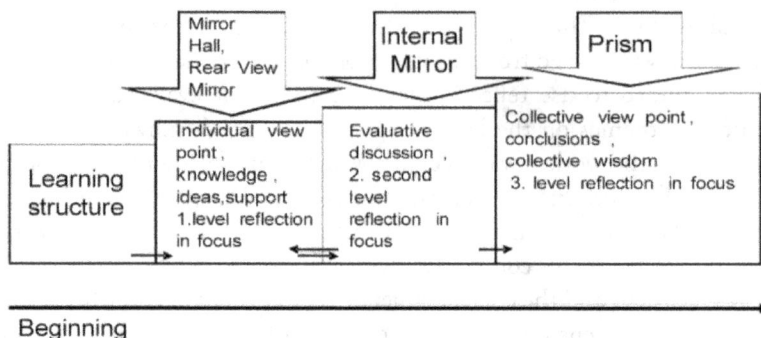

may benefit people outside the team.

With regard to direct impacts, previous observations from first piloting (Yliruka, 2006) were confirmed in the sense that direct peer evaluation impacts and use needs were similar in various sectors. From a single worker's perspective, the evaluation practice supports a social worker's basic work due to the optional working methods suggested by the peer group. The method provides the social worker with the opportunity to discuss a difficult case without rushing and in a way that provides team members with the possibility of understanding the client process which a member is or was going through. Mirror also offers an opportunity to auto-analyse one's working processes. The method helps the worker document and observe his/her work and provides support for coping in difficult client work situations.

For the peer group, Mirror proposes a structured and economical way of analysing client issues. In a multifaceted client case, the method helps to raise essential issues for follow-up and produce in-depth peer evaluation. Mirror provides insight on a colleague's thinking since, in addition to facts, subjective interpretations are also analysed. The approach prevents participants from arriving at hasty interpretations and conclusions on a colleague's work and creates an opportunity to share success stories. A discussion generates collective understanding of social work and insight, creates an excellent opportunity to keep the core issues of social work on the agenda and enables the exchange of the relevant knowledge and expertise (Yliruka, 2006).

From effectiveness to deeper understanding

The teams did not formulate direct effectiveness assumptions, that is suppositions on whether a client's well-being had improved due to the process. However, the workers did draw conclusions on what seemed essential to successful social work and on what they had personally learned from the process. One might say that they sought *evidence for themselves* on the client's work's effectiveness. This does not refer to attempting to prove that they had made no errors, but to constructing an understanding of social work and its prerequisites and dealing with imperfection. These types of conclusions were written in the Rear View Mirror forms. While they can be categorised as first-degree learning results, they also indicate second-degree results in that the workers' knowledge formation and reflection structure had developed as a shared practice.

> *I think it is particularly important to go back to the client cases and to review what was really done after the team session. This enables us to illustrate social work processes, which is in accordance with the spirit of the times anyway.* (E-mail 6.3.08)

> *Bearing the child's benefit clearly in mind adds meaning to one's work.* (K16)

> *The network formed by the authorities may provide resources for this type of client relationship.* (K16)

> *Consistency and limitation will yield results in the long term.* (K16)

> *'I have learned that one should observe how deep one goes into the client process. To succeed in one's work, one should at times attempt to come closer and at times to back off. I have the desire to go deep in the client process in order to understand the issues and persons involved.* (K16)

An illustration of generative learning includes an example of how the client process became clear to the worker and how the process was then documented. The worker utilised his/her Mirror case description in order to justify the organisation of a seminar.

> *Thanks to the case, I was able to promote the idea of organising a seminar and raising the interest of the Criminal Sanctions Agency.* (Kr3)

Another example of a generative result lay in some workers reporting having shown their Mirror summaries to their clients in the spirit of open documentation (Wilczynski 1981). A third example of generative impact was the creation of an immigrant parents group (Lindblom & Maahi 2008, 7).

How does Mirror support renewal? According to Engeström (1995), teams should be capable of identifying contradictions as a source of expansive learning in the team. A more harmonious approach is suggested by the organisational knowledge creation model by Nonaka & Takeuchi (1995). Emphasising trust, emotional elements and communal learning states, this model proposes that new knowledge is generated through alternating between tacit and explicit knowledge. Models of developmental evaluation, in turn, focus on mirrors which catalyse the work community's reflection on its activities. One of the most effective mirrors is the voice of the client (Vataja et al. 2007, 367).

In the Mirror method, retrospective and evaluative monitoring functions as the mirror, while joint conclusions form the development engine. Furthermore, Mirror constituted a team tool for evaluating whether the social work measures conducted had been sufficient, and for testing a planned working strategy. For instance, one team discussed whether a family's situation should be influenced by reinforcing the role of the family network or by investing in the inclusion of the family's father. The team also discussed whether a Family Group Conference or some other methodical approach would be worth considering.

Reviewing structural factors in peer evaluation also revealed a type of non-functioning co-operation with other bodies providing assistance, a problem which was not solvable within the team. Seikkula & Arnkil (2005, 17) underline that in a multiple problem case, several actors will take an interest in the client. Each specialised body, acting within the framework of its own basic task, will then attempt to trigger change. If the desired progress is not achieved within the overall situation, the workers involved will increase their efforts to change one another. This forms a repeated interactive pattern involving both clients and workers. Perceiving the existence of such patterns is the key to changing them. With Mirror, a team may indeed observe the need for a multi-professional forecasting dialogue, designed to open up this type of problem, or organise a collaboration meeting on co-operation issues.

Some teams also noted, however, that there is a risk that the team's ability for renewal might weaken over time. The teams therefore tried to keep their boundaries flexible and promote individuals' personal development through further studies, for instance. One team made conscious efforts to include students and workers from other teams in their peer evaluation meetings. By offering a method-learning opportunity to visitors, the team also received outsiders' input through their peer evaluation. Indeed, Wenger (1998, 256) suggests that richness of boundary processes is an indication of learning within a community.

As a consequence of piloting, additional meanings were attached to the working method. Mirror also became *support for supervisors' duties.* In the midst of organisational reform and continuous personnel changes causing pressure, Mirror was seen as an operating method supporting continuity. Supervisors also emphasised the importance of joint discussion as a tool for providing them with insights on an individual worker's support and guidance needs. This feeling was mutual: one worker reported that Mirror had been a means of having their voice heard within the team, in addition to providing personal understanding of the client case. In the peer evaluation feedback form, the worker noted that prior to the peer evaluation they were unable to assess whether a situation was difficult or not, or whether their working method was effective in the client case. They had been previously vaguely concerned about their Mirror case, but were unable to present the issue in a manner that would have led to any measures being taken by others, or to him/her obtaining case-related feedback. For the worker, the conducted peer evaluation discussion produced guidelines for the future, provided analytical help in working with the client, and made the worker feel that they had been heard.

Figure 4 illustrates the importance of Mirror work for a team. For all team members, the working method provides a learning structure. Motivation for self evaluation mainly derives from a single member's own work and the desire to seek support for it. The Mirror Hall is an aid for such an analysis (1. level reflection). Also the use of Rear View starts from the individual worker's view point. Peer evaluation generates material for 2. level reflection, supported by the Internal Mirror. Over time, the method enables reaching inductive conclusions on larger themes based on an individual case, through monitoring the client process. Such conclusions can be noted down on the Prism form (3. level reflection).

The following case illustrates the Mirror process. It is based on the true events, taken from different cases. This narrative illustrates experiences of the method on a more general level.

Merja

Social worker Merja self-evaluated her work. She chose to look more closely at her work with the children who had been taken into custody, and her work with their family care worker and biological parents. Merja was pondering, what would be the best way to support the growth of children and the relationship with their biological parents as well as the family care worker at her work. She evaluated the strengths and risks in the situation and the chosen methods and arguments behind them. In addition to that she evaluated the nature of the client relationship and her own role in it. She also scrutinized her abilities and resources to work in the situation. She concluded that there was not enough time to attend to a matter carefully and that she would need further training on family care.

In the peer evaluation meeting social workers had a common discussion based on Merja's self evaluation. The conclusion was that there was a need to step backwards: it was important to assess the appropriateness of the whole placement in foster care. The involvement of a peer worker was also suggested. The discussion was vivid and multifaceted: different viewpoints were expressed. The workers were not under pressure in the meeting since there was a lot of time for discussion. Peers gave Merja positive feedback about the clear presentation, keeping child perspective in focus, and about Merja's ability to see various solutions, in spite of a difficult situation. Some of the social workers became irritated by the fact that Merja had had so little support for her work. All the workers expressed the level of their concern at level 4 (scale 1-4). Merja's own evaluation was 2-3.

After the peer evaluation discussion Merja was relieved, as she understood that her peers had found the situation challenging. She thought that the whole team had affirmed, that social work should not be done in great haste, and that the welfare of the child should always be a prime factor. Also, one should not try to tackle difficult cases alone. Instead, one should seek for support. Merja was a bit annoyed at the self evaluation,as she thought it to be a bit time consuming. However, considering the outcome of the process, she was satisfied. The peers thought that the common work in the peer evaluation meeting gave a shared sense of support to slow down social work processes in order to do the work well.

In the formative evaluation Merja evaluated the case another time in the peer group. She went through the client process thoroughly, reflecting on it with the first self evaluation done in the beginning of the process. Merja thought that her own thinking had clarified in the process. Due to that, she had been able to work in a more client-oriented way with all parties involved – , more than before, when she had been worried about her own role in the process. She had not made use of all the suggestions that were made in the previous peer evaluation meeting. The most important outcome was, that by taking time for reflecting, she felt she was able to act more sensibly in the case. She could express herself more openly in her discussion with the family worker and also reflect her own role in it. That enhanced discussion about important matters. Also, the family care worker was more able to give voice to her own concerns, such as tiredness. Merja thought that she was now more able to undertake a good assessment of the situation. She felt that she was now professionally sure about herself. Concretely, she was sure that it was good to continue supporting the family care worker with family work.

Merja reconsidered her need for immediate training about family care, since the client process had clarified sufficiently. The situation did not burden her anymore, even though she acknowledged some challenging areas such as creating a good working relationship with the biological parents.

In the formative meeting the team discussed what was to be learned about the case and themselves as a group. They were pleased with the fact that Merja's case had progressed methodically and that Merja had benefitted from their reflection. They thought that Merja's ability to work independently had strengthened. When Merja had gone though the suggestions made earlier and evaluated what had worked and what had not, this helped them also to understand more about the social work. The team wrote down on the Prism-form as a mutual conclusion that it was important to try to have influence on the foster care system. Children with special needs have to be placed with the families who have the needed resources. The superior thought that this is an important subject to put forward in the service system.

Conclusions

The Mirror project offered a varied range of experiences and knowledge of the factors and methods supporting work communities in social welfare; ones which promote the proactive, continuous development of work practices and conditions, the organisation and improvement of work and innovation within work communities, and resolving the question of how to establish these as a regular part of social work. This pilot project improved the Mirror method in an inclusive way, thus supporting renewal in social work organisations.

The study illustrated that adaptation of such a method will have different non-linear consequences in different kinds of socio-material networks. Nonetheless, the objectives of the project were achieved commendably: the method proved both suitable for various social welfare sectors, and useful – provided that the critical elements were met by the teams. In the pilot teams, the method enhanced the methodical nature of the work. The Mirror method was anchored in eight out of ten pilot teams, and was also disseminated to other teams that adopted it autonomously. The method supported the documentation of social work, contributed to the evaluation of working methods' functioning, and helped in drawing conclusions on one's own work and abilities. Furthermore, it enhanced the adoption of better working methods and assisted in coping at work.

References

Alasoini, Tuomo (2007): Ohjelma ja projekti informaatio-ohjauksen välineenä. Oppimisverkostoihin perustuvan projektitoiminnan mahdollisuuksia ja haasteita. Helsinki. Työministeriö, 2007. Raportteja / Työministeriö, Tykes; 59.

Bereiter, Carl & Scardamalia Marlene (1993): Surpassing ourselves: an inquiry into the nature and implications of expertise. Chicago: Open Court.

Bakhtin, Mihail Mihajlovic (1982): The dialogic imagination. Austin: University of Texas Press.

Carpenter, Margaret (1999): Job rewards and concerns for social workers. The impact of changes in funding and delivery of mental health services. Smith College Studies in Social Work70(1) pp. 70-84.

Chelimsky, Eleanor (1997): The coming transformations in evaluation. In Chelimsky, Eleanor & Shadish, William R. (eds.) Evaluation for the 21st Century. A Handbook, 1-26. Thousand Oaks, London, New Delhi: Sage.

Engeström, Yrjö (1995): Kehittävä työntutkimus. Perusteita, tuloksia ja haasteita. Helsinki: Hallinnon kehittämiskeskus.

Engeström, Yrjö (2004): Ekspansiivinen oppiminen ja yhteiskehittely työssä. Tampere: Vastapaino.

Eräsaari, Risto (2002): Avoimen asiantuntijuuden analytiikka. In Pirttilä, Ilkka & Eriksson, Susan (eds.) Asiantuntijoiden areenat. Jyväskylä: SoPhi.

Fook, Jan (2002): Social Work. Critical Theory and Practice. London: Sage.

Gimbel, Ronald W. & Lehrman, Sue & Strosberg, Martin A. & Ziac, Veronica & Freedman, Jay & Savicki, Karen & Tackley, Lisa (2002): Organizational and environmental predictors of job satisfaction in community-based HIV/AIDS services organizations. Social Work Research 26 (1) pp. 43-55.

Hakkarainen, Kai (2000): Oppiminen osallistumisen prosessina. Aikuiskasvatus 2(20) pp. 84-98.

Hakkarainen Kai & Paavola Sami & Lipponen Lasse (2003): Käytäntöyhteisöistä innovatiivisiin tietoyhteisöihin. Aikuiskasvatus 21 (1) pp. 4-13.

Hakkarainen, Kai & Palonen, Tuire & Paavola, Sami & Lehtinen Erno (2004): Communities of networked expertise. Professional and educational perspectives. Sitra's publication series, publ.no. 257. Exford: Elsevier ltd.

Järvinen, Minna-Kaisa (2007): Asiakas-työntekijäsuhteen dialoginen arviointi kriminaalihuollossa. Lisensiaatintutkielma, sosiaalityön erikoistumiskoulutus, marginaalisaatiokysymysten erikoisala. Tampere: Tampereen yliopisto.

Karvinen-Niinikoski, Synnöve, & Salonen, Jari & Meltti, Tero & Yliruka, Laura & Tapola, Maria (2005): Konstikas sosiaalityö 2003: suomalaisen sosiaalityön todellisuus ja tulevaisuudennäkymät. Helsinki : Sosiaali- ja terveysministeriö. Sosiaali- ja terveysministeriön selvityksiä 2005:28.

Koivisto, Juha (2007): What evidence base? Steps towards the relational evaluation of social interventions. The Policy Press. 4 (3) pp. 527-37.

Kuittinen, Matti (2007): Tiimit ilman tiimityötä eli mihin kariutui tiimien suuri lupaus? Psykologia 2007 (1) pp. 55-61.

Koivisto, Juha (2007): What evidence-base? Steps towards relational evaluation of social interventions. Evidence and Policy, 3(4) pp. 527-537.

Latour, Bruno (1987): Science in Action. How to follow scientists and engineers through the society. Harvard University Press, Cambridge, MA.

Liikanen, Hanna-Liisa & Kaisla, Susanna (2007): Gerontologisen sosiaalityön menetelmistä. Gerontologisen sosiaalityön kehittämishanke pääkaupunkiseudulla 2005-2007. Pääkaupunkiseudun sosiaalialan osaamiskeskus Helsinki: Socca, Heikki Waris-instituutti. Työpapereita 3/2007.

Macdonald, Geraldine (2000): Evidence-based practice. In Davies M. (ed.) The Blackwell Encyclopedia of Social Work. Blackwell, Oxford.

Mannerström, Kaija & Nurhonen, Aili & Mustonen, Tiina & Yliruka, Laura (2005): Itse- ja vertaisarvioinnin malli tukemaan aikuissosiaalityötä. Sosiaaliturva 7, 24-26.

Meltti, Tero & Kara, Hanna (2009): Sosiaalityöntekijöiden työolot, -ympäristö ja työhyvinvointi sekä niihin vaikuttavat tekijät. In Laura Yliruka, Juha Koivisto & Synnöve Karvinen-Niinikoski (eds.) Sosiaalialan työolojen hyvä kehittäminen. Helsinki 2009. Sosiaali- ja terveysministeriön julkaisuja 2009:6, pp. 22-39.

Mönkkönen, Kaarina (2002): Dialogisuus kommunikaationa ja suhteena. Vastaaminen, valta ja vastuu sosiaalialan asiakastyön vuorovaikutuksessa. Kuopion yliopiston julkaisuja E. Yhteiskuntatieteet 94.

Nonaka, Ikujiro & Takeuchi, Hirotaka (1995): The Knowledge- Creating Company: New York: Oxford University Press.

Nowotny, Helga (2000): Transgressive Competence. The Narrative of Expertise. European Journal of Social Theory 3(1) pp. 5-21.

Parton, Nigel & O'Byrne, Patrick (2000): Constructive social work: towards a new practice. Basingstoke: Palgrave.

Polanyi, Michael (1983): The Tacit dimension. Gloucester: Doubleday & Company, Inc.

Raeithel, Arne (1983): Tätigkeit, Arbeit un Praxis. Frankfurt am Main: Campus.

Rasanen Leena (2009): Työyhteisön kehittämistä ja työhyvinvointia tukevat johtamisen käytännöt. In Laura Yliruka, Juha Koivisto & Synnöve Karvinen-Niinikoski (eds.) Sosiaalialan työolojen hyvä kehittäminen. Helsinki 2009. Sosiaali- ja terveysministeriön julkaisuja 2009:6, pp.59-76.

Ruch, Gillian (2005): Relationship-based practice and reflective practice: holistic approaches to contemporary child care social work. Child and Family Social Work 2005 (10) pp. 111-123.

Rossiter, Amy & Prillentensky, Isaac & Walsh-Bowers, Richard (2000): A postmodern perspective on professional ethics. In B. Fawfett, B. Featherstone, Fook Janis & Rossiter Amy (eds) Practice and Research in Social Work: Postmodern Feminist Perspectives. London: Routledge.

Saaristo, Kimmo (2000): Avoin asiantuntijuus: ympäristökysymys ja monimuotoinen ekspertiisi. Nykykulttuurin tutkimusyksikön julkaisuja 66. Jyväskylä: Jyväskylän yliopisto.

Seikkula, Jaakko & Arnkil, Tom Erik (2005): Dialoginen verkostotyö. Helsinki: Tammi.

Shaw, Ian (1999): Evaluoi omaa työtäsi. Reflektiivisen ja valtuuttavan evaluaation opas. Helsinki: Stakes Työpapereita 4/1999.

Sosiaalibarometri (2007): Eronen, Anne & Londén, Pia & Perälahti, Anne & Siltaniemi, Aki & Särkel, Riitta. Helsinki: Sosiaali- ja terveysturvan keskusliitto ry.

Tynjälä, Päivi & Nuutinen, Anita & Eteläpelto, Anneli & Kirjonen, Juhani & Remes Pirkko (1997): The Acquisition of Professional Expertise – a challenge for educational research. Scandinavian Journal of Educational Research (41) pp. 475-491.

Vataja, Katri (2008): Does the choice of method make a difference? Comparison of two self-evaluation methods harnessed for organizational development. Paper presented at the EES Conference 1-3 October 2008, Lisboa, Portugal.

Wenger, Etienne (1998): Communities of practice: Learning, meaning and identity. Cambridge: Cambridge University Press.

Wilczynski, Brahna Lauger (1981): New life for recording: involving client. Social work 26 (4 July).

Yliruka, Laura (2000): Sosiaalityön itsearviointi ja hiljainen tieto. Helsinki: Stakes, FinSoc. Työpapereita 2/2000.

Yliruka, Laura (2005): Sosiaalityön itsearviointi kontekstuaalisena käytäntönä. In Mirja Satka, Synnöve Karvinen-Niinikoski, Marianne Nylund & Susanna Hoikkala (eds.) Sosiaalityön käytäntötutkimus. Helsinki: Palmenia, 124-143.

Yliruka, Laura (2006): Kuvastin reflektiivinen itse- ja vertaisarviointimenetelmä sosiaalityössä. Helsinki: Stakes. Työpapereita 15/2006.

Unpublished literature:

Haapamäki, Elise & Yliruka, Laura (2006): Kuvastin työyhteisökyselyt.

Kaisla, Susanna (2006): Itäisen kehittämisryhmän internet-päiväkirja 22.6.06. http://www.socca.fi/gero/ryhmat/ita.html (accessed 7.10.2008).

Säiläkivi, Suvi (2007): Kuvastin työyhteisökyselyt.

Internet sources:

Pääskynen Kari (2004) Hidas-prosessi. In Mönkkönen Kaarina (ed) Innovaatioilla Savon koulutuskuntayhtymä Pohjois- Savon ammatillinen instituutti, sosiaali- ja terveysala. ESR- projekti Tavoite 1- ohjelman unpublished report. http://www.paaskyset.com/hidas4/ (accessed 7.10.2008)

Vataja, Katri & Seppänen-Järvelä, Riitta (2007): Sosiaalitoimistojen kehittämisen hyvät käytännöt - Tutkimusavusteinen kehittämishanke (2005–2007). Unpublished report. https://groups.stakes.fi/NR/rdonlyres/57C4EFF0-042E-488B-97CE-38843F92578E/0/HYKEloppuraportti.pdf (accessed 7.10.2008)

Presentations and reports on Mirror

Lindblom, Bengt & Maahi, Katri (2008): KUVASTIN - Reflektiivinen itse- ja vertaisarviointimenetelmä lastensuojelun sosiaalityössä *www.vantaa.fi/i-liitetiedosto.asp?path=1;220;4720;4743;75601;75613 (viitattu 7.10.2008)*

Liikanen, Assi & Kaisla, Susanna (2007): Gerontologisen sosiaalityön menetelmistä. Helsinki: Socca.

Notes

1   Throughout the chapter 'case' refers to the worker's self evaluation of his/her own work with the client, not to the client him/herself.

2   If no answer was obtained for the follow-up survey, the researcher sent an e-mail or called the team's contact person.

3   The Mirror Hall form needs to be used. The team ensures that the Mirror Hall themes are discussed, that positive feedback is given systematically and that advising discourse is avoided in the discussions (see Yliruka 2006, 43).

4   In her study, Minna-Kaisa Järvinen (2007) analysed the client and worker's expertise within the Probation Service. A client and a worker both have various angles on their co-operation relationship. The client's co-operation orientations – of obligation, crisis and change – describe the client's relationship with co-operation and change. In turn, the worker's working distances – close-, interim- and remote-distance work – describe the worker's distance to the client's change efforts. The combination of these client and worker angles form various states of co-operation, differing from each other in terms of co-operation, activity, change, the use of networks and dialogism. Järvinen qualifies these states of co-operation as obligatory, remote control, interim-distance, acute and active states.

7
Action research in local authority practice:
A path to learning and professional development for work with at-risk families
Karin Kildedal

Introduction

For several years, there has been recurring criticism of the social work performed by Danish local authorities involving children and adolescents for not being sufficiently qualified and not meeting the standards set by politicians and legislation. This criticism has led to growing political and societal pressure to professionally upgrade social work in this area, to ensure that the work is based on research more than seems to have been the case so far. From a research point of view, one way to make practice more knowledge-based could be the use of interactive research targeting professional development of social work practice in local authorities. Action research is a particularly well-suited form of research as it requires commitment to action from both the field and the researcher involved.

In this chapter I will discuss the challenges and opportunities of action research when used for the professional development of social work practice, compare action research to other types of interactive research, and introduce action research approaches based on democratic and learning theory principles. The chapter also reports on a concrete action research project in a large Danish local authority, involving the professional development of social work practice with at-risk families. Lastly, the chapter will reflect on the advantages, disadvantages and challenges posed by applying action research as a method for the professional development of social work practice.

Interactive research – practice research – practitioner research – action research

Traditionally, the context in which research is carried out is one in which the strength of the research is determined by its ability to pass peer review within its scientific field (that is, whether it is accepted by fellow researchers). Interactive practice-oriented research, on the other hand, is carried out in a context in which the strength of the research is determined by its ability to create practical insights which can help develop new products in a specific workplace. The concept of interactive research refers to research aiming to interact with practice in such a way that the research produced is applied in practice. Interactive research is based on a range of different methodological approaches, using concepts like practice research, practitioner research and action research. Within these concepts, there are various strands and directions, sharing some similarities yet clearly distinguishable in other respects. This chapter will primarily focus on action research, and it starts out by clarifying how action research differs from practice research and practitioner research.

Epstein (2001) defines practice research as a research approach based on the application of research-inspired principles, designs and data collection methods to investigate practice in order to come up with answers to questions that may enlighten practice. In reality, however, the process usually starts with researchers doing some research, trying to cooperate or interact with practice in various ways, hoping to persuade practice to apply their research results and further develop the practice field in question. There is rarely any pre-agreed commitment from practice to apply the research results, which means that the scope for researchers to bring about changes in this field is limited.

Practitioner research can be defined as research in which the practitioner researches their own practice by using scientific methodology to produce results that may help change or upgrade practice. Practitioner research is often carried out, headed or supervised by a qualified researcher (Jarvis 2002; Ramian 2010; Kildedal 2009).

By contrast, action research can be described as a formally agreed binding interaction between field and researcher, with the express intention of changing or developing a given professional practice, based on the assumption that knowledge about the field's learning profile can help choose actions that will change the state of affairs or practice of a given field. A characteristic of action research is that the researcher participates actively in finding solutions to practical problems in cooperation with others, and that for the researcher this participation also constitutes a learning process (Gustavsen & Sørensen 1995, 55).

Action research started in the USA in the 1940s as a protest against the traditional positivistic research approach of the time. Kurt Lewin (1997), among others, maintained that traditional researchers had a rigid, preconceived conception of human reaction. Lewin stressed the importance of engaging with real-life problems and studying them in their context, and he developed an action research model which has formed the basis of a large number of projects. The model describes the phases of an action research project, the point of departure being a real-life problem with which the 'client' contacts the researcher, in order to gain help in finding a solution. Based on a general idea of the nature of the problem, followed by more detailed examination of it (research), a course of 'actions' (initiatives or measures) are planned, to be continuously adjusted and adapted on the basis of the ongoing research into the 'actions' (Lewin 1997)

In the 1960s and 1970s, action research spread to Europe, and, especially in Scandinavia, it became an important part of a new kind of critical, action-oriented social science research. However, action research soon split into two directions: a leftist progressive strand and a technocratic-functional tradition. The former approach aimed to find new ways of solving societal problems, and was often described as 'liberation sociology research', implying strong opposition to the Establishment. This direction was characterised by solidarity with the underprivileged groups of society and a tendency to blur the boundaries between researcher and social or political activist. The other direction, the technocratic- functional tradition, usually has as its primary objective to 'further develop or implement a politically decided concept or programme', aiming to 'develop social technologies to solve specific social problems' (Clausen et al. 1992, 17). Since then, action research has further branched out into a multitude of rather diverse directions.

Action research in the field of social work draws mainly on the technocratic-functional approach, but today tends to place a stronger emphasis on dialogue and democratic aspects instead of merely helping to 'further develop or implement a politically decided concept or programme', which today is, however, also an important part of action research. Action research into at-risk families will, for instance, always be subject to certain restrictions when it comes to developing professional social work practice, consisting of the policy context as expressed in rules, regulations and ministerial circulars specifying clearly, both the legal and the ideological, intentions, which both field and action researchers must abide by.

Organisational learning is a must - for social work to develop professionally

Organisational learning implies that an organisation can only learn if its members, individually as well as a group, take part in a number of learning processes. These learning processes are necessary for the learning outcomes to become embedded, both in the individual member and in the organisation as a whole. That is, organisational learning can only occur if its members recognise that a situation is problematic, or that the organisation is in need of general professional development. In either case, nothing will happen unless the members commit themselves to change on behalf of the institution (Argyris et al. 1985; Senge 1999). As an organisation can only learn through the individuals who embody it, what is needed is a learning theory perspective focusing on the individual in the agency as the only active force capable of effecting change. Consequently, action research requires working methods that initiate learning and reflection processes aimed at motivating staff to want to become involved, to change the organisation in the desired direction.

Peter Senge (1999) has developed a theory on organisational learning which may be very useful in this connection. In his theory, Senge describes five disciplines needed for an organisation to become and remain a learning institution. The cornerstone is systems thinking – also called the fifth discipline - which is about seeing 'the whole' rather than the parts, in order to understand complex interrelationships in an organisation. Senge calls it a framework for looking at connections between the parts rather than the parts themselves, and studying patterns of change rather than focusing on 'snapshots' of change. It is within this framework that the learning structures that are apparent in the way the organisation works must be investigated, before deciding where and how to initiate learning processes.

Senge refers to the other four disciplines as the core disciplines. They include: personal mastery, mental models, building shared visions, and team learning. Personal mastery relates to individual staff members' personal development and thus also to the individual's competences and abilities to create results. Whether an organisation is able to learn depends on whether its staff collectively possesses sufficient levels of 'personal mastery', and whether they are willing to use it to learn, individually as well as collectively , in order to help develop their agency. . Personal mastery also plays a role in the next discipline, working with 'mental models'. Mental models are deeply ingrained assumptions and generalisations that affect how a person understands the world. They can sometimes constrict an individual's way of thinking, making them unable to see any alternative to how things are usually done. To effect change, these mental models need to be brought to the surface, challenged, tested and discussed in order to change them and make it possible to do things differently.

The next discipline 'building shared visions' concerns the need for all members of the organisation to share a vision for the future, one that can motivate them to become involved and help move the agency in the direction dictated by the shared vision. Having a shared vision is vital for a learning organisation, says Senge, because only a shared vision can create the focus and energy needed to create individual, and in the long-term, organisational learning. But according to Senge, it is the learning taking place in the agency's teams that is the main driver for change, as these teams are in effect a sort of micro-cosmos for learning in the entire institution. Insights gained in organisational teams, transformed into new competences, are likely to spread to other individuals and other teams in the agency. Team results often set the tone, thus establishing a standard for shared learning throughout the entire organisation (Senge 1999).

The reason why Senge's theory on teams as the pivot for organisational learning is so interesting in this context is the fact that the staff in local authorities are usually organised in teams, which are the hub of practical social work. It is these teams that discuss the complex of problems surrounding families who either contact the local authorities for help to solve a wide range of social problems, or who are contacted by the system in response to reports about concerns over the wellbeing of a specific child. It is in these teams that knowledge and experience is put into practice, to arrive at a solution judged by professionals to be the best in a given situation. The process and the outcome must be justified professionally, based on extensive knowledge about the field. However, as mentioned above, social work is often criticised for being performed without sufficient theoretical foundations, which makes the need for evidence-based social work all the more acute. Action research can help develop the quality of knowledge and ultimately the social work performed in a local authority.

To achieve this end, it is essential to start by developing competences through cooperation with the teams responsible for the work performed. By using the cooperation with these teams as the pivot for organisational learning new knowledge will be generated, this will then become embedded in the concepts and thoughts of the agency (its shared memory). It has been customary in local authority practice to seek new knowledge mainly by having individual staff members participate in professional upgrading or continuing education. However, not all local authorities have arrangements for turning this 'acquisition' of new knowledge into shared knowledge, and in many cases it probably never does. As a consequence, new knowledge often only forms part of the individual's competences, not of the organisation's shared memory. To ensure that new knowledge becomes part of the organisation's shared knowledge, learning processes should instead be planned and organised round the local authority's social work team structure.

Forms of knowledge in action research into local authority practice

In the following the focus will be on the types of knowledge that may be applied to solving a real-life problem that a local authority might contact an action researcher about, to enlist his or her help in upgrading the level of professionalism in their social work with at-risk families

'In action science we seek knowledge that will serve action', writes Argyris (et al.) in *Action Science* (1985, 36) and continues:

> The actions scientist is an interventionist who seeks to promote learning in the client system and to contribute to general knowledge. This is done by creating conditions for valid inquiry in the context of practical deliberation by members of the client system.

According to Argyris, this has three implications: *First* that knowledge must be designed with the human mind in view, and by taking account of the limited information-seeking and processing capabilities of human beings in the action context. *Second* that knowledge should be relevant to the forming of purposes as well as to the achieving of purposes already formed. It will not do to assume that intentions and goal are given. And the *third* implication is that knowledge must take account of the normative dimension, in answering the practical question: 'What shall I do?' (Argyris et al. 1985, 37).

So, as Argyris' approach states *the first knowledge* a researcher needs is knowledge about the staff members' learning potential and the level of their motivation for development. Throughout the 1980s and 1990s, many public organisations, not least local authorities, were subjected to so much restructuring that researchers in the field have talked about a veritable boom in public administration initiatives aiming to bring about change in the public sector (Antonsen & Beck Jørgensen 2000). Many local government staff report 'change fatigue' in the wake of these constant demands for change and reorganisation. In the local authority that will be used as an example later on, the following statement was made in one of the opening interviews, 'We're so fed up with all the things that keep on coming at us from the top. We've been invited to so many weddings, but hardly ever to a funeral!' What the person is saying is that in recent years there has been an abundance of change and development projects initiated, implemented and run by management, but that many of them just fizzle out, without ever being formally closed. Bearing in mind that development and change can only ever occur if the staff members feel committed to the process, it is sometimes a good idea for the researcher to start out by 'researching' the way the staff members see the situation and how they feel about the project. This type of research can be done by interviewing selected staff members to hear their evaluation of the present competences available in the organisation and the types of learning processes that might motivate new learning in the specific context; an added benefit is that it provides a good basis for the future cooperation. Once the project has started, the learning processes applied during the realisation of the project must be researched on an ongoing basis to evaluate which learning processes, and thus which 'actions', prove the most suitable.

The second kind of knowledge, Argyris (1985) says, must be relevant to forming the purposes of the specific project. In action research projects about professional development of social work with at-risk families, this means that the existing knowledge about professional social work in this area must be researched, but it also means that it is necessary to introduce various forms of new knowledge in order to successfully develop the quality of social work. Argyris mentions two concepts that may be used as a point of departure for studying and working with knowledge forms: *espoused theory* and *theory-in-use*. Espoused theories are those that an individual claims to follow, and theory-in-use is the often tacit cognitive maps by which human beings design action (Argyris et al. 1985). Action research into social work requires that the researcher, together with the field, investigates what the espoused theory is, while at the same time trying to make the theory-in-use explicit. In social work with at-risk families, the purpose is often to make professional social work more knowledge-based by designing new espoused theories and transforming them into theory-in-use, to create a better alignment of the two theories and the actions resulting from them.

Nonaka and Takeuchi (1995) have identified *four learning processes* that demonstrate how competence can change from tacit – or silent – knowledge into explicit knowledge.

Figure 1
Four learning processes

Learning process	Situation	Effect on competence
Socialisation	Everyday work	From tacit to tacit
Externalisation	Dialogue and reflection	From tacit to explicit
Combination	Strategy processes	From explicit to explicit
Internalisation	Trying out with new things	From explicit to tacit

The figure shows that in the course of everyday work a mutual *socialisation process* takes place during which primarily tacit knowledge is transferred: 'learning by doing' by working with others. To develop more competences, there has to be an *externalisation* of the tacit knowledge. This can happen via dialogue with co-workers, reflection and interpretation of experiences from work. *Combination* implies that the organisation combines their own experiences (the externalised knowledge) with theory (e.g. through education of staff members). In addition, these theories must be coupled with the organisation's intentions and goals, which in this case will always be subject to the state's goals and intentions as expressed in the current legislation in the field. *Internalisation* occurs when the outcome of the newly acquired knowledge is converted into new plans and work routines (Nonaka & Takeuchi, here in Marnburg 2001).

To make sure that the acquired knowledge does not remain individual knowledge only but is converted into shared memory, the combination process must take place in a professional community. In this case, that would be the teams already existing in the organisation and which constitute the force field for learning (Senge 1995). The combination processes must be characterised by dialogue because this process is the most important element in a democratic system, and is the very cornerstone of any dynamic development founded on information-based decisions (Marnburg 2001).

The third implication mentioned by Argyris is that knowledge must take account of the normative dimension by answering the practical question: 'What shall I do?' (Argyris et al. 1985, 37). When working with at-risk families, social work has to take its starting point in the ideologies expressed in legislation and ministerial circulars. The 'profession' furthermore requires that social work must be based on 'evidence-based knowledge'. The homepage of the Danish SFI Campbell institute[1] states that although 'evidence' is usually defined as 'hard facts', solid well-documented knowledge, when it comes to social work the concept of evidence is more complex. Here, evidence can be understood as 'the best current knowledge' available on a particular issue. Therefore it is vital to make an effort to find this knowledge and not just settle for the most easily accessible or most convenient knowledge on offer. The best current knowledge is found by being systematic in the search for it. A thorough critical review of the knowledge available in a field will often reveal that the degree of evidence varies considerably; but also that a high degree of evidence is not always easy to obtain. In such cases the best current knowledge may, for instance, be statements from experts or one's own or colleagues' personal experiences. According to the international Campbell Collaboration, the most reliable evidence is obtained from systematic and well-designed effect measurements, especially several measurements which together may offer a reliable estimate of whether an intervention has an effect or not. A systematic research review is usually the best qualitative form of evidence-based research, since it will be the result of a systematic effort to reduce potential sources of error.

So, in social work evidence-based knowledge is understood as more than simply research results. Here 'evidence' has a broader meaning; also, it is not limited to knowledge about effect only. Effect is just one of the many questions that evidence-based policy and practice may wish to obtain more knowledge or evidence about. Therefore action research works with and researches into knowledge about the learning potential of the organisation and its staff, i.e. the espoused theory in force and the current theory-in-use, just as it seeks to involve different forms of evidence-based knowledge and combine it with the knowledge already available. Furthermore, the researcher will seek to develop new knowledge that may be applied in similar systems

How to handle different forms of knowledge at the practical level

Using the knowledge forms mentioned above, I will now classify the various forms of knowledge: 'Big' theories, understood as theories recognised by professionals as the best current knowledge in a given field;

empirical knowledge from research, and finally experience from actual practice. However, in social work there is a fourth type of knowledge that is also very important: interpersonal knowledge produced in interactions between families and social workers (Kildedal 2005). On the basis of the above understanding of the types of knowledge, an action researcher can operate with three categories of knowledge:

+ *Local knowledge* (espoused theory, theory-in-use and interpersonal knowledge).
+ *Pre-existing or prior knowledge* ('big theories', evidence-based empirical research results)
+ *Co-generated knowledge/theory* (knowledge/theory generated and applicable in both the specific and similar systems)

The special thing about this type of action research (development of the professional level in social work) is that in order to upgrade the knowledge platform for the practical social work, the researcher must strive not only to do research to uncover local knowledge but also to combine pre-existing knowledge with it. This will be the case when the work performed is not sufficiently knowledge-based and an infusion of new information is needed, or when an action research project is to be used to develop a new knowledge base to provide a team with a shared professional platform.

To accommodate the democratic aspect and the learning-theory approach as well as integrating various forms of knowledge in the project, it is a good idea to design the process in such a way that the researcher and the participants become joint 'owners' of the project. It is also important to establish a framework that allows continuous interaction between researcher and field on the knowledge and learning generated in the course of the process. The interaction between researcher and field may be summed up as follows:

The middle column of the model shows the elements of action research that are joint activities involving both the researcher and the field. Generally speaking, they represent the democratic elements of action research: cooperation on management of the process based on the research performed, conflict management and planning of the implementation of the outcome of the project. To the right are the researcher's tasks, which primarily involve doing the research and making the results available to the field. To the left, the participants' tasks, which are to produce the data that the researcher collects and uses for analysis. As should be evident by now, in this type of action research the researcher has a special obligation to provide the organisation with relevant knowledge that can interact with the knowledge present within it already. Finally, it is the researcher's duty to seek to develop general knowledge, applicable in similar contexts.

Figure 2
Interaction between researcher and field

The tasks of the participants *Develop practice*	Joint tasks *Cooperate, plan and manage*	The tasks of the researcher *Do research*
Produce data Generate new knowledge Test new knowledge Decide new knowledge platform	Formulate problems, goals and sub-goals Manage the process Study learning processes Solve any conflicts arising Support the process	Collect data Analyse data Generate new knowledge Describe new knowledge platform
Convert knowledge into practice Implement shared knowledge platform	Facilitate development processes Support implementation	Research into learning processes Support conversion process
Retain and further develop new knowledge platform	Close cooperation between researcher and field	Generate general knowledge

The middle column of the model shows the elements of action research that are joint activities involving both the researcher and the field. Generally speaking, they represent the democratic elements of action research: cooperation on management of the process based on the research performed, conflict management and planning of the implementation of the outcome of the project. To the right are the researcher's tasks, which primarily involve doing the research and making the results available to the field. To the left, the participants' tasks, which are to produce the data that the researcher collects and uses for analysis. As should be evident by now, in this type of action research the researcher has a special obligation to provide the organisation with relevant knowledge that can interact with the knowledge present within it already. Finally, it is the researcher's duty to seek to develop general knowledge, applicable in similar contexts.

A case-study: Action research into local authority practice

In the following I am going to describe an action research project in a large Danish local authority, which was carried out on the basis of the principles outlined above. The background for this project was strong criticism in the press of the local authority's social work in a few concrete cases. This resulted in a situation where social work performed in the local authority in general was presented as being of inferior quality and open to criticism from all sides. The politicians responsible for the local authority's social policy decided to have the quality of the social work involving at-risk children and families investigated and, if necessary, initiate measures to improve and develop quality. An agreement was signed between the local authority and the Aalborg University, represented by me, to initiate an action research project to investigate and evaluate the professional quality of social work, and to contribute towards quality improvement. The project lasted just over a year. The first six months were spent 'researching' the field, and based on the outcome of this research an intervention course was planned. The project was followed by a coordinating group and a steering committee who were involved on an ongoing basis in the analysis of the research results and in the planning of the learning process based on these results. First, a document analysis of 47 randomly selected case files was made, followed by a number of focus interviews with social workers and department heads from the four teams responsible for the work performed. Both the investigation of the professional quality of the case files and the interviews were carried out on the basis of a memorandum on professional standards required in social work. Basically, the memorandum stated that the 'profession' of social work requires an explicit theoretical foundation, relevant ethical considerations, systematic description, analysis and evaluation, and consistency between this part of the work and the remedies and measures initiated. Furthermore it stated that the analysis of the case files would also focus on observance of good administrative practice as described in the legal definitions of the act. The memorandum had been discussed in advance with the steering committee and with key persons in the local authority, who had all given their approval of its perspective.

The conclusion regarding the analysis of the case files was that the files to some extent complied with good administrative practice, but that there were major shortcomings in their description of the professional content of the case work. There was little consistency in the way descriptions, analyses and evaluations were recorded in the case files, and there were very few indications of the knowledge on which decisions were made. Consequently, as they showed so much variation and so many inconsistencies and irregularities, it was not possible to give an overall evaluation of the quality of the professional social work performed on the basis of the case files. It was, however, possible to conclude that the electronic design of the case files was not at all supportive of professional case filing, as there were no guidelines or suggestions on how to use professional terminology in the files. The electronic file consisted of blank pages only, and it was left entirely to the individual case workers to devise a structure of their own.

The interviews focused on examining the social workers' and their supervisors' perception of their own professional standard. Again the memorandum was used as a starting point for the staff's own evaluation of their compliance with the criteria for professional standards stated in it. This part of the research showed that both the social workers and their department heads felt that the individual social worker had high professional standards, but the interviews also revealed that there was no common or shared knowledge base for their work. The interviews showed that by and large social work was performed at the discretion of the individual social worker, based on his or her own professional standards; that is, quality very much depended on the competences of the individual social worker. Another conclusion was that the department heads had too many purely administrative duties and said they lacked time for professional supervision of the department's professional work.

The final analysis of the level of professional quality in the local authority was presented in the context of three categories, the first category being a professional unit in which the staff generally have poor qualifications, usually due to years of insufficient professional upgrading or continuous education. In such a unit there is a lack of knowledge, and development will require an infusion of knowledge. The second category is a professional unit that has a shared professional platform (theories and values), which has been fully implemented so that all staff members perform their work on the basis of this shared platform. The third category is characterised by individual staff having a high level of professional standard but the unit having no common professional foundation. Therefore the staff lack a common language, and metaphorically they act like little semi-autonomous 'satellites', each flying as they see fit. To develop and improve professional standards in such a unit, it is necessary to make sure all the 'satellites' start flying in some kind of formation.

The overall conclusion to the investigation of the level of professional quality in the local authority was that it fitted into the third category.

There was no indication that the professional standard for social work in the local authority was poor – in fact, the opposite might be said to be the case. It was concluded that 'there is an insufficient common professional foundation for the social work performed, which means that the conditions for improving and developing professionalism are not available' (Kildedal & Verwohlt 2009)[2]. On the basis of the investigation, it was decided to continue the project, in order to develop and implement a shared professional platform. And this became the starting signal for the 'action part' of the research project.

'Actions' during the process

The goal for this part of the project was to find a common knowledge base, to be put in writing, and to decide a plan for implementation at the end of the project. Using the theories described above as the basis for the next steps, it was decided to use the four teams in the organisation as the point of departure; that they should become the pivot of the process. Due to the size of the local authority, it was not expedient to involve all staff members in the process of formulating the shared professional platform. But bearing in mind the importance of making the process democratic, a model was designed around a 'learning circle' consisting of a social worker and a department head from the four teams, plus representatives from the local authority's day-care and residential care institutions for children and adolescents. These representatives were included because there was a need to sort out a number of professional issues related to cooperation between the two parts of the local authority administration. Dialogues between the participants in the learning circle, and between the participants and their colleagues back in their own teams, constituted the fundamental idea of the learning circle, inspired by both the democratic and the learning theory approach. The intention was to involve as many as possible in the development of the shared professional platform, to secure the commitment of all staff members and to motivate them to take ownership of the platform eventually formulated.

The work in the learning circle became the pivot of the process of assembling and discussing wishes and requirements in relation to the shared professional platform, deciding which to include and finally formulating the shared professional platform. The process revolved around a series of dialogue meetings, discussing and working with forms

Figure 3
Learning circle meetings

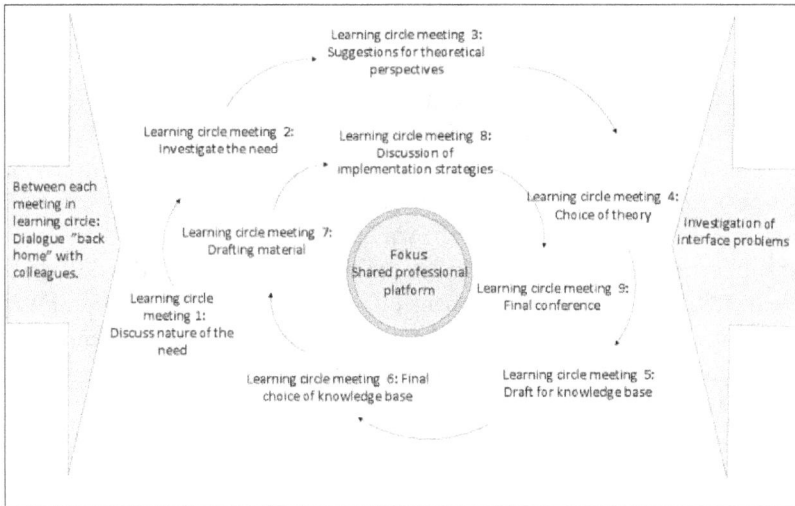

of knowledge and uncovering local knowledge (theory-in-use, espoused theories etc.) and suggestions for how to transform the new knowledge into actions in future. At this stage, the cooperation between researcher and the participants in the learning circle also included discussions on which forms of pre-existing knowledge (big theories, empirical research results etc.) should be included in the designing of the new platform. The process is outlined in the model below.

As can be seen in the model, the setup of the learning circle included eight meetings and a final conference. About 16 persons participated in each learning circle meeting, and some 250 (the entire staff) were invited to the final conference. Before finally arriving at a result acceptable to all parties involved, a wide range of research methods had been applied. To set the work in motion, a questionnaire survey among social workers was used to learn more about the knowledge base they were working from at the start of the process, and what they thought should be included in a future shared professional platform as well as the requirements it would need to fulfil.

Analyses of the questionnaires showed, among other things, that the present 'local knowledge' had its roots in a systems approach, which then became the starting point for the following part of the work. The next steps in the process took place through both written and face-to-face dialogues between researcher and learning circle, and between the learning circle and the four teams. The written part mainly consisted of minutes or a summary of discussions at the learning circle meetings, listing a range of issues to be discussed in the four teams, to give them a chance to voice their opinion to their representative in the learning circle.

Through this process, a shared professional platform was eventually produced, based largely on a systems approach. This platform was formulated as a 25-page document, which was presented at a final conference for all involved staff members and made available in print and electronically. At the conference the document was presented orally to the entire staff, and the management then presented the implementation strategy. This strategy outlined the training programmes and other forms of support to aid implementation in the teams and in the individual staff member's daily work. Development of an electronic case file system was also initiated, using the terminology of the document, and intended to create more consistency in the description of social work with at-risk families across the local authority.

Reflections on theory vs. practice

Finding an answer to the Argyris' question 'What shall I do?' is by no means easy (Argyris et al. 1985). Finding out what constitutes the best current knowledge about the field is in itself quite a challenge, and once it has been uncovered, the next question is how to convert it into professional social work actions targeting at-risk families. In fact, this is *the* challenge in the profession of social work. In this connection it makes sense to return to Senge's theory about teams as the pivot and driving force in an organisation working with 'conversion processes' (that is, turning theory into concrete, practical action) and using it as a starting point for deliberations on how to take the next step, 'converting' new theories into actions.

Practical social work can be described as the process of deciding which actions, out of a number of possible alternatives, to choose in a complex world and, says Payne (2006), this explains why a theory or a perspective should always be accompanied by a model offering explicit guidance. However, new knowledge far from always points to a model or includes guidelines on what to do, so in real life it is often left to practical social work to convert knowledge into action. As Payne points out, it is one of the characteristics of professional social work that it involves combining and converting different forms of knowledge, values and experience into practice. He goes on to say that there is general agreement that practice must necessarily be eclectic, but that care must be taken to avoid relying on theories that conflict or stray too far from main theory applied. Therefore it is vital that an eclectic approach is applied in a consistent and carefully designed manner, testing the choices and decisions made in a team of professionals rather than doing it on an individual, more or less arbitrary basis (Payne 2006, p.50).

When testing decisions in a team of colleagues, the individual social worker must be able to account for the knowledge that his or her decisions are based on and the likely outcome of the action, and to argue why this particular solution is to be preferred over alternatives. To be able to do this, the teams responsible for making decisions must develop work routines and use working methods that draw on the agreed knowledge base or shared platform in their argumentation.

Professional development of social work: Who is being targeted in action research?

This chapter started out by describing a learning theory approach to action research, arguing that inspiration from theories on learning organisations could be useful in an action research project intended to develop professional social work practice. As explained above, the approach points back to a technocratic-functional line of thought also referred to as the socio-technical approach to action research. This approach, in combination with a learning theory perspective, is well suited for working with local authority practice in social work.

However, it also makes sense to consider the perspective of Reason and Bradbury (2001):

> Actions research is a participatory, democratic process concerned with developing practical knowledge in the pursuit of worldwide human purposes, grounded in a participatory worldview, which we believe is emerging at this historical moment. It seeks to bring together action and reflection, theory and praxis, in participation with others, in the pursuit of practical solutions to issues of pressing concern to people, and more generally the flourishing of individual persons and their communities. (Reason & Bradbury 2001, 1)

The reason why this perspective makes sense in this context is that it revolves around the question: Who is action research supposed to help? Ultimately, what action research into social work with at-risk families aims to do is improve conditions for these families. In this type of project, it does so in an indirect way, by supporting the professional development of the frontline staff working with these families. Looking at it in the light of Reason and Bradbury's definition, for the researcher the perspective 'worldwide human purposes' is to help produce highly qualified, knowledge-based social work that will eventually benefit at-risk families, through a high professional standard of the help and support they are offered. When Reason and Bradbury state that the purpose of engaging in action research is to 'produce practice knowledge that is useful to people in the everyday conduct of their lives', the knowledge they talk about is, of course, the knowledge of the professionals, but definitely also the knowledge generated in the interaction between social worker and field, referred to above as interpersonal knowledge. This type of knowledge builds on the very essence of social work: that it is the individual human being who 'possesses the most profound knowledge of himself', and that social work is essentially about facilitating developmental and learning processes in people. When working with at-risk families, knowledge about the learning processes of the individual human being and the individual family can only emerge if the social worker seeks consciously to create a 'learning environment' when interacting with the family. In that way an action research project based on a learning theory approach can also be seen as an 'exemplary' approach because the participants add to their own experience by working with learning processes that they may later use in their daily work with at-risk families.

One of the main challenges of working with action research is ensuring that the project becomes a participatory, democratic process. When researching in a local authority context, creating democratic processes is indeed a challenge. Here the researcher will find him- or herself placed between, at one end, the staff members and, at the other, the political and strategic management. In this field of tension, there is a potential for conflict between the participants and the researcher, between the researcher and the management, as well as among the participants. This aspect of action research means that the researcher, in addition to his or her competences in research, may also need competences in conflict management. In the case above, local authority practice, the conflict is often about staff wanting extra resources if the development process involves changes that they see as demanding more time. The response from management and politicians will often be that the development process must take place within the existing framework, which then determines the conditions that the researcher works under. The dilemma for the action researcher, in this as in many other situations, is that they can offer advice but not make decisions; the researcher is unable to fulfil the demands of the staff, even if agreeing that the demands are reasonable.

Action research differs from other types of research especially in two ways: the research is participant-oriented, which means that to an agreed extent the participants are involved in the research, and the researcher is actively involved in initiating the development processes. As for the former, the implication is that there has to be a close, democratic interaction between researcher and field. As for the latter, the implication is that the researcher is physically present in many and very diverse situations. As a result, the competences of the action researcher play a major role in the success and outcome of the action research project. The role of the researcher can be discussed from the following positions: the researcher plays a high-profile role (runs the project); or the researcher and field play equal roles (a participatory design); or the researcher has a low-profile role (contributes, but the project is run mainly by others) (Gustavsen & Sørensen 1995).

In the type of action research discussed here, the researcher plays a high-profile role. This role makes great demands on the researcher's competence in working with processes; on the one hand conducting the research using democratic principles, on the other striving to achieve the goals agreed with the field beforehand. This type of project will often be initiated on the basis of a formal agreement with the management, implying obviously that the management expects certain results which the researcher is expected to deliver. This means, at a practical level, that the first meetings with the persons expected to 'develop' are extremely important. It is vital that the researcher tries very hard to build up a relationship of trust with the participants, bearing in mind that there is an inherent conflict between the strategic management's wishes for speedy, effective results and the very nature of the human learning process. It is possible to force through a learning process, but lasting and constructive results can only be achieved if the learners want to achieve them and, as stated above, organisational learning is only possible if the members of the organisation want to participate. This is where the researcher's own learning process comes into the picture. The researcher will have to work with those of his or her own competences required by the specific field and the people involved in it, which will affect the researcher's cooperative competences and teach him new ways of handling conflicts or managing processes.

When Reason and Bradbury write that

the wider purpose of action research is to contribute through this practical knowledge to the increased well-being – economic, political, psychological, spiritual of human persons and communities and to a more equitable and sustainable relationship with the wider ecology of the planet of which we are an intrinsic part' (Reason & Bradbury 2001, p.2)

it follows that the action researcher needs to see him- or herself in a much wider perspective. So action research is also about communicating the knowledge acquired about at-risk children and families, be it in an educational context or in articles or statements to the press, to influence socio-political decisions made regarding at-risk families. Action research into social work is thus to be understood as more than just one single project: the real issue is the sum of help and support offered to families at risk. Reason and Bradbury also talk about action research 'as a way of being part of the world'. This way of putting it makes a lot of sense to someone like me, who is strongly involved in the socio-political aspects of social work and who sees the objective of her professional life as a commitment to help improve the conditions of children and families at risk.

References

Argyris, C., Putnam. R. & McLain Smith. D. (1985): Action Science. Jossey-Bass Publishers.

Antonsen, M. & Beck Jørgensen T. (eds) (2000): Forandringer I teori og praksis – Skiftende billeder fra den offentlige sektor. Jurist og Økonomforbundets Forlag.

Clausen, C., Lorenzen, B. & Baungaard Rasmussen, L. (1992): Deltagelse i teknologisk udvikling. Fremad.

Epstein, I. & Blumenfield, S. (eds) (2001): Clinical Data-Mining in Practice-Based Research. Birmingham: The Haworth Social Work Practice Press.

Gustavsen, B.& Sørensen B.A. (1995): Aksjonsforskning. In Eikeland O. & Finsrud, H.D. (eds): Forskning og handling – Søkelys på aksjonsforskning.

Jarvis P. (2002): Praktiker-forskeren: udvikling af teori fra praksis. København: Alinea.

Kildedal, K. (2005): Aktionsforskning – Èn af vejene til udvikling af det sociale arbejdes praksis. In Munch (ed.) Forskning og socialt arbejde. UFC Børn og unge.

Kildedal, K. (2009): Undersøgelse af den socialfaglige praksis i Århus Kommune. Et Aktionsforskningsprojekt del 1 og 2 (available in Århus Kommune).

Lewin, K. (1997): Resolving Social Conflicts. – Field Theory in Social Science. Washington: American Psychological Association.

Marnburg, E. (2001): Den selvudviklende virksomhed - Idépilarer i lærende organisasjoner. Gyldendal: Norsk Forlag.

Payne, M. (2006): Teorier I Socialt arbejde. Hans Reitzels Forlag.

Ramian, Knud (2010): http://knudramian.pbworks.com/FrontPage

Ramian, K. (2002): Practitioner Research on Mental Health Rehabilitation in Collaborative Research Networks. 4th International Conference on Evaluation for Practice. Tampere.

Reason, P. & Bradburry H. (2001): Handbook of Action Research. Sage Publications.

Research in Action/forskning and Handling. Arbeidsforskningsinstituttets skriftserie. Sverige.

Senge, P. (1999): Den femte Disciplin. Klim.

Notes

1   (http://www.sfi.dk/Default.aspx?ID=268)

2   The report may be downloaded at: http://www.aarhuskommune.dk/ files/aak/aak/content/filer/magistratens_1._afdeling/socialafdelingen/ organisationsindgangen/undersoegelser/Kildedal_til_udlevering.pdf

8

Approaching practice research in theory and practice

Erja Saurama and Ilse Julkunen

Introduction

This chapter examines different conceptions of knowledge and ways of producing knowledge in social work in relation to practice research. The objective is to create a review of the different thoughts and perceptions that we have formed in our numerous activities in this field of study. The chapter will describe our connection to practice research and, particularly, to its methodology. We will also evaluate different influences that practice research has taken from other fields of study. Through different examples we will attempt to illuminate the process of creating knowledge in practice research towards the end of the chapter. Our approach to the subject is hence practice-oriented and the point of departure is practice-based. In contrast, the literature on the topic is mainly interdisciplinary and theoretically constructed from many different areas of social sciences. The aim has been to keep our approach sensitive to all of the ideas that have been created within the broad framework of practice research. The chapter does not attempt to give a conclusive definition of practice research because strict definitions, or even attempts to define the subject matter, may culminate in restricting rather than unlocking different paths to discussing the phenomena. Our view is that practice research in social work is still a novel subject trying to find its characteristic form and content.

This chapter has been written by carrying out a dialogue, not only amongst ourselves, but also with different communities of practice research. The Heikki Waris –Institute (Finnish-speaking) and the Mathilda Wrede Institute (Swedish-speaking) are organizations in Helsinki that focus on social work research and teaching. The operations of these institutes are directed towards the everyday life of social work[1]. Both institutes organize and invest resources in teaching practice research, but in this paper we will concentrate solely on research. The *Research & Write* study group (organized conjointly by the Waris and Wrede Institutes) has become an innovative arena for collective learning. Our thinking has benefited greatly from different discussions in both of the Institutes. Naturally, the first critical audience for this chapter works in these Institutes.

There is no one definition of practice research; in different contexts it has been understood and defined in various ways. Different terms are also used when describing practice research in social work: practice-based research (Epstein 2001; Johnsson & Svensson 2005), practitioner research (Shaw 2005) and practice research (Satka et al. 2005). To draw the line is not unambiguous, but one division that can be established is whether the conductor of practice research is an active practitioner, a social worker, or whether the process of producing knowledge is seen in a larger perspective. Some researchers place their focus particularly on the practitioner. For example, Knud Ramian (2004) demands that a social worker carrying out research needs to spend 80 % of his or her time at work in practice. Generally speaking, researchers do not have a preference or they do not recommend any particular methods or approaches, although many of them mention different participative principles such as action research and ethnography (McCrystal 2000). A short overview of the discussion reveals that the following qualities are seen as relevant in practice research:

1. Problem-solving is connected to practices within social field, or as Epstein (2001) describes: 'to be able to answer questions that derive from practice and to be able to answer in such a way that it informs practice'.
2. The research process is characterized by its orientation to change, i.e. transformative nature.
3. The research is conducted in an interactive manner with various actors involved in the research process.
4. The roles of the researcher and the practitioner overlap and the researcher is both the subject and the object.
5. The production and implementation of knowledge overlap.

In the first Finnish book of practice research in social work (Satka et al. 2005), the development of practice research is described, introducing conceptual and methodological tools in social work and its research. The book defines practice research in social work as an approach that studies and solves problems related to practices in the social field, having an applicable nature and serving many different interests. According to the book, the function of practice research in social work is to strengthen an innovative culture of research and knowledge formation in the social field. It is particularly the culture of creating knowledge that is seen to separate practice research from the more conventional field of social research[2].

Practice research is conducted at the institutes of practice research in Helsinki and is heuristically located at the intersection of two worlds, that is where the practice of developmental social work and the academic world, through scientific research on social work, meet. The practical side of social work wants to put resources into enhancing services, the university for its part wants to improve the quality of teaching social work as a subject and strengthen its substance and theory basis. Practice-based knowledge formation and research-based practice form a dialectic connection that can be best put to use in the practices of social work and the social field of study. An indirect objective is to introduce the knowledge formed in practice to the academic world and to further improve the theoretical basis of social work as a subject matter.

Foundations of practice research

What we understand as practice research in social work has its own particular origins. The methodological interests of the 1980s in studying humans and the social world were a window of opportunity also for the development of social work. Different new empirical methods concerning the actor, interaction and speech became popular at the same time as social work, as an academic discipline, was framed in different universities. The different phases of the development of social sciences – the decline of logical empiricism (and science based on its methods), the rise of qualitative and narrative research and the so-called linguistic turn – have further trained researchers of social sciences, including social work, and equipped them with different methodological approaches and abilities to reflect upon the theoretical basis and commitments of their research. The mental distance between the researcher and the subject of research has diminished, the relationship between the objectivity and subjectivity of research has become more problematic and, by and large, the question of the nature of knowledge and the methods of acquiring knowledge has become a common part of research activity. The question of the 'voice' of the subject, their point of view and the framework of different meanings has become an interesting challenge in the research process. Simultaneously, a new relationship has been established between science and the society surrounding it. We may remark that the perspective of critical welfare research has broadened or even switched, to study the interaction between an actor, civil society and the different communities within it (Williams & Popay 1999; Juhila 2006).

A research approach that emphasizes the importance of the relation to practice has counterparts in prévious history, when the groundwork of social work was just starting to be put in place. We can find crucial influences from pragmatic epistemology, according to which knowledge is *a posteriori*: Knowledge is something that comes about after practice, action and experience. What is relevant is the conscious and logical analysis of experience and perceptions as well as testing knowledge in practice. (Bertilsson & Christiansen 2001, 467-472.) In fact, it is an interesting detail that the operational field of some of the pioneers and pragmatists, such as Jane Addams and George Herbert Mead was the same: the industrialized city environment of early twentieth century Chicago and its settlement movement.

On the one hand, pragmatic tradition was a constant reminder that scientific research does not offer a privileged view into the world as it is, but that we also need to take seriously other points of view of human practices, such as morality and religion (Pihlström 1998). On the other hand, pragmatic tradition is not a united front either. Charles S. Peirce, who has been mentioned as the father of pragmatism, was a conservative and he opposed practical applications of science, whereas another famous pragmatist John Dewey was a utilitarian, defending the function of science to produce intelligent tools with which to develop civil society. Peirce, however, softened his views later when developing the idea of abductive reasoning (Bergman 2008). In fact, the principle of abductive reasoning has been adopted largely into western research from the pragmatic philosophy of science (Peirce 2001). What Peirce meant by abduction was reasoning 'backwards', that is a search for a hypothesis that would explain a new or strange phenomenon perceived in practice. Peirce himself had a certain basic model of research according to which ideas are first sought abductively, then clarified deductively and finally tested inductively. The search for ideas starts with research material and through analysis of perceptions (Paavola & Hakkarainen 2006, 271.) Compared to hypothetic-deductive reasoning, the difference concerns the material-based approach, i.e. looking for ideas in research material. Deductive reasoning does not produce new knowledge, but verifies it and gives it a truth-value. The difference from inductive reasoning is in the implementation of already existing knowledge while explaining the phenomenon. In fact, most of the qualitative research in social sciences could probably be included within the limits of the different degrees of abductive reasoning – pure inductive research is impossible. Abduction has particularly been considered as a method of invention (Paavola & Hakkarainen 2006, 272). As the demand for innovations runs high today, the interest to this 'third way' of reasoning has also grown.

The pragmatist John Dewey (1929/1999) criticized in his time the European, Cartesian philosophy of science which separated practice and knowledge, which according to him had developed into the rule of rational thinking, scientific knowledge and even scientific superstition, compared to practical wisdom and acquired skills.

> Are the objects of the affections, of desire, effort, choice, that is to say everything to which we attach value, real? Yes, if they can be warranted by knowledge; if we can *know objects* having these value properties, we are justified in thinking them real. But as objects of desire and purpose they have no sure place in Being until they are approached and validated through knowledge. The idea is so familiar that we overlook the unexpressed premise upon which it rests, namely that only the completely fixed and unchanging can be real. The quest for certitude has determined our basic metaphysics. (Dewey 1929, 17-18)

What Dewey wanted to do was to restore the value of the needs of practical life in the field of knowledge formation; although practice is uncertain, chaotic and volatile, it is nevertheless the reality within which people have to solve the problems they face. Dewey pointed out that the method of becoming conscious of something is the same whether it concerns common life or scientific work. In both cases, the question is about problem solving and science is also work in practice.

Science has been seen as mankind's way out of uncertainty and the objective of science is the pursuit of certainty (Dewey 1929/1999).What has followed is that reality has started to be understood as parallel to scientific knowledge:

> There are certain things which are alone inherently the proper objects of knowledge and science. Things in the production of which we participate we cannot know in the true sense of the word, for such things succeed instead of preceding our action. What concerns action forms the realm of mere guesswork and probability, as distinct from the warrant of rational assurance

which is the ideal of true knowledge. We are so accustomed to the separation of knowledge from doing and making that we fail to recognize how it controls our conceptions of mind, of consciousness and of reflective inquiry. For as it relates to genuine knowledge, these must all be defined, on the basis of the premise, so as not to admit of the presence of any overt action that modifies conditions having prior and independent existence. (Dewey 1929, 18.)

Dewey's pattern of inquiry (1938) is based on a pragmatic paradigm that sees commonsense as well as scientific knowledge as a means to improve human practices. It emphasises that the *scientific goal is to create knowledge of the practical world*, that is, knowledge capable of practical application. With reference to practice research what is relevant is Dewey's criticism that only when experiences and the perceptions of the actors can be based upon research results do they become real, hence only then would they be regarded as subjects of social reform.

An operational and pragmatic element is involved in all acquisitions of knowledge. Since the research process is only possible in a context that has already been shaped by different operational conventions, the individuals or the communities they form need to already have certain skills at the outset of the research, which they can develop further as the research progresses. There are no ways of operating without the appropriate skills that can be used and applied in a conventional manner to cope with certain assignments. Hence, there is no research without skills. Thinking can be perceived only in texts; to acquire knowledge requires research operations regulated by skills. Theories are formed and tested always with an eye on practice. There is no 'pure' science without the motivation offered by technical applications, or without the testing of the theories enabled by the technical arrangements of tests. Nevertheless, pragmatists do not claim that knowledge would equal skill or that science is the same as technical operations. They only inform us that the boundaries are tied to the context and that they are imprecise in the end.

What is also relevant from the point of view of practice research is the active and changing nature of learning. According to Dewey, knowledge is not something similar to the passive reviewing of facts, but something that is skillfully operating in the practical context, solving problems and reaching for goals that are valued as worthwhile. Learning does not have any perennial, a-historical nature, and the nature of learning can change over time as different learning-related practices and skills develop. Acquiring knowledge is to learn how to operate skilfully and learn through practice. 'Learning by doing' is a good description that encapsulates the entanglement of knowledge and action underlined by pragmatism. However, learning through practice has also been criticized as a naïve perspective, because it does not result in a deeper conceptual understanding, but it also requires a different kind of learning in order to support the development of understanding (cf. Hakkarainen et al. 1999; 2004).

Empirical methods emphasizing the concept of reflexivity of pragmatism have prevailed mainly in pedagogy (Mezirow 1991) and in organization research (Schön 1983). In social sciences, the methods of action research and participative observation, that have their roots in the Chicago school, have maintained their place at the margins of social research for decades. Pragmatism as a practical research orientation has, however, been neglected.

Research has different kinds of epistemological functions. There are many different ways of conducting research and the question of what kind of interpretation research needs or entails, has everything to do with the intellectual functions and interests of the research (Ronkainen 2007). The social nature of knowledge is illuminated by Jürgen Habermas' (1965) division between the technical, practical and critical interests of knowledge. Habermas highlights that critical consciousness is formed when an actor has to confront other traditions and ways of life and faces existential dichotomies. People need a perspective on their own existence and on the existing institutional phenomena. Understanding, in other words, includes the transference and extension of this perspective. A human being sees things differently after he or she understands them; even our self-perception might change. Understanding or being aware is therefore the object of critical thinking, and critical consciousness even has an existential dimension; 'self-knowledge' can develop as a person obtains a perspective on his own existence. According to Habermas, all kinds of communal consolidation are ultimately tied to the question of how the understanding of social reality is reached. We may even claim that Habermas' objective is to build a bridge between the culture of experts and common life, and therefore to enrich and challenge different perspectives that might have originally been taken for granted.

Habermas' theory of communicative action (1987) rules out authority-based institutions except when there is a good argument for them, and offers perspectives on how critique and change could be extended to be within the reach of actors. Shotter and Gustavsen (1999) have developed this theory further and turned dialogical criteria into operational practice, according to which free communication without domination is possible. They have formed a criterion, which is known as a method of discussion and democratic dialogue in the Nordic research of work life and organizations (see also Gustavsen 1996 2004). The point of departure for a perspective that underlines the importance of democratic dialogue is that real operational changes require the involvement and participation of several different parties. A democratic dialogue can also be seen as one particular tool that enhances self-understanding regarding practice. In social work practice research the creation of knowledge is tied to practices and their development. It emphasizes interaction and the equal discussion between different parties in order to enable change. In the creation of knowledge and aspirations for participation, collective and innovative practice research can greatly benefit from ideas developed in different fields of study regarding action research and the dialogical approach. Such fields of study are in accordance with the above-mentioned pragmatism: ethnography, action research, action theory and developmental work research. In action theory a practice can be studied as a construct, which consists of activity, action and operation. In this case, practice is a collective activity that has its own social motive and history. The science of action is usually applied to action research and its development in different organizations. The approach is based on Chris Argyris's work, which was influenced by Donald Schön. Relying on the science of action, workers are encouraged to turn into reflective practitioners (Heikkinen et al. 2006).

The turns in knowledge production

In our attempt to develop the concept of practice research we have also been influenced by sociological science and technology research, which studies the practices of producing scientific knowledge and technical innovations. In this field the focus is particularly on birth process, transformation and transference of scientific knowledge. Hence we have reached the world we live in today; a discussion of the ever changing role of knowledge is part of our time.

Human beings and different organizations function in a changing technological, human, institutional, economic and natural environment. In a worldwide scale, we are entering a new global, information-guided and networked environment. Welfare society is also adapting to the challenges of the new era. According to the analysis of Castells and Himanen (2001, 181), the changes are apparent in the multiplicity of web-based information environments as well as in the transformation into a new kind of expertise. In this world, production of knowledge is no longer demarcated within the boundaries of universities and research institutes, since an increasing number of organizations, such as the R&D departments of companies, consultants, development units of public administration, etc. have started to produce knowledge for their own purposes. The number of monopolies of knowledge is in decline.

Gibbons, Nowotny and Scott (1999) discuss two different models of knowledge production. The first is based on the perceptions acquired by the methods of natural science that are mainly produced by academic staff. The other model is a reference to knowledge that is more heterogeneous, temporary, socially relevant and reflective. It is usually also locally contextualized. In the first model, external knowledge and expertise appear to be superior, and objective compared to the traditions of practitioners and their knowledge that is based on practice. In the second model, the point of departure is more equal and interactive. We may say that today expert knowledge is understood to be socially determined, which means that experts are thought to be functioning within social contexts, such as work groups and communities. In practice research we are in search of a third way of knowing, in which academic knowledge and expert knowledge based in practice are seen as mutually relevant and in a dialogue, so that both accept and value the unique nature of the other party.

Knowledge formation arising out of practice means in fact the use of a methodological approach that is in accordance with abductive reasoning. This model is very close to the view of knowledge formation in social work expressed by Aulikki Kananoja (1984):

> A question has risen whether knowledge is born also in the manner that a social worker in her own work perceives things systematically, gathers these perceptions into a constant whole, gives the perceived knowledge different meanings and, subsequently, in her own work tests whether these new meanings are reliable.

Both the epistemology criticized by the pragmatists and their own analyses were products of their time. However, what is particularly interesting today is that practice and conscious action have once again become crucial issues. Hans Joas has continued developing the pragmatism and modern analysis of it in his book *The Creativity of Action* (1996). What Joas brings to the surface is particularly the importance of creative and collective action as a new focus in social sciences.

Ulla Mutka (1998) in her book, *The Fourth Turn of Social Work*, discusses the state of social work, and its ways of conception and self-understanding. The problem, according to Mutka, has been the superiority and primacy of scientific knowledge compared to experimental knowledge. She asserts that the confusion and hesitance brought about by the development of civil society that is typical of our age is necessarily calling for more versatile ways of knowing, which simultaneously is developing the basis for different ways of defining expertise.

A relevant topic of discussion in social work research is knowledge formation arising from practice with the help of the so-called critical reflection (for example, Karvinen et al. 2000, Fook 2002).This additionally has a larger connection to postmodernism as well as to different discussions in social sciences in which knowledge and knowledge formation are analyzed critically, hence bridging the gap between knowledge, knowing and practice (see Karvinen-Niinikoski 1999) Karvinen-Niinikoski emphasizes the epistemological turn that concerns knowledge production and the significance of practice turn: scientific knowledge cannot be viewed as independent, but it is thought to be shaped in continuous interaction with other forms of knowledge and in the practice of common life among the practitioners.

One strong basis of practice research in social work is thus the building of a new relationship between knowledge, knowing and practice. Present day experts need to be able to cross different kinds of borders and to connect different elements in order to meet the challenges that the development of our society produces. This creates pressure also for the knowledge formation process itself; how to develop research problems so that they would better meet the burning challenges set for research. The communal demand for practice research is based on local needs to develop new knowledge constructions and the desire for developmental work. The development as local action is however not enough, what is also required is the construction of development work more intensively and consciously using the different tools of research.

Development means creating something new and looking forward. The challenge in knowledge production is to see what kind of problem framework or choice of possible worlds ought to be set as the target: what is the focus of the work now and what will it be in ten years. At its best, practice research can function in processes of change as a communal practice that can unite three functions of social sciences – constancy (upholding continuity), critical (challenging the existing) and constructive (renewal) – and benefiting all of these in a fruitful way. Science can then be seen as a social practice that is based upon a dialogue between science and its subject.

In social work, a reflective attitude has slowly become the dominant attitude in practices relating to the job as well as studying for it, but research problems based on experience in the development of working methods of social work are relatively new. In the processes of social work and the processes of scientific thinking there are many similarities related to creative problem solving. Social work seeks solutions suitable for its users while research seeks answers to the research problems (Pohjola 1994). One of the recent ideas is that in fact many of the epistemological and methodological analyses are quite similar to those that are raised in service user work. This concerns the similarities not only in the processes, but also in the principles and methods (Laine & Saurama, 2009).

Experiences of practice research

In our attempts to conduct practice research , we have been able to use the above mentioned textbook *Practice research of social work* (Satka et al. 2005) as a tool. It condenses practice research as follows (cf. 10-11):

1. the proposed problems to be solved are related to the practices of the social field and the purpose is to serve the different interests of the field
2. there exists an immediate connection to developmental work that enables us to build a new kind of relationship with the prevailing conceptions and theories in social sciences
3. the methodological innovativeness of the practitioners reaches from the theories of social science to the development of work methods
4. all the participants are vessels of knowledge and they have a right to participate in the production of knowledge
5. the work commits to bringing forth the experiences and knowledge of marginalized individuals and of those citizens that are unable or too weak to defend themselves.

Practice research attempts to create a reflective relationship to the prevailing conceptions and theories existing in social sciences that are created through its connection to practice. Practice research uses tales, metaphors and dialogical encounters that analyze the living reality in a coherent and proper manner. It is characteristic for knowledge gained from practice and the experience of individuals to be personally touching. This research tendency has taken as one of its objective to particularly expose the experiences and knowledge of individuals pushed to the margins (Satka et al. 2005). In other words, practice research is value-laden. It is attached to practice and its development, it attempts to make social work more visible, aims to continuously re-evaluate its conceptions, operates in a communal manner, and takes seriously the ethics of the social work field.

A crucial aim in practice research is to find ways of producing knowledge that cross boundaries. In different institutes the researcher/ social workers study the methodology of practice research and through their own empirical projects they seek to contribute to improving and spreading the concept. We have sought to apply the criteria of democratic dialogue and critical and expansive learning to the whole process of knowledge formation. The researcher/social workers also try to participate in direct work with clients as much as possible. However, according to our own experience the idea of a researcher who would devote 80 % of her time to client work is simply unrealistic (cf. Ramian 2004). Our starting point is not that the researcher/social worker needs to strictly spend a certain amount of their time in working directly with users, but to ensure that the work is relevant in practice by operating in an open and collective manner.

Participatory and collective knowledge formation in practice means that all participants are involved: the users of services, other citizens, professionals, providers of services and different actors in administrative and voluntary sectors. Promoting the participation of the customer in the process of creating knowledge in practice research has strong intellectual support. Anne-Marie Lindqvist's (2008) thesis on participation in the context of care and research studies participation in practice and also the role of research through the users of social work – in her case, the participation of disabled individuals. The users became co-researchers. The research process itself became part of the research material in which the researcher was involved as both the subject and the object. Half of the thesis consists of analysing how participation is implemented at different phases of the care context, the other half on how participation was implemented within the research context. The research process was open and it included regular dialogues between the actors in practice. Users also participated in the research reference group. What is clear is that the participation of the users brings a critical point of view to the research as it simultaneously enlightens the plurality and complexity of the concrete implementation in practice.

What we are therefore doing when formulating the concept of practice research is looking for a multilateral and collective way of creating knowledge. We aim to consciously work in an interactive and abductive manner. The possible conceptual tools, different situations and the information that they offer play a crucial role in this. The reasoning involved is usually carried out as a communally decentralized process, as well as relying on the available literature. What needs to be taken into consideration when planning the upcoming research is firstly the participation of service users in knowledge production, secondly the role of developmental and peer groups, and thirdly the participation of management and awareness of the goals of the undertaking. This method of working ensures the applicability and relevance of the knowledge being produced. Researcher/social workers create within the field developmental teams made up of social workers dealing with users. These pilot groups analyze their own work (for example, Koskinen 2007; Myllärniemi 2007; Lindroos 2008; Sjöblom 2008; Muukkonen 2008). The reasearcher/ social workers develop and test ideas together with their pilot group. Later the forthcoming material will be used in their research. The material and its interpretations is also returned to the field to be reviewed by the developmental team, in which case the results and interpretations transform from subject-bound into a communal perspective. Different field and writing periods are divided according to the needs of different research and developmental projects. When the ideas are expressed for the use of the community at large, new conceptualizations are created that can then be developed further, compared and/or tested in practice (Hakkarainen et al. 1999).

Regarding the research conducted at universities, the developmental orientation has meant that it is a challenge to traditional research, regardless of how empirically or inductively oriented it is. Practice research means creating new meanings which are different from the traditional basis of research which studies what has already taken place – something that has already found its meaning and is part of past reality (cf. Sulkunen 1997). An example would be how to study the flow of phenomena or something that has not yet become part of the semiotic world. To understand the deeper meaning of this question has also resulted in recognizing the need to develop the methodology of practice research.

When social work is analyzed as an academic subject matter and as an object of scientific research, the question of the flow of action and the participation of the actors in action that becomes knowledge cannot be answered within the traditional methodology of research.

Conceptualization means making something visible and verbalizing the feelings, perceptions and unconscious actions that still have no words for describing it. When words are transformed into concepts, these may already be part of a theory. Parallel processes of knowledge acquirement – perceptions, systematizing and analyzing perceptions and constructing, testing and evaluating new operational models – are what we mean when we use the term practice research. It is not a *de facto* research method, but more of a paradigm or a culture of knowledge formation that includes the whole process of knowledge formation in practice. The interest of knowledge is tied to practice without excluding different ways of carrying out practice research. Practice research does not require a certain kind of method, because that might classify research in much too narrow a way. The aim is more experimental in the spirit of Charles S. Peirce (1931): 'I sincerely believe that a bit of fun helps thought and tends to make it pragmatical'.

In the Finnish institutes of practice research and in the different projects that have been carried out and developed, the ratio between development and research varies,. There is a continuum where there is no set boundary. Nevertheless, experience has proved that the goals change during the process. In some cases the point of departure is visible, while the process progresses critically towards creating new practices (Koskinen 2007; Myllärniemi 2007). Some projects aim more purely and boldly towards modelling. These cases call for earlier ground work and they also require an extensive amount of knowledge formation so that the project can be taken towards the systematizing of action (e.g. Ervast & Tulensalo 2006; Lindroos 2008). Other research projects study critically the research project as well as the phenomenon itself (Lindqvist 2008; Sjöblom 2008), attempting to develop the methodology of practice research and exposing the experiences of people in the margins and of citizens with lesser abilities to defend themselves.

What is interesting from the action-based and methodological perspective is this orientation in research to commit itself to openly seeking for something new, and the willingness to accept and analyze change. We have been able to find many similarities with the pragmatic scientific tradition, although we are not committed to following any particular school or tradition. In the Institutes we are concerned with how to carry out action research, and with being able to make sure that the results of different projects are relevant in practice. Perhaps the most important point about practice research is that the researchers have worked or are currently working in practice *and* have been trained for research as well.

It is both, a resource and a challenge. Many years ago Edith Abbott and Sophonisba Breckinridge had already emphasized the capabilities of researchers in the work of the Hull House settlement in 1920s Chicago. They defended a view that social workers hold significant scientific abilities and that research should not be conducted only by social scientists (see Shaw & Bryderup 2008). Researcher/social workers offer a different perspective on research which researchers working from the outside do not possess. At the same time, a multiparty, communal and critical process of learning enhances the birth of novel mental commitments.

When the researcher, the subject, is also part of the object that is studied, an interesting question is raised, namely how to study one's own actions. The Mertonian norms of science say that a researcher needs to seclude him or herself from the subject matter and neutralize her own influence on the field of study. We have identified this problem realizing that a researcher needs to be able to perform different kinds of mental transformations during the research. When gathering the research material, discussing, perceiving and interviewing, he or she might well identify him or herself with the work group and users, but the analysis of the material, must be based upon tried research methods. The researcher should also be reflective about her own role in the field. The gathered analyzed material and the analyses are returned as if in a hermeneutic securely sealed circle to the developmental team to be reviewed at the point at which they become externalised. In other words, the researcher is responsible for the *analysis* of the research process, whereas the other participants act as vessels and *interpreters* of knowledge.

Can the practice of social work be approached in any other way than as research concerning one's own work? Different models of knowledge production prevail in our Institutes and we encourage our researcher/ social workers to try new methodological applications and new points of departure. One example concerns boys in child protection who are approached in their everyday school communities and, in a sense, studied ethnographically at close range. What is relevant in this case is how the researcher/social worker uses his experience of child protection, how he is in regular interaction with the child protection worker, and how he tests the possible conceptual creations and develops them further. This kind of research process is open-ended and it crosses different boundaries. In this concrete project an analogous example is the well-known Barneby Skå community in which about 70-80 troubled young men between the age of 7 and 15 lived. Gustav Jonsson and Anna-Lisa Kälvestan who built the research community in Skå balanced practice and research, and wanted to learn more about what kind of phenomena they were working with and what kind of results the community produced. Their point of departure was interesting: the idea was not to produce material about youngsters in the Skå community, but to study ordinary boys living in Stockholm. In this way they were able to form a theoretical framework that functioned as a mirror for the practice (Börjesson 2004; Vinterhed 1977). By studying in an innovative manner the family relations of the children and the communities (for example by using the drawings of the children) the researchers managed to form a significant theoretical basis for child protection practices (Jonsson & Kälvestan 1964). The material of the research was huge – altogether 222 boys participated – and it is known as the first qualitative research in Swedish social work, although as a whole it was quantitatively oriented as it was customary at the time.

Reflections

Practice research is open to different kinds of interesting epistemological considerations. Conceptualization requires much expertise from the researcher: it calls for methods of thinking learned in scientific research, systematization and research logic, approved research methods, and good background knowledge of relevant literature – but most of all, what is required is different fora where knowledge formation can be developed and tested communally. Unsurprisingly, Hakkarainen, Lonka and Lipponen (1999) point out that meta-conceptual awareness is possible only through being actively part of the research process. Through the process of communal learning an individual can become aware of his own mental commitments and gradually start to change them.

Our view is that practice research is at a stage of dynamic development in which it is important to maintain a searching, bold and innovative attitude towards conducting practice-based research. It means that the relevant actors are actively studying and carrying out collective discussions and also building their own community. We have invested considerable resources in building a trustworthy and secure research community. Regular meetings, group tutoring, study groups and development seminars as well as a willingness to present the results of different projects to outside visitors, create a shared spirit and a development-oriented atmosphere. It can already be remarked that an experience of ten years has brought 'the field' and 'the university' closer together. The research-orientation of social workers has increased, students feel that they are better equipped when they graduate and teachers have found new connections to actors who work in practice.

The research capabilities of social workers are the instrumental resource on which practice research depends. The premise of implementing practice research is fundamental to the educational system of Finnish social work which offers social workers, in addition to the skills to work with service users, the resources to carry out research. The knowledge produced by the users and the employees can become part of the research process, either in a material or an interpretational framework, although the commitment to the research process might vary.

Social work research is versatile by nature and it is supposed to be so. This research can be practised academically when developing theoretical analyses and conceptions. This research is also required as knowledge producing action that arises more directly from practice and also returns to the field. As a social actor, social work has a significant role in the lives of citizens. The interventions of social work require social expertise and that the gathered database of knowledge is applied sensitively while questioning what is perceived as self-evident.

Our approach towards the concept of practice research has been (and is) very open-ended. We have brought forward the following critical points: the relationship between the subjects and objects of knowledge, the relationship between research and development, and the collective nature of knowledge formation, and particularly, user-participation. A crucial part of the conceptual awareness of practice research is that different kinds of knowledge related to the organization of reality are in equal standing with each other. They have different roles in human conduct. The ideal is that research and practice-based expertise meet each other as equals.

We would also want to emphasize that different dimensions can be seen in the transformative nature of practice research and how practice research is involved in the whole process of knowledge formation – changing both it and the culture around it. If and when the goal is to change and develop existing practices, the information of the actors in practice is relevant: who is speaking and from whose perspective? When the user's expertise concerning his/her own life and the experience of employees are considered as forms of knowledge, a whole new horizon is visible for piecing together the reality of social work and a new cultural way of outlining the knowledge formation of social work. But most of all, we must go back to basics. We need to ask what knowledge is, what research is, and what they mean in the context of social work. We are particularly interested in the question of what the research that takes place in changing different practices for the better is. Our answer is – at least for the time being – that this concerns a world where the object under review is a larger entity than merely the research and its methodology.

References

Alasoini, Tuomo (2006): *Tuntosarvia ja tulkkeja: Oppimisverkostot työelämän kehittämistoiminnan uutena muotona.* Helsinki: Työministeriö.

Argyris, Chris & Schön, Donald A. (1987): *Theory in practice: increasing professional effectiveness.* San Fransisco: The Jossey-Bass Publishers.

Bergman, Matts (2008): *Meliorismi ja klassisen pragmatismin yhtenäisyys.* Lecture at Erkki Kilpinen seminar 31.10.2008, University of Helsinki.

Bertilsson & Christiansen (2001): Toimittajien loppusanat. In Charles S. Peirce. *Johdatus tieteen logiikkaan ja muita kirjoituksia.* Tampere: Vastapaino.

Börjeson, Bengt (2004): *Från Skås försök. En diskussion om relationen kunskap och social praktik.*

Castells, Manuel & Himanen, Pekka (2001): *Suomen tietoyhteiskuntamalli.* Helsinki: WSOY.

Dewey, John (1929): *The Quest for Certainty. A Study of the Relation of Knowledge and Action.* The Collected Works of John Dewey. Later Works: Volume 4.

Dewey, J. (1938): *Experience and Education,* New York: Collier Books. (Collier edition first published 1963).

Epstein, Irwin (2001): *Mining for silver while dreaming of gold. Clinical data-mining in practice-based research.* Taylor & Francis.

Ervast, Sari-Anne & Tulensalo, Hanna (2006): Sosiaalityötä lapsen kanssa. Kokemuksia lapsikeskeisen tilannearvion kehittämisestä. *Soccan ja Heikki Waris -instituutin julkaisusarja nro 8.* Helsinki: Yliopistopaino.

Fook, Jan (2002): *Social Work. Critical Theory and Practice.* London: SAGE Publications.

Gibbons, Michael, Nowotny, Helga & Scott, Peter (1999): *Re-thinking science: knowledge and the public in an age of uncertainty.* Cambridge: Polity Press.

Gustavsen, Björn (1996): Action Research, Democratic Dialogue, and the Issue of 'Critical Mass' in Change. *Qualitative Inquiry* 2 (1) pp. 90–103.

Gustavsen, Björn (2004): Making knowledge actionable: From theoretical centralism to distributive constructivism. *Concepts and Transformation,* 9 (2) pp. 147-180.

Habermas, Jürgen (1965): Erkenntnis und Interesse. In Habermas, Jürgen (1968),

Technik und Wissenschaft als 'Ideologie'. Suhrkamp, Frankfurt am Main, pp. 146—168. (Tieto ja Intressi. Suom. Paavo Löppönen). In Tuomela, Raimo – Patoluoto, Ilkka (eds) (1976) Yhteiskuntatieteiden filosofiset perusteet 1. Gaudeamus, Helsinki.

Habermas, Jürgen (1987): *The Theory of Communicative Action. Vol. 2. Life World and System: A Critique of Functionalist Reason*. Cambridge: Polity Press.

Hakkarainen, Kai, Lonka, Kirsti & Lipponen, Lasse (1999): *Tutkiva oppiminen. Älykkään toiminnan rajat ja niiden ylittäminen*. Porvoo: WSOY.

Heikkinen, Hannu L. T., Rovio, Esa & Syrjälä, Leena (eds) (2006): *Toiminnasta tietoon. Toimintatutkimuksen menetelmät ja lähestymistavat*. Helsinki: Kansanvalistusseura.

Joas, Hans (1996): *The Creativity of Action*. Cambridge: Polity Press.

Johnsson, Eva & Svensson, Kerstin (2005): Theory in social work: Some reflections on understanding and explaining interventions. *European Social Work*, 8 (4) pp. 419–433.

Jonsson, Gustav & Kälvestan, Anna-Lisa (1964): *222 Stockholmspojkar, en socialpsykiatrisk undersökning av pojkar i skolåldern*. Stockholm: Stockholm universitet.

Juhila, Kirsi (2006): *Sosiaalityöntekijöinä ja asiakkaina. Sosiaalityön yhteiskunnalliset tehtävät ja paikat*. Tampere: Vastapaino.

Kananoja, Aulikki (1984): Sosiaalityön kolmiyhteys – tutkimus, käytäntö, opetus. *Sosiaalityön vuosikirja 84*. Sosiaalityöntekijäin liitto.

Karvinen, Synnöve (1993): Reflektiivinen ammatillisuus sosiaalityössä. In Riitta Granfelt, Harri Jokiranta, Synnöve Karvinen, Aila-Leena Matthies & Anneli Pohjola: *Monisärmäinen sosiaalityö*. Helsinki: Sosiaaliturvan keskusliitto.

Karvinen, Synnöve, Pösö, Tarja & Satka, Mirja (eds) (2000): *Sosiaalityön tutkimus. Metodologisia suunnistuksia*. Jyväskylä: SoPhi.

Koskinen, Anna-Kaisa (2007): 'Vaihtoehtoinen tarina' – Mitä on sosiaalinen muutostyö? *SOCCA:n ja Heikki Waris-instituutin julkaisusarja nro 14*. Helsinki: Yliopistopaino.

Laine, Terhi & Saurama, Erja (2009): Semiotic analysis in the study of social work. *Social Work and Society*, 7, 2, http://www.socwork.net/sws/article/view/77/336

Lindroos, Michaela (2008): Att utforska världsbilder i samtal – en praktisk forskning i mångkulturellt socialt arbete. *FSKC rapporter 1/ 2008*.

Lindqvist, Anne-Marie (2008): Delaktighet i en forsknings- och omsorgskontext ur ett medborgarperspektiv för personer med utvecklingsstörning. *FSKC Rapporter 5/2008*.

McCrystal, Patrick (2000): Developing the social work researcher through a practitioner research training programme, *Social Work Education*19 (4) pp. 359-374.

Mezirow, Jack (1991): *Transformative dimensions of adult learning*. San Francisco: Jossey-Bass higher and adult education series.

Mutka, Ulla (1998): *Sosiaalityön neljäs käänne. Asiantuntijuuden mahdollisuudet vahvan hyvinvointivaltion jälkeen.* Jyväskylä: SoPhi.

Muukkonen, Tiina (2008): Suunnitelmallinen sosiaalityö lapsen kanssa. *Soccan ja Heikki Waris –instituutin julkaisusarja* nro 17.

Myllärniemi, Annina (2007): *Lastensuojelun perhetyö ammattikäytäntönä* – jäsennyksiä perhetyöstä toimintatutkimuksen valossa. *Soccan ja Heikki Waris -instituutin julkaisusarja* nro 15.

Paavola, Sami & Hakkarainen, Kai (2006): Entäpä jos...? Ideoiden abduktiivinen kehittely tutkimusprosessin olennaisena osana. In Kristina Rolin, Marja-Liisa Kakkuri-Knuuttila & Elina Henttonen (eds) *Soveltava yhteiskuntatiede ja filosofia.* Helsinki: Gaudeamus.

Peirce, Charles S. (1931): The collected papers.Vol V. *Pragmatism and Pragmaticism.* Cambridge MA: Belknoap Press

Peirce, Charles S. (2001): *Johdatus tieteen logiikkaan ja muita kirjoituksia.* Tampere: Vastapaino.

Pihlström, Sami (1998): *Pragmatism and philosophical anthropology: understanding our human life in a human world.* American university studies. Series 5, Philosophy; 186. New York: Lang.

Pohjola, Anneli (1994): Tiedontuotanto sosiaalityössä. In Riitta Granfelt, Harri Jokiranta, Synnöve Karvinen, Aila-Leena Matthies & Anneli Pohjola (eds) *Monisärmäinen sosiaalityö.* Helsinki: Sosiaaliturvan keskusliitto.

Ramian, Knud (2004): *Praksisforskning som laeringsrum i socialt arbeid.* http://www.ceps.suite.dk/laeringsrum%20i%20praksis.pdf

Ronkainen, Irene (2007): *Tiedon tehtävät ja tulkinnan taju.* Lapin yliopisto.

Satka, Mirja, Karvinen-Niinikoski, Synnöve & Nylund, Marianne (2005): Mitä sosiaalityön käytäntötutkimus on? In Mirja Satka, Synnöve Karvinen-Niinikoski, Marianne Nylund & Susanna Hoikkala (eds) *Sosiaalityön käytäntötutkimus.* Helsinki: Palmenia-kustannus.

Schön, Donald (1983): *Reflective Practitioner. How Professionals Think in Action.* New York: Basic Books.

Shaw, Ian (2005) Practitioner Research: Evidence or Critique? *The British Journal of Social Work,* 35(8) pp. 1231–1248.

Shaw, Ian & Bryderup, Inge (2008): Visions for Social Work Research. In Inge Bryderup (ed) Evidence Based and Knowledge Based Social Work. Research Methods and Approaches in Social Work Research. Danish School of Education. Aarhus University. Shotter, John & Gustavsen, Björn (1999): *The role of dialogue conferences in the development of learning regions: doing from within our lives together what we cannot do apart.* Centre for Advances Studies, Stockholm School of Economics.

Sjöblom, Stina (2008): 'Har de blivit hjälpta så att de blivit stjälpta?' En studie i socialarbetets potential och gränser inom handikappservice. *FSKC rapporter* 2/2008.

Sulkunen, Pekka (1997): Todellisuuden ymmärrettävyys ja diskurssianalyysin rajat. In Sulkunen, Pekka & Törrönen, Jukka (eds) *Semioottisen sosiologian näkökulmia. Sosiaalisen todellisuuden rakentuminen ja ymmärrettävyys.* Tampere: Gaudeamus, pp.13–53.

Vinterhed, Kerstin (1977): *Gustav Jonsson på Skå – en epok i svensk barnavård.* Stockholm: Tiden.

Williams, Fiona & Popay, Jennie (1999): Balancing Polarities: Developing a New Framework for Welfare Research. In F. Williams, J. Popay & A. Oakley (eds) *Welfare Research. A Critical Review.* London: UCL Press.

Notes

1. The research and teaching facilities are based in the city of Helsinki Social ServicesDepartment and different operations are coordinated on contract basis. The department has established six researcher/social worker posts at the Heikki Waris –Institute and two at the Mathilda Wrede –Institute. The idea is that social workers coming from the field work in two year projects. The subjects of research are agreed upon in the boards of the institutes that are formed by the different parties involved. The University of Helsinki funds the professorships and the lectureships in practice research. Also other municipalities in the region participate in the funding.

2. Characteristic of the rapid adaptation of the concept of practice research is that it was coined only while writing the textbook that brought the different themes together. After the book was published, while reflecting upon it, different actors started asking 'is what I am doing practice research?' The actors asking this question were also the authors who participated in writing the book. This is a distinctive example of how concepts affect reality – and in this case – how they restrict it.

Appendix:
The Salisbury Statement

Background to developing a statement on practice research

Professionals in the early 21st century are required to practise more effectively amid the increasing challenge of uncertainty and complexity. The widespread call for evidence-based practice is a major response to this. Yet contemporary approaches to research often fail to produce adequate evidence or knowledge about practice for use in variable situations. How is professional practice to be researched better, to provide a basis for improved practice? This question affects us all, and is answered in both similar and different ways across a range of countries and professions.

Mapping the range of answers to this question is an important step in developing research for better practice. In June 2008, a group of interested professionals came together (organised by SPRING – the Southampton Practice Research Initiative Network Group) in Salisbury, UK, to begin this mapping by formulating an international statement on practice research. The group comprised academics and practitioners from a range of countries (the Nordic countries, Italy, Canada, the USA, Israel, Singapore and the UK). This group formed the backbone of the group known as the 'Salisbury Forum'. The group was comprised primarily of social workers, but tried to formulate a statement which might be applied more broadly in all professions where the research of practice is important.

The statement is not intended to be definitive or conclusive, but simply aims to begin tracing the contours of practice research at this point in time as it continues to evolve. We have tried to word it in an inclusive manner, so that various perspectives and differences are recognised. We hope that the statement will provide a basis for continued discussion. We have written it so that various professionals, from different countries and contexts, will be able to use this statement to continue to craft their own thinking and positions on practice research; to increase the profile of practice research; and above all to undertake more and better practice research.

Practice Research: The Salisbury Statement

Practice research: why is it important and why now?

The current global context demands effective practice from professionals. Economic and social changes mean more accountability is required yet the climate is of increasing unpredictability which compounds the difficulties in achieving accountability. There needs to be a shift in the way practice is researched so that it provides relevant knowledge for better practice in complex and uncertain situations.

A major problem is a mainstream assumption that research leads practice. But research also needs to be practice-minded in order to better study and develop knowledge which emerges directly from the complex practices themselves. Practice research, involving equal dialogue between the worlds of practice and research is important as a concept, since it seeks to develop our understanding of the best ways to research this complexity. It is important at this time in history given that concerns with new accountabilities now converge with doubts about the adequacy of scientific knowledge as a sole basis for improving practice.

What is it?

There is no definite consensus on the meaning of the term 'practice research' and other related terms (e.g. 'practitioner research') are often used instead. Following is an example of a statement about practice research which captures some of the nuances involved:

> Practice research involves curiosity about practice. It is about identifying good and promising ways in which to help people; and it is about challenging troubling practice through the critical examination of practice and the development of new ideas in the light of experience. It recognises that this is best done by practitioners in partnership with researchers, where the latter have as much, if not more, to learn from practitioners as practitioners have to learn from researchers. It is an inclusive approach to professional knowledge that is concerned with understanding the complexity of practice alongside the commitment to empower, and to realise social justice, through practice.

Practice research involves the generation of knowledge of direct relevance to professional practice and therefore will normally involve knowledge generated directly from practice itself in a grounded way. The following identifies some of the specific aspects involved.

Clearly there has been thinking and practice regarding the linking of practice and research for some time, and this has taken particular paths of historical development in different settings (eg. the case study approach was seen as an early method for researching practice in some countries). Much of the contemporary meaning turns on the issue of how to bridge the gap between the world of research and the world of practice.

Several specific issues are involved in determining how best to bridge this gap:

+ Whether and how practitioners are involved in practice research. This involves questions of whether practitioners are both users and creators of knowledge, and whether this means they MUST be involved in research to make it meaningful practice research.

+ Whether all research which is useful to professionals is practice research or are there also other sorts of research which are necessary for effective practice.

+ How practice is understood and the different aspects incorporated (e.g. different types, methods, settings). How practitioners use and develop knowledge (and what types of knowledge) is a central question. What is the nature of complex practice experience, and how is this best represented through research? Practice research at some level needs to be able to represent the concerns of everyday practice.

+ How the concept of research is understood – the particular approach to ways of knowing (epistemology) which underpins research, and how concepts like 'rigour' and 'trustworthiness' relate. In particular, the conception of research may need to allow for the creation of knowledge through day to day practice experience, 'Inquiry', or 'research-minded practice' may be more appropriate terms.

+ How the concept of knowledge is understood underpins both the above issues. In particular, what types of knowledge does practice research focus on, and whether it should involve exposing the tacit/implicit dimension of practice are key issues. _ How practice research relates to research in other disciplines (e.g. social science) or dominant professions (e.g. medicine) is a key question, including whether it simply draws from and modifies these, or whether there is a need to develop new and different paradigms/methods

Why is it done?

Broadly and simply, practice research aims to directly improve practice, by generating relevant professional knowledge. However there is a multitude of complicating perspectives on exactly what is involved in this:

+ Who is it for? There are many different interest groups involved (practitioners, service users, academics, researchers, policy makers, managers, the general public) who may represent contradictory interests. Which ones take primacy, and whether practice research must always benefit (and involve) the service users directly are major issues on which perspectives will differ.
+ The drivers of practice research. This is linked with the above question. Questions of whether it must be driven by concerns which derive directly from practice, or whether it is possible that less direct concerns may also be relevant provide different perspectives.
+ The value base of practice research. Should there be a value base tied directly with the value base of the relevant profession (i.e. In the case of social work should it aim at change towards greater justice (social and personal)?
+ In developing the relationship between practice and research the following principles/practices are important:

  o Collaboration
  o participation
  o ethical reflexivity and critical reflection
  o contextuality and
  o the dynamic, fluid or relational nature of research

+ Practice research may also contribute to the development of the profession through generating its distinctive knowledge and expertise.

How is it done?

What methods are relevant to practice research? Whilst it is acknowledged that the actual problems and questions which arise from practice should drive its research, it is also appropriate to ask whether particular methodologies or methods are preferable.

Both existing and new methods may be relevant in continuing to develop the ways in which the complexities of practice are researched. An inclusive approach (recognising multiple perspectives) is important in articulating paradigms therefore purely quantitative or purely qualitative approaches are seldom applicable. Practice research may often require creating new methods or innovatively using existing methods in ways which are congruent with the principles of collaboration, complexity, dialogue, relationality and contextuality. For example, methods such as participatory action research, or involving reflection and reflexivity, may lend themselves more readily to the purposes of practice research

If there is to be dynamic dialogue between practice and research, the methods for devising research problems and questions directly from practice, and the relative roles of practitioners and researchers require further attention. How does each of the different parties in the research process (practitioner, academic, service user, policy maker, manager) make a differing (or similar) contribution based on their specific position and expertise?

What next?

What is now needed to further develop practice research?

+   Structures, processes and conditions to support practice research – a range of different structures and conditions may be needed depending on the interest group and resources available. Different countries have tried different initiatives (e.g. In Finland the Centres of Excellence; in other Nordic countries the HUSK partnerships between government, academia and service users). Within organisations, spaces (physical and intellectual and protected time) need to be made available for exchange of practice research ideas. Social capital needs to be built to enable practice research, and to encourage educationalists to train practitioners to be more research - minded, and researchers to be more practice-minded.
+   Research funding bodies need to recognise the emergence of new models for researching practice.
+   New paradigms/epistemologies? Perhaps new ways of talking about practice research need to be developed in order to recognise the emergent nature of a practice research approach
+   Call for action. The time has come for further systematic and

collaborative action. Educationalists, practitioners, researchers, managers and employers all have an intrinsic part to play in developing practice research, so collaborative efforts in a number of spheres are vital.

Having the resources and structures is not enough. What should animate these is a culture which supports the engagement of practitioners and researchers; where their different skills can be valued 7 and exchanged; and where equal value is given to the challenge of making knowledge more generalisable and to the recognition and valuing of specific and local knowledge.

A vital part of developing the concept of practice research is the need to keep doing it, and from these practices, to continue to develop our understanding.

Membership of the Forum

The following were part of the Salisbury Forum Group that provided the foundation of this Statement:

Gurid Aga Askeland, Norway
Mike Austin, USA
Tony Evans, UK
Sylvia Fargion, Italy
Mike Fisher, UK
Jan Fook, UK
Ilse Julkunen, Finland
Aulikki Kananoja, Finland
Synnöve Karvinen-Niinikoski, Finland
Rhoda MacRae, UK
Edgar Marthinsen, Norway
Matts Mosesson, Sweden
Joan Orme, UK
Helen Pain, UK
Jackie Powell, UK
Gillian Ruch, UK
Mirja Satka, Finland
Riki Savaya, Israel

Ian Shaw, UK
Tim Sim, Hong Kong
Lars Uggerhøj, Denmark
Helen Welsh, UK
Bessa Whitmore, Canada
Laura Yliruka, Finland

www.ingramcontent.com/pod-product-compliance
Lightning Source LLC
Chambersburg PA
CBHW050438280326
41932CB00013BA/2157

* 9 7 8 1 8 6 1 7 7 1 3 0 8 *